When Reason Goes on Holiday

Philosophers in Politics

NEVEN SESARDIĆ

Encounter Books
New York • London

First American edition published in 2016 by Encounter Books, an activity of Encounter for Culture and Education, Inc., a nonprofit, tax exempt corporation.
Encounter Books website address: www.encounterbooks.com

Manufactured in the United States and printed on acid-free paper. The paper used in this publication meets the minimum requirements of ANSI/NISO Z39.48–1992 (R 1997) (*Permanence of Paper*).

FIRST AMERICAN EDITION

LIBRARY OF CONGRESS CATALOGING-IN-PUBLICATION DATA
Names: Sesardic, Neven, 1949– author.
Title: When reason goes on holiday: philosophers in politics / by Neven Sesardic.
Description: New York: Encounter Books [2016] | Includes bibliographical references and index.
Identifiers: LCCN 2016011693 (print) | LCCN 2016023313 (ebook) | ISBN 9781594038792 (hardcover: alk. paper) | ISBN 9781594038808 (Ebook)
Subjects: LCSH: Political science—Philosophy—History—20th century. | Philosophy—Political aspects—History—20th century. | Political atrocities—History—20th century. | Right and left (Political science)—History—20th century.
Classification: LCC JA83 .S455 2016 (print) | LCC JA83 (ebook) | DDC 320.01–dc23
LC record available at https://lcn.loc.gov/2016011693

Interior page design and composition: BooksByBruce.com

“It is curious that the greatest intellectual gifts sometimes carry with them the inability to perceive simple realities that would be obvious to a moron.”

—E. T. Jaynes

Contents

Credits

Figure 2.1 Praising successes of Soviet agriculture during the Holodomor
SOURCE: © Gerd Arntz, Picture Statistics, Moscow 1934, c/o Pictoright Amsterdam 2016 (reprinted with permission).

Figure 2.2 The concern for minorities in the USSR
SOURCE: *Vsesojuznyj institut izobrazitel'noj statistiki sovetskogo stroitel'stva i chozjajstva pri CIK SSSR: Na strojke socializma. Dostiženija pervoj pjatiletki,* Moscow: IZOSTAT, 1933.

Figure 4.1 Carnap protests against the imaginary Gulag
SOURCE: *Daily Worker,* January 28, 1952.

Figure 4.2 *Daily Worker*: Save the Rosenbergs!
SOURCE: *Daily Worker,* January 14, 1953.

Figure 5.1 Gödel's membership card
SOURCE: Dawson, J., et al. (eds.), *Kurt Gödel: das Album.* Wiesbaden: Vieweg, 2006, p. 48 (reprinted with permission of Springer).

Figure 5.2 Gödel goes with the flow
SOURCE: Dawson, J., et al. (eds.), *Kurt Gödel: das Album.* Wiesbaden: Vieweg, 2006, p. 66 (reprinted with permission of Springer).

Figure 7.1 Lakatos biography
SOURCE: http://web.archive.org/web/20130511032620/http://www2.lse.ac.uk/philosophy/LakatosAward/lakatos.aspx.

Figure 7.2 Éva Izsák (1925–1944)
SOURCE: Yad Vashem (reprinted with permission).

Figure 10.1 Book burning during the Cultural Revolution
SOURCE: akg-images / Zhou Thong (reprinted with permission of AKG-Images).

Figure 11.1 Angela Davis and Erich Honecker, 1972
SOURCE: Bundesarchiv, Image 183-L0911-029 / Photo: Peter Koard (reprinted with permission).

Acknowledgments

Many colleagues and friends read earlier drafts and helped with useful comments. I owe special thanks to my former graduate student Nathan Cofnas who went through several versions of the manuscript and suggested many significant improvements. I also received valuable feedback from Tomislav Bracanović, Rafael De Clercq, Zvjezdana Dukić, Berislav Horvatić, Andrew Irvine, Tomislav Janović, Paisley Livingston, David Papineau, Sean Scully, Ante Sesardić, Peter Singer, David Stamos, Matej Sušnik, Omri Tal, and Daniel Wikler.

When I was finishing the first version of the book manuscript and when I started thinking about a potential publisher, I decided that my first choice would be Encounter Books. So I was thrilled when Roger Kimball offered me a book contract. I would also like to thank the production manager Katherine Wong for helping with many details and Dave Baker of Super Copy Editors.

Preface

Analytic philosophers emphasize the importance of logic, clarity, and reason. This is what made studying philosophy especially attractive for many of us who lived under communism. When we saw how much these philosophers valued intellectual integrity and uncompromising pursuit of truth, we found their approach inspiring and we tried to emulate it. This helped us preserve our sanity in the world of constant lies that surrounded us.

It was therefore a huge disappointment when I started to discover that a number of the most prominent Western philosophers who were rightly admired for their scholarly contributions actually abandoned reason altogether when they turned to politics. I realized that some of the thinkers I once regarded as models of rationality rushed into supporting ill-conceived and inhumane political causes. Some were even apologists for the mendacious communist regime that so obviously trampled on human liberty and that was abhorred by those of us who experienced it firsthand.

My disappointment led to curiosity about the extent of this betrayal of reason by philosophers and its many manifestations. I tried to learn more about this strange phenomenon that has received surprisingly little attention. The results of that research are presented here.

CHAPTER ONE

The Wisdom That Failed

"Many would be wise if they did not think themselves wise."

—BALTASAR GRACIÁN

Should philosophers be kings, as Plato suggested? Or, to paraphrase William F. Buckley, wouldn't it be better to be ruled by the first 2,000 people listed in the telephone directory than by the most illustrious of Socrates' intellectual descendants?

The evidence presented in this book shows that, despite their declared love of wisdom, surprisingly many leading philosophers have shown embarrassingly poor judgment in their excursions into politics. The disastrous way some of the most influential contemporary philosophers have engaged in politics should make us think twice before following their advice. This also raises a question: How could people who are obviously very clever and sophisticated in a field that is intellectually demanding be so foolhardy in practical affairs?

Indeed, twentieth-century philosophers have a bad track record in choosing sides in some momentous political debates. Many contemporary philosophers have disgraced themselves by defending totalitarian political systems and advocating political ideas they should have easily recognized as distasteful and inhumane. To give just three well-known examples, Jean-Paul Sartre championed Stalinism and later Maoism, Martin Heidegger actively supported and celebrated Nazism, and Michel Foucault publicly expressed enthusiasm for Khomeini's Iranian Islamic revolution.

How could the very people committed to gaining the deepest knowledge about the world and human existence get things so wrong? Could this have something to do with the fact that the three philosophers just named (plus many others with similar unfortunate involvements in politics) belong to the so-called continental tradition in philosophy?

The terms *continental* and *analytic* describe two different schools in philosophy that have been in conflict roughly since the beginning of the twentieth century. The distinction between them is notoriously hard to draw in clear and explicit terms, but philosophers usually have no problem assigning most of their colleagues into one of these two traditions. A provisional self-characterization of the analytic style of doing philosophy is the claim that the analytic approach "involves argument, distinctions, and... moderately plain speech" (Williams 2006, viii). In one of the best historical accounts of the rise and development of analytic philosophy, this approach is described as being committed "to the ideals of clarity, rigor, and argumentation" and to the goal of "pushing rational means of investigation as far as possible" (Soames 2003, xiii–iv). Basically, then, the trademarks of analytic philosophy would be clarity of thought, precision, and logical coherence, as well as the honest and persistent effort to avoid obscurantism, pretentious writing style and false profundity.

This opens the path for the argument that analytic philosophers are better protected from committing political blunders because of their training in clear and logical thinking, whereas continental philosophers, lacking this kind of training and consequently being prone to empty rhetoric, undisciplined thought, and obscurity, will be much more exposed to the risk of making fools of themselves in politics. This is what many analytic philosophers tend to think.

We Will Teach You How to Think, They Said

The American Philosophical Association (APA), which is heavily dominated by analytic philosophy, seeks to attract philosophy majors with the following message:

> The study of philosophy serves to develop intellectual abilities important for life as a whole, beyond the knowledge and skills required for any particular profession. Properly pursued, it enhances analytical, critical, and communicative capacities that are applicable to any subject matter, and in any human context (APA 1992).

This is a remarkably strong and bold statement about the alleged effects of studying philosophy: The pursuit of philosophy is claimed to enhance students' analytical, critical, and communicative capacities, which can then be applied to *any subject matter and in any human context.*

The main problem here is that the APA provides no evidence at all for the wonderful improvements in thinking that philosophy supposedly can produce. Moreover, many scholars actually insist that the currently available empirical evidence comes nowhere near to establishing such a sweeping and resolute causal claim. In contrast to the APA's assurance that studying philosophy improves reasoning skills, psychologists tell us that after a hundred years of debate "the issue of whether generalizable reasoning skills transfer to reasoning contexts outside of formal schooling *remains an open question in the opinions of leading researchers*" (Barnett & Ceci 2002, 615; emphasis added). What the APA advertises is additionally problematic because it seems to promise something like "far transfer" (i.e., transferring what one learns in one context to other very different subject matters and contexts). And the prospects of achieving far transfer are notoriously questionable (see Holyoak & Morrison 2005, 788–90, and references therein).

All in all, therefore, it appears that the APA is involved in false advertising, which can be explained by ignorance, self-serving intellectual dishonesty, or some combination thereof.

In a recent discussion about the value of philosophy, the executive director of the APA, Amy E. Ferrer, said this:

> Philosophy teaches many of the skills most valued in today's economy: critical thinking, analysis, effective written and verbal

> communication, problem solving, and more. And philosophy majors' success is borne out in both data—which show that philosophy majors consistently outperform nearly all other majors on graduate entrance exams such as the GRE and LSAT, and that philosophy ties with mathematics for the highest percentage increase from starting to midcareer salary—and anecdotal evidence indicating that philosophy and other humanities majors are increasingly successful and sought after in the business and technology sectors (quoted in Jaschik 2015).

Ferrer's defense of the value of studying philosophy is fallacious. It is based on the logical mistake *post hoc, ergo propter hoc.* Briefly, the statistical correlation between studying philosophy and all these good outcomes does not mean that the former causes the latter. It may well be that those who embark on philosophy studies are simply smarter to begin with and that their subsequent success is in no way (or not mainly) the result of what they learned in philosophy courses.

This pretty obvious alternative explanation for the good performance of philosophy majors is not recognized by the APA as a possibility that deserves any consideration. The same blind spot reappears in a letter that was signed by three officers of the APA (including the well-known Stanford philosopher Michael Bratman) and published on the APA website. Again, the authors first provide statistical data about above-average accomplishments of philosophy majors and then jump to the conclusion that studying philosophy "*trains* students' general cognitive skills, *improves* their ability to reason" and thereby "*make[s]* philosophy majors highly flexible in the job market" (APA 2014; emphasis added). The three italicized words all assert causal influence and they can be justified only if something more than a merely statistical correlation is provided. The fact that even very prominent philosophers do not sufficiently appreciate the warning that correlation does not imply causation—perhaps the most hackneyed principle of critical thinking—is not the best advertisement for the value of philosophy for critical thinking.

The British Philosophical Association (2016) also promises on its website that the philosophy student will develop the capacities to "think well about important issues" and "learn to be an independent and flexible thinker," and that these skills will "both be of value throughout one's life and in demand by many employers." Again, no evidence is provided that studying philosophy can really bring about these magnificent effects. Moreover, given all that we currently know there is no good reason to accept these optimistic claims.

In 2010 more than a thousand people, including a number of well-known philosophers, signed a petition titled "Make Reasoning Skills Compulsory in Schools" (Burgess 2010). The petition was addressed to Michael Gove, the UK Education Minister. The petition urged the government to make philosophy classes compulsory from a very early age, arguing that this "would have immense benefits in terms of boosting British school kids' reasoning and conceptual skills, better equipping them for the complexities of life in the 21st century."

In support of this radical proposal they offered two pieces of evidence.[1] One was a collection of articles written by a group of people, *all* of whom are philosophers and philosophy educators, and who—as we learn in the book introduction—were "all firmly committed" to the view that philosophy should be a compulsory part of the school curriculum (Hand & Winstanley 2009, xiii–xiv). Besides this highly biased source produced by true believers, the petition invoked a 2007 study by two researchers at Dundee University allegedly showing that "confronting core philosophical debates as the nature of existence, ethics and knowledge can raise children's IQ by up to 6.5 points, as well as improve emotional intelligence."

There are three major problems here. First, the public campaign to force all children in the UK to take philosophy classes

---

1 They also cited the UNESCO publication *Philosophy: A School of Freedom* (2007), but far from advocating compulsory philosophy classes that book actually urges restraint and caution in this matter. It recommends that those who think about introducing philosophy into primary-school curricula should first initiate trial projects "so that the success of these practices can be evaluated in relation to national educational objectives" (17).

essentially relied on *only one* scientific study. (Consider an analogous case: If two researchers announced that in their sample of 177 children, taking a certain new medicine was statistically associated with better health, would anyone seriously consider the proposal that, on that basis alone, all children in the country immediately start taking the medicine regularly?)

Second, it is unclear whether the supporters of the petition were aware that the authors of the study in question themselves explicitly cautioned the reader that the results "should not be over-interpreted or accepted uncritically." (It is hard to think of a more extreme way to over-interpret and uncritically accept a study than to prescribe a national curriculum based on its tentative conclusions.) The authors pointed out that their study suffered from methodological imperfections and warned that sampling was not entirely random, that the possibility of the Hawthorne effect (also known as the observer effect) could not be ruled out and that differences between experimental and control classes could be influenced by factors that were not measured (Topping & Trickey 2007, 283).

And third, even if the gains were genuine, whether they would be sustained after the experiment ended would be unclear. Obviously there would be little point in modifying the national curriculum for elementary schools if the good effects dissipated soon after any such intervention came to an end (which frequently happens with reported increases in childhood IQ).[2] So before starting a massive educational reform, it stands to reason that the durability of those effects should be confirmed in the first place, preferably by independent research teams.

Surprisingly, despite all these self-evident reasons against joining the campaign, a number of well-known philosophers (including Simon Blackburn, Jonathan Glover, Bill Brewer, A. C. Grayling, Duncan Pritchard, Peter Simons, Jon Williamson, Bob Hale, John Dupré, Robert Hopkins, Brian Leiter, Jennifer Saul, and Helen Beebee) not only supported the hasty and ill-thought-out proposal but were ready to defend it publicly by putting their

2 "In fact many interventions have been shown to raise test scores and mental ability 'in the short run' (i.e., while the program itself was in progress), but long-run gains have proved more elusive" (Neisser et al. 1996, 88).

signatures on the petition. Even more oddly, among the names of the supporters we also find leading philosophers of science who should have immediately realized that there is simply no way that the presented evidence could justify the extravagant proposal of the petitioners. (Two of those philosophers of science, Alexander Bird and James Ladyman, are past editors-in-chief of the *British Journal for the Philosophy of Science*, arguably the world's best journal in the field.)

One would have expected philosophers to be careful about making such confident public assertions about philosophy's benefits for two reasons. First, since it is obviously in their interest to spread the belief that studying philosophy pays off so well, they should be acutely aware of the possibility of self-deception. Second, they should be concerned about the well-being of their prospective students who could be lured into choosing philosophy by false advertisements, but might later come to regret their massive investment of time and money in something that does not lead to the promised results.

Russell's Paradox: A Genius with a Streak of Foolishness

The belief that studying philosophy, when it is geared toward developing analytical skills and conceptual clarity, also enhances rationality and critical thinking in practical affairs of everyday life (including politics) dates from the early days of analytic philosophy.

In a book still frequently assigned to undergraduate philosophy students, Bertrand Russell expressed a similar view about the practical usefulness of philosophy: "The essential characteristic of philosophy... is criticism. It examines critically the principles employed in science *and in daily life*" (Russell 1912, 233; emphasis added). This sounds nice, but there was little trace of critical examination in many of Russell's own actions and especially in his political statements. George Trevelyan, Russell's undergraduate classmate at Cambridge, once said about him: "He may be a genius in mathematics—as to that I am no judge; but about politics he is a perfect goose" (Monk 2000, 5). Similarly George Santayana said:

"Along with his genius he has a streak of foolishness" (quoted in Eastman 1959, 192). Illustrations of Russell's political irrationality could easily fill a whole chapter in this book, but since many of these episodes are probably already widely known I will give only a few examples of his ludicrous political outbursts.

In an article published on October 30, 1951, in the *Manchester Guardian*, Russell said that the United States was as much a police state as Hitler's Germany or Stalin's Russia. He continued:

> In Germany under Hitler, and in Russia under Stalin, nobody ventured upon a political remark without first looking behind the door to make sure no one was listening… [W]hen I last visited America I found the same state of things there… [I]f by some misfortune you were to quote with approval some remark by Jefferson you would probably lose your job and perhaps find yourself behind bars.

It should be stressed that Russell's anti-Americanism and his political silliness date back to the time of the First World War. In his January 1918 article (for which he went to prison), he stated that if the war continued "[t]he American Garrison will be occupying England and France" (Russell 1918). This confidently predicted occupation of England and France by the U.S. Army of course never happened, but Russell did not allow himself to be embarrassed by such a silly prophecy. In the same article he claimed it was "completely false" that the mass of Russians were against the Bolsheviks (although in fact more than 75 percent voted against them in the election of 1917). He also said it was completely false that Bolsheviks dared not permit the Constituent Assembly to meet (although in fact the Constituent Assembly did meet but was expressly dissolved by Bolsheviks).[3]

---

3 As one of the participants of these events reported: "In England there was once a 'Long Parliament.' The Constituent Assembly of the RSFSR [Russian Soviet Federative Socialist Republic] was the shortest parliament in the entire history of the world. It ended its inglorious and joyless life after 12 hours and 40 minutes." (www.marxists.org/history/ussr/government/red-army/1918/raskolnikov/ilyin/ch01.htm#bk04)

On November 27, 1965, Russell sent the following message to the Tricontinental Conference (an event that took place in Havana in January 1966 and that was described in a report to the Committee on the Judiciary of the U.S. Senate as "probably the most powerful gathering of pro-Communist, anti-American forces in the history of the Western Hemisphere"):

> In every part of the world the source of war and of suffering lies at the door of US imperialism. Wherever there is hunger, wherever there is exploitative tyranny, wherever people are tortured and the masses left to rot under the weight of disease and starvation, the force which holds down the people stems from Washington (quoted in Monk 2000, 467).

Russell biographer Ray Monk correctly observes that here Russell comes close to saying the USA "is responsible for literally *every* evil in the world" (ibid.). Although Russell was very old at the time, Monk argues that the senility excuse for his signing such statements is not convincing because a lot of evidence shows that Russell was "in full awareness of what he was doing" and that he "remained in possession of his mental faculties until his dying days" (Monk 2000, 455).

On June 11, 1966, Russell sent the following message to Hanoi:

> I extend my warm regards and full solidarity for President Ho Chi Minh and for the people of Vietnam. I convey my great wish that the day may not be far off when a united and liberated Vietnam will celebrate its victory in a free Saigon (quoted in Flew 2001, 119).

So Russell expressed "full solidarity" with the Vietnamese Communist leader who was already at the time responsible for labor camps, reeducation, torture, and mass executions under the slogan "Better ten innocent deaths than one enemy survivor" (Courtois et al. 1999, 568–69; Rosefielde 2009, 110–11). Could Russell have known (or reasonably suspected) in 1966 the truth about Ho Chi Minh's murderous past? Actually, yes. In *From Colonialism to Communism: A Case History of North Vietnam*, published in the United States in 1964, Hoang Van Chi estimated that around half a million people lost their lives due to Ho Chi Minh's policies in the fifties. The book had an immediate impact and any responsible person making public statements about Vietnam should have known about it. Russell did not live to see his "great wish" come true; the Communist "liberation" of Vietnam led to hundreds of thousands deaths.

His anti-Americanism was so notorious that even W. V. Quine, who had a great deal of respect for Russell as a philosopher, once said: "I was never drawn to socialism and communism as [Russell] was, much less to the views he held in his declining years when he was demonstrating against the United States in favor of Soviet Russia" (quoted in Borradori 1994, 34). The *New York Times* published an amazingly biased letter from Russell about the Vietnam War in 1963, to which the editors appended a response saying the letter "reflects an unfortunate and—despite his eminence as a philosopher—an unthinking receptivity to the most transparent Communist propaganda." The editors expressed their own serious reservations about U.S. policy in Vietnam but said that Russell's letter represented "something beyond reasoned criticism" and in some parts amounted to "arrant nonsense."

Russell had taken an anti-American stance earlier, during the Cuban missile crisis of 1962. Here is his crucial argument from a leaflet released on October 23, 1962, reprinted in his autobiography (1967–69; 2009, 625):

> YOU ARE TO DIE
> Not in the course of nature, but within a few weeks, and not you alone, but your family, your friends, and all the inhabitants of Britain, together with many hundreds of millions of innocent people elsewhere.
> WHY?
> Because rich Americans dislike the Government that Cubans prefer, and have used part of their wealth to spread lies about it.

Monk makes an apt comment about the pamphlet: "Its over-simplification of the issues involved would have been startling had [it] come from a schoolboy; from one of the greatest thinkers of our age, [it was] truly astonishing" (Monk 2000, 442).

Communist Temptations at Oxford

J. L. Austin, one of the key figures in ordinary language philosophy (a school of thought that flourished at Oxford in the 1950s and 1960s), argued that philosophy has beneficial consequences in the political domain:

> In Austin's generation, the social and political implications of the teaching of philosophy, and of the forming of habits of thought in a ruling class, were certainly not unnoticed, and he was acutely conscious of them. He seriously wanted to 'make people sensible' and clear-headed, and immune to ill-founded and doctrinaire enthusiasms. He believed that philosophy, if it inculcated respect for 'the facts' and for accuracy, was one of the best instruments for this purpose (Hampshire 1992, 244).

Notice that the author of the text just quoted, Stuart Hampshire, who is also a well-known British philosopher, seems to agree with Austin and, furthermore, associates the belief about the political implications of the teaching of philosophy not just with Austin but more widely with "Austin's generation."

And yet Austin's famously meticulous analysis and his sharp logical mind did not save him from "ill-founded enthusiasms." For after visiting the Soviet Union in the mid-thirties he said that he "was impressed by his experience" and that he had "admiration for the great men who had worked against gigantic odds, Marx and Lenin for example" (Berlin 1973, 6). Being "impressed" with the Stalinism of the mid-thirties is not easily reconcilable with being "clear-headed." On a different occasion Isaiah Berlin reports that Austin "came back from the Soviet Union *deeply impressed* by the discipline and the austerity of life and so forth, and remained under the influence for some time" (Hampshire & Berlin 1972, from

0:06). For many details about ordinary life under Stalinism in the thirties and how deeply *un*impressive it was, see Sheila Fitzpatrick's *Ordinary Stalinism.*[4]

Another example of the belief that philosophy can help the forces of reason comes from philosopher A. J. Ayer, who in his famous book *Language, Truth, and Logic* (1936, 35) claimed that the task of philosophy is to *define rationality*. But someone whose main task is to try to understand the nature of rationality should be the first one to spot irrationality and be on guard against it. Yet just a few months after the book was published Ayer had a baffling bout of irrationality in politics. Over one weekend in February 1937 Ayer was "wrestling with the choice" of whether to join the Communist Party of Great Britain (Rogers 1999, 136). It was a very strange moment to be considering this move. Just a few weeks earlier, thirteen Old Bolsheviks had been sentenced to death in a farcical Moscow show trial. The verdict had been openly celebrated by the British Communist Party.

Any reasonable person must have had serious doubts about the credibility of the accusations and the whole judicial procedure. The London *Times* reported on January 26, 1936:

> The guilt of all the prisoners was already officially announced before the public proceedings began.... The Soviet Press is duly crying for death to the "wriggling hypocrites," the "mischievous vermin," the "venomous Trotskyist vipers."... The whole process is loathsome. All that can be said of it is that guilt may sometimes be established, innocence never.... The general atmosphere can only be compared to the inquiries that were made into witchcraft in the fifteenth and sixteenth centuries, when wretched old men and women were persuaded that they too had departed from the Absolute Good as laid down by authority and that their harmless or venal practices were the result of communing with the Evil One.

---

4 A good illustration is the following joke that was popular in the Soviet Union precisely in the thirties: There is a ring at the door at 3 o'clock at night. The husband goes to answer. He returns and says: "Don't worry, dear, it is bandits who have come to rob us."

But despite all these worrying features and also the bizarre fact that the accused were very eager to confess and help the prosecutors make the case for their death penalty, the British Communist Party took the hard Stalinist line and—only a few days before Ayer's "to join or not to join" moment—claimed in its newspaper the *Daily Worker* that "the scrupulous fairness of the trial, the overwhelming guilt of the accused, and the justness of the sentences is recognized" (Redman 1958, 48). Only several months earlier, at the end of another show trial in Moscow in which sixteen Old Bolsheviks were sentenced to death, the title of the editorial in the Party's newspaper was "Shoot the reptiles!"

And this is the political party that Ayer was on the verge of joining. He decided not to only at the last moment. The funny thing is that apparently Ayer was not bothered much by the Party's slavishly praising all aspects of Soviet totalitarianism; his reason for not joining was that he "did not believe in dialectical materialism" (Ayer 1977, 187). Apparently Ayer had no major disagreements with Stalin's politics at the time—only with his philosophical opinions.

But why did Ayer want to join the Communist Party in the first place? According to his friend Philip Toynbee, it was just his "desire for reasonable activity" (ibid.). So relying on this report, we discover something interesting: A well-known philosopher who believed that philosophers can best explain the meaning of the word *rational* or *reasonable* regarded becoming a card-carrying member of an organization that fully supported Moscow's policies during the Great Terror of the thirties to be a reasonable activity.

Bad Arguments and Bad Politics: What Causes What?

Michael Dummett, too, believed in the salutary influence of philosophy on political attitudes. Speaking about Gottlob Frege's political views that he found so shocking (for more about Frege's case, see pp. 188–192), Dummett said "Frege's philosophy ought to have kept him from holding such views but it didn't" (quoted in Warburton & Edmonds 2010). Here again is the idea that philosophy can (or should) protect people from bad political opinions.

Also, according to Dummett, philosophers in particular "have a duty to make themselves sensitive to social issues" and to do something about them. "If you are an intellectual, and particularly if you aim to be a philosopher, and therefore to think about very general questions, then you ought to be capable of responding to general burning issues, whether the public is ignoring them or has fastened its attention upon them" (Dummett 1996, 194). But, as documented in chapter 9, it appears that Dummett's philosophy didn't keep him from making a fool of himself in politics, either.

Dagfinn Føllesdal, a philosopher who had a distinguished career at Harvard and Stanford, also stresses the political benefits of analytic philosophy:

> We should engage in analytic philosophy not just because it is good philosophy, but also for reasons of individual and social ethics... In our philosophical writing and teaching we should emphasize the decisive role that must be played by argument and justification. This will make life more difficult for political leaders and fanatics who spread messages which do not stand up to critical scrutiny, but which nevertheless often have the capacity to seduce the masses into intolerance and violence. Rational argument and rational dialogue are of the utmost importance for a well-functioning democracy. To educate people in the activities is perhaps the most important task of analytic philosophy (1997, 15–16).

Despite his usual sensitivity to rational argument in philosophy, Føllesdal lowered his guard considerably when turning to politics, e.g. when he was bamboozled into allowing his name to be used in a political conflict in a foreign country, although he should have been aware that he was poorly informed about what was happening there (see p. 173).

Many more examples could be given of analytic philosophers who have argued that the critical ability supposedly cultivated by philosophical education is the best antidote to political follies and fanaticism. I happen to disagree with them. I have found no good evidence that being trained in analytic philosophy boosts political rationality. On the contrary, my aim in this book is to show that some of the leading analytic philosophers have held political views that are both deeply troubling and manifestly irrational. At the same time, in contrast to their highly problematic political beliefs and activity, their academic contributions to philosophy usually carried the marks of extremely careful thinking and the highest intellectual rigor.

Wittgenstein famously said that "philosophical problems arise when language goes on holiday" (1967: I, §38). This book deals with another phenomenon: When philosophers enter politics it is often *reason* that goes on holiday.

In the text that follows I will drop the qualifier *analytic* when talking about philosophers, since virtually all of my examples will be analytic philosophers. The illustrations will include some of the greatest names of contemporary Anglo-American philosophy such as Neurath, Carnap, Wittgenstein, Putnam, Davidson, Dummett, Lakatos, Parfit, and many others, as well as Einstein, who, besides being a physicist, has been embraced by many philosophers as one of their own.

I will explore in detail the individual cases of these very distinguished philosophers and their highly dubious political views or actions. I will also briefly address the politicization of some leading philosophical institutions.

The bleak record will cast additional doubt on the hypothesis that reasoning skill in philosophical matters transfers to political judgment. Perhaps it is not the way philosophers argue that influences their politics but, rather, the opposite. Maybe it is philosophers' politics that affects their intellectual standards (for the worse) and leads them down the path of irrationality when they enter the political domain.

CHAPTER TWO

Otto Neurath: A Philosopher and the Commissars

"Neurath must be rediscovered!"

—Rudolf Haller

Among the historical roots of contemporary analytic philosophy is logical positivism, a movement that started in Central Europe in the period between the two world wars. It is mainly associated with the group of philosophers known as the Vienna Circle. Some of the leading positivists (Rudolf Carnap, Carl Gustav Hempel, Hans Reichenbach, Herbert Feigl, and Philipp Frank) immigrated to the United States in the thirties and had a huge and lasting influence on the development of philosophy there and beyond.

Despite a lot of recent research on the development of logical positivism, there are still many misconceptions about it, particularly about its politics. Here is an example of how even one of the cognoscenti, philosopher Clark Glymour, can go astray:

> There is a larger reason I do not find the positivists embarrassing: the contrast case on the continent. The positivists... wrote with scientific and liberal ambitions, and at least with a passing connection with mathematics and science; in a time in which philosophy on the continent was embracing obscurantism and vicious, totalitarian politics they stood for liberal politics (Glymour 2011).

True, there was a strand of liberal politics among positivists. But it is incorrect to ascribe that attitude to the movement itself. The Vienna Circle did have its (classical) liberal wing, represented mainly by Moritz Schlick. It seems he hated anything that smacked of political agitation, explaining: "We have no need for agitation, we leave that to political parties. In science we simply describe what we have found out and we hope that we got it right" (Neider 1999, 313).

But another, larger group of philosophers, represented by Neurath, Carnap, Hahn[1] and others, had more radical political views; some of them leaned toward socialism or even, more worryingly, communism—in theory and sometimes, as we will see, in practice as well. Contrary to what Glymour says, "vicious, totalitarian politics" was by no means absent from the positivists' thinking.

Let us first illustrate how politics sometimes crept, unexpectedly and rather crudely, into important programmatic documents that were supposed to present the positivist philosophy to the world. This is from the famous manifesto of the Vienna Circle from 1929:

> This development [the increased appreciation of empirical science] is connected with that of the modern process of production, which is becoming ever more rigorously mechanized and leaves ever less room for metaphysical ideas. It is also connected with *the disappointment of broad masses of people* with the attitudes of those who preach traditional metaphysical and theological doctrine. So it is that in many countries the masses now reject these doctrines much more consciously than ever before, and along with *their socialist attitudes* tend to lean towards a down-to-earth empiricist view (Neurath 1973, 317; emphasis added).

What is the evidence that "broad masses of people" ever had any idea about traditional metaphysics, let alone that they were disappointed with it? Also, how do "their socialist attitudes" become

1 According to Karl Menger, also a Vienna Circle member, Hahn was "a convinced socialist" and he "always articulated his unpopular leftist convictions freely and forcefully" (Menger 1994, 58).

relevant for the manifesto defending the scientific worldview? And, finally, how can the alleged fact that "masses" lean toward empiricism advance the case of logical empiricism? All this is left unexplained.

We know that most of the group members enthusiastically supported the manifesto although the first draft was written by its most radical member, Neurath. Carnap and Hahn also had some input, while other members were indirectly involved: Herbert Feigl, Philipp Frank, Friedrich Waismann, Victor Kraft, Karl Menger, and Kurt Gödel, who all officially belonged to the Circle. The manifesto was dedicated to Schlick, but he was not at all happy with the leftist rhetoric of some parts of the document, believing as he did that philosophical insights should be strictly separated from political views and value judgments. Menger had the same concern, and for this reason he decided to distance himself from the Circle, asking Neurath to list him henceforth as "only among those *close* to the Circle" (from Menger's "Introduction" in Hahn 1980).

The Ernst Mach Society, an organization that was also associated with logical positivists and that was led by Schlick, was outlawed by the Austrian Chancellor Dolfuss in 1934. When Schlick protested to the police, arguing that the Society was completely apolitical, he was criticized by both Neurath and Carnap, who "did not feel comfortable" having the Society described as "politically neutral" (Stadler 1992, 376). The police searched Neurath's offices in Vienna in his absence, most likely (as his future wife Marie suspected) because he had been denounced as a Communist (Reisch 2005, 32). See pp. 25–32 for more details.

Another member of the Vienna Circle, mathematician Karl Menger, had this to say about Otto Neurath:

> [Neurath] looked at everything—ideas as well as facts—through an often distorting lens of socialist philosophy and with an eye to the possible effects of the ideas and facts on a socialization of society. I have never seen a scholar as consistently obsessed with an idea and an ideal as Neurath (Menger 1994, 60).

Here is how Karl Popper saw Neurath:

> In my opinion he was a kind of Marxist, he supported a kind of politics which I regarded as very wrong. Furthermore, he was especially naive, in the best sense of the word. His attitude to communism was naive, decidedly naive (from an interview with Popper in Stadler 2015, 269).

Heinrich Neider, another contemporary of Neurath who knew him personally, confirms this impression:

> With him knowledge and thought were always just an aid to the actual doing, which for him ultimately was the revolution. He had a revolutionary past and he actually always saw himself as a revolutionary (Neider 1999, 298).

When Neurath visited New York in 1936, Ernest Nagel introduced him to many philosophers sympathetic to logical positivism. Knowing that Neurath "was always on the lookout for talent both intellectually and *politically compatible* with the Unity of Science movement" (Reisch 2005, 66; emphasis added), Nagel sent him a list of American philosophers who had attended a reception in Neurath's honor and brief information about each philosopher's political views. Nagel concluded that they "without exception have left sympathies in politics."

Neurath's tendency to mix politics with philosophy of science is recognizable in many of his writings. Here is an illustration from his essay "Personal Life and Class Struggle" from 1928:

> Scientific attitude and solidarity go together. *Whoever joins the proletariat can say with justification that he joins love and reason.... Marxism*... announces to the proletarian front that *it has become the carrier of the scientific attitude.* The time should not be far off when this will become clear to many serious bourgeois thinkers.... To many bourgeois it may seem degrading... if one looks at [science] from the point of view of the *class struggle.*

> The *proletariat* appreciates science properly only as a means of struggle and *propaganda in the service of socialist humanity*. Many who came from the *bourgeoisie* are worried whether the *proletariat* will have some feeling for science; but what does history teach us? It is precisely the *proletariat that is the bearer of science without metaphysics* (Neurath 1973, 252, 297; emphasis added).

The best way, though, to see how radical Neurath's political views were is to look at his attempts to realize his ideas in practice. Let us briefly consider two such episodes: one in Munich, the other in Moscow.

Neurath in Munich

In the chaos at the end of World War I in November 1918, Kurt Eisner, the head of the Independent Social Democratic Party, declared a free state of Bavaria. Neurath saw this as a window of opportunity for applying his political theories to the real world. He went to Munich, discussed his economic ideas with Eisner and others, and also presented his ideas in a talk to the Workers' and Soldiers' Council.

Here are the main goals, in Neurath's own words:

> In order to be able to control money and credit transactions, it would be mandatory to introduce a moneyless payment system. This would also prevent the hoarding of money and tax evasion.
>
> . . . An economic plan would have to be the basis for all measures taken by the large organizations which are to be created. It would be mandatory to trace the movements of raw materials, energy, people and machines on their way through the economy. Therefore one needs a universal statistic that provides comprehensive overviews for entire countries and even the whole world. All specific statistics have to be incorporated into it.
>
> . . . Wages in kind and barter would again become important tools on this higher level of socio-economic organization.

> . . . [T]he central bank would have to organize agriculture, mining and industry simultaneously, supply farms with industrial products and administer agricultural production.
> . . . Socialization should not be simply from the bottom up; rather, one has to form the organizations from the top down since this would be the only way to secure that everything receives its appropriate position (quoted in Cartwright et al. 2008, 44–45).

The central bank organizing agriculture, mining, and industry simultaneously? A universal statistic keeping track of movements of raw materials, energy, people, and machines "throughout the whole world"? Workers being paid in kind and then presumably, without money, praying to God (or the bureaucracy in charge) to find a way to exchange their "wages," on favorable terms, for something they *really* needed? And bureaucrats (perhaps philosopher kings?) at the top, making sure that "everything receives its appropriate position"?

Some readers will probably react to these proposals in the same way as Max Weber, who placed Neurath politically on the "extreme left" and proclaimed his economic ideas to be an "amateurish, objectively absolutely irresponsible foolishness" (quoted in Neurath 2004, 24). According to the well-known economist Lujo Brentano, Neurath's economic plans for the future were similar to "the economic organization that may have existed in ancient Egypt, where everyone's life was directly or indirectly micromanaged by the King" (Sandner 2014, 124). The prominent Marxist Otto Bauer described Neurath as a representative of "a military and authoritarian socialism" (ibid., 134). Even the socialist Karl Kautsky was appalled and said, first, that the ideal for Neurath's proposals would be "the prison or the barracks, whose inmates get everything they need in natura" (quoted in Nemeth et al. 2008, 66), and second, that the envisaged level of state control would have to include coercion and forceful police action "with results which would be as poor as in Russia today" (ibid., 68).

But when Neurath presented his program amid the turmoil of revolutionary Munich in January 1919, the workers, soldiers, and some politicians liked it. In March, under the newly formed Hoffmann government, he was appointed director of the Central Economic Administration, a body with many important prerogatives. In April even more radical elements took power and declared the Bavarian Soviet Republic.[2] The ousted government fled the city, but Neurath stayed and kept his position.

One of the revolutionary activities Neurath was involved in was the socialization of newspapers. The justification for this move was that it was intolerable that "many members of the public are forced to read a newspaper that is politically, spiritually and intellectually alien and disgusting to them" (quoted in Cartwright et al. 2008, 49). In what way were members of the public "forced" to read something that they found "disgusting"? Isn't it more likely that this was just an excuse for the government to take away freedom of the press? Nancy Cartwright and her coauthors in their study of Neurath try valiantly to exonerate him by arguing that he was actually "opposed to censorship" (ibid., 50) and that "he stressed both then and at other times that there was no intention to limit freedom of expression in any way, but rather the converse" (246). Unfortunately, a documented public statement of his suggests the opposite:

> I will make energetic use of the authority given to me by the parliament.... The bourgeois newspapers are allowed to provide only a small part of political news. They have no right to express a political opinion. They may offer instructional or entertaining articles to the public. But only free men, i.e. socialists from the majority party up to communists, have the right to freedom of the press (quoted in Noske 1920, 136).

This kind of selective application of the freedom of the press has an eerie resemblance to Herbert Marcuse's infamous suggestion—in the true spirit of Newspeak—that genuine (or "liberating")

2 Physicist Werner Heisenberg, who was involved on the side of the forces that crushed the Bavarian Soviet Republic, later said: "Pillage and robbery, of which I myself once had direct experience, made the expression 'Räterepublik' [Soviet Republic] appear to be a synonym for lawless conditions" (Cassidy 2009, 53).

tolerance should extend only to one half of the political spectrum: "Liberating tolerance, then, would mean intolerance against movements from the Right, and toleration of movements from the Left" (Marcuse et al. 1969, 109).

Given that Gustav Noske was Neurath's enemy at the time (he was in charge of the army that suppressed the Bavarian revolution), perhaps his report of Neurath's statement should not be immediately taken at face value. Yet it is not very likely that Noske made this up out of whole cloth; if he had, Neurath would have in all likelihood vigorously reacted. But to the best of my knowledge, Neurath never disputed this damaging attribution of which he must have been aware. Besides, other sources also point out that Neurath's role in this affair was not something to be proud of, e.g., that "the government was *under the control of the extremists,* and was *forced,* for example, to undertake *under the direction of Dr. Neurath* the immediate socialization of the Bavarian newspaper publishing companies" (Lutz 1922, 139; emphasis added).

Although Neurath was offered a six-year contract at the beginning of his term as director of the Central Economic Administration, he managed to stay in office only about one month. The Bavarian Soviet Republic collapsed within weeks, which should not be surprising in light of all known facts. Among many other worrying circumstances, some very strange individuals were appointed to key positions in the government—in some cases the lunatics were running the asylum.

At one point the foreign minister of the short-lived Soviet Republic was Franz Lipp, who on one occasion sent a cable to Lenin, explaining to him that Bavaria's former prime minister had fled from Munich to Bamberg and had taken the key to the ministry toilet with him. (Lenin actually did respond but didn't offer any advice about how to recover the missing toilet key.) On another occasion Lipp sent the following letter to his colleague, the transport minister: "My dear office mate! I have declared war on Württemberg and Switzerland because these dogs did not lend me 60 locomotives at once. I am certain that we will win. Besides I will beg of the Pope, with whom I am well acquainted, for this victory" (quoted in Noske 1920, 136).

The fact that Neurath could be busily pursuing his plans for far-reaching political reforms amid this level of insanity tells us something about his own irrationality and foolishness. The Munich revolutionaries were a laughingstock around Germany at the time, and for us today certain events bring to mind Monty Python skits—with the difference that the Bavarian Soviet Republic had deadly consequences. Many people lost their lives in these events, on both sides.

While some of the revolutionary leaders were imprisoned for years or executed, Neurath got off with a relatively short sentence of eighteen months and a more lenient incarceration (at a so-called "fortress"). He served only a small part of his sentence.

Neurath was lucky to be treated so kindly. Defending himself in court, he had argued, ridiculously, that he was not involved in politics at all.[3] The court rejected this outright and in its verdict insisted that "with his high intelligence he must have been aware that through remaining in his high government office, instead of stepping down, he was in fact aiding and abetting this treasonable government" (Nemeth & Stadler 1996, 20–21). So the court linked Neurath's guilt to his being smart: He should not have allowed his reason to go on holiday. He himself admitted his responsibility in a lecture he gave in Vienna in 1920: "Though I had not intended support of the Soviet Republic I should have known that my behavior did in fact give such support" (Neurath 1973, 27). Yet some philosophers claim there was little reason to identify Neurath with the Bavarian Soviet government itself (e.g., Rudolf Haller in Uebel 1991, 26).

Neurath in Moscow

In Vienna in the 1920s, Neurath and the artist Gerd Arntz developed a method of visual presentation of statistics, which was later to be called ISOTYPE (International System of Typographic Picture

---

3 Max Weber was a witness at the trial, and although he had put in many good words for Neurath in the hope of making a lighter sentence more probable, he still couldn't help expressing surprise that Neurath did not admit the obvious and simply say: "Yes, that corresponded to my beliefs and I stayed because the government wanted to realize those ideas that I regarded as correct" (quoted in Neider 1999, 307).

Education). The main idea was to use pictures to simplify information and to present facts in a way that practically anyone could understand.

In September 1929 and February 1930, Neurath contacted VOKS, explaining the advantages of his pictorial statistics for the Soviet Union.[4] In an internal memo, VOKS concluded that Neurath's graphs would certainly be of great use for their propaganda abroad, but for the time being his asking price remained a sticking point (Köstenberger 2013, 276–77). Eventually the Soviet government accepted Neurath's overtures and invited him to establish and run an institute in Moscow that would apply his method to spread mass information in the service of the regime. The Institute of Pictorial Statistics (IZOSTAT) was born. Neurath was contractually obliged to spend two months a year at the institute in Moscow, which he did from 1931 till the end of 1934.[5]

As was usual in the Soviet Union, in addition to an administrative director IZOSTAT also had a so-called red director, basically a person appointed by the Communist Party to oversee the work and to be vigilant for the smallest signs of "counter-revolutionary activity." In addition, the responsibility for IZOSTAT was very early assigned to the Central Executive Committee, the highest governing body of the Soviet Union at the time. In charge of "methodological direction" was a special commission headed by Avel Enukidze, the secretary of the Presidium of the Central Executive Committee and one of Stalin's most trusted friends. Neurath was completely okay with all these arrangements, which left no doubt that he and members of his team would be kept on a tight leash by the Communist Party.

In a way, Neurath was the right person for the job because, like his employers, he believed statistics to be an instrument of class struggle. In an article from 1927, "Statistics and Proletariat," he

4 VOKS was an abbreviation (in Russian) for All-Union Society for Cultural Relations with Foreign Countries, which was "primarily a propaganda arm of Soviet power working in close contact with the Party hierarchy, Comintern, Commissariat Ministry of Foreign Affairs *and secret police*" (Clark 2011, 39; emphasis added).

5 Departing Moscow, Neurath could not return to Vienna because the police were looking for him there. He received a warning in a coded message sent to him from Vienna that said "Carnap is waiting for you." This meant he should avoid Austria and Germany and go to Holland via Prague, where Carnap was teaching at the time (Sigmund 2015, 264).

wrote: "Statistics is a tool of proletarian battle, statistics is a necessary element of the socialist system, statistics is a delight for the international proletariat struggling with the ruling classes" (quoted in Mayr & Schreder 2014, 137).

It appears the leaders of the Communist Party had put great faith in IZOSTAT. In Neurath's own words: "Our method met with exceptional success in the Soviet Union. In 1931 the Council of People's Commissars decreed that 'all public and co-operative organizations, unions and schools are directed to use picture statistics according to the method of Dr. Neurath'" (quoted in Cartwright et al. 2008, 71).

And indeed, the graphs produced under Neurath's directions soon appeared everywhere: in railway stations and theater foyers, on postcards, and in magazines. And, most importantly, they appeared on a daily basis in newspapers like *Izvestia* and *Pravda*, the official newspaper of the Communist Party of the Soviet Union (Stadler 1982, 217).

What was it the People's Commissars especially liked about "pictorial statistics"? Perhaps the illustration in Figure 2.1 (from Arntz et al. 1979) can help explain this.

As Chris Chizlett (1992, 303) pointed out about this and many other graphs produced by IZOSTAT, it is noteworthy that no source is given for the information presented. In fact, according to the testimony of Gerd Arntz, Neurath's main collaborator at the time, the statistical data were simply provided to IZOSTAT by the Soviet authorities and it was *impossible* to check their veracity (Sandner 2014, 231).

The particular graph reproduced in Figure 2.1 is supposed to represent the increase in crop spraying in the Soviet Union from 1931 to 1934.[6] The pictorial representation is indeed extremely simple and appears to leave no doubt about what it says, namely

6 Robin Kinross (1994, 73) thinks that since the graph is not signed "Institut IZOSTAT" and is not up to their usual standard in some other respects, it should not be taken to represent the work of Neurath's group. But his view is refuted by the fact that Neurath's main collaborator, Gerd Arntz, did include this very graph in the book describing the approach to symbols and statistics that he developed together with Neurath (Arntz et al. 1979). Let me add that in order to reprint the graph (Figure 2.1) here, I had to ask Gerd Arntz Estate for permission. It was also reproduced in Stadler 1982 (259).

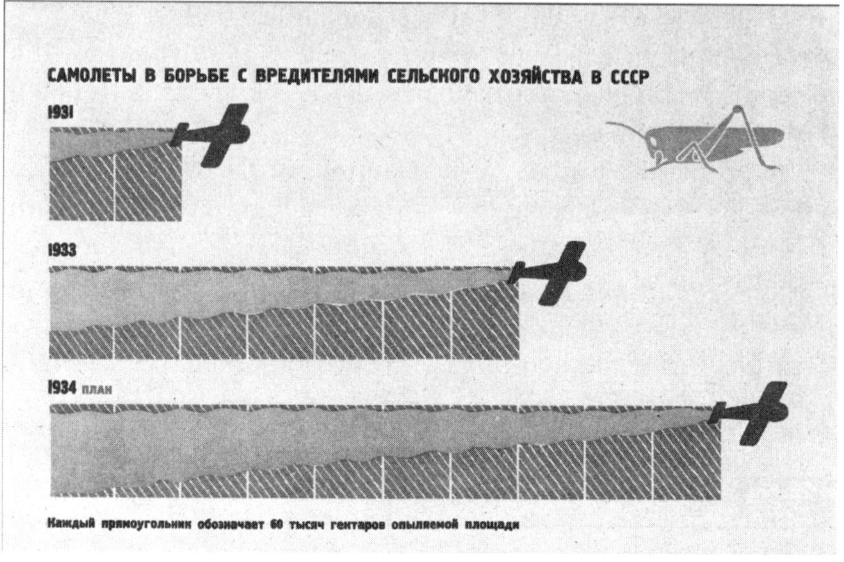

FIGURE 2.1: Praising successes of Soviet agriculture during the Holodomor

that there was considerable and impressive progress in crop spraying over this three-year period. The size of the sprayed acreage in the whole country first more than tripled and then increased another 40 percent. Splendid!

But a closer examination leads to a very different conclusion. First, notice that the year 1932 is skipped in the graph. Why? And second, the output for the year 1934 is not about what really happened but only about what was *planned.*[7] So although the picture manages to create a belief in steady and remarkable improvement, this is basically sleight of hand.

But the graph is a lie in a much more troubling way. The years that it covers include the infamous period of the great famine in the USSR. It took an especially big toll on Ukraine, where it is often referred to as "Holodomor" (murder by hunger). Scholars agree that the number of people who perished in the famine across the

7 This was not an isolated case. Neurath and his associates used to include in their graphs similar projections based merely on the wishful thinking of the Soviet government: "This visual statement of future success was a typical feature in IZOSTAT charts" (http://isotyperevisited.org/2009/09/the-second-five-year-plan-in-construction.html)

whole Soviet Union was at least 6 million (Courtois et al. 1999, 159; Naimark 2010, 70).

Hence it turns out that Neurath worked for the Soviet government and prepared graphs showing the wonderful successes of crop spraying at the very time when millions of people were starving, as a direct result of the actions of that very government.

This seems so bizarre and inhumane that the question must be raised whether he was possibly unaware about what was going on around him (in the country, let us recall, in which he lived two months a year). Ignorance as an excuse appears to be suggested by what Marie Reidemeister, Neurath's future wife, allegedly said to him some time after they had left the Soviet Union for good: "Tell me, how can you explain that they made such fools of us in Moscow? For we had not noticed anything of all those scandalous states of affairs" (quoted in Neider 1999, 330).

It is very hard, however, to square the ignorance hypothesis with what was generally known at the time, both inside and outside the Soviet Union. There were many correspondents reporting about the situation in the USSR, in very dramatic terms. For example, in 1933 Malcolm Muggeridge described what he saw with his own eyes and concluded: "The particular horror of their [Bolshevik] rule is what they have done in the villages. This, I am convinced, is one of the most monstrous crimes in history, so terrible the people in the future will scarcely be able to believe it ever happened.... It is impossible to describe the horror of it" (Muggeridge 2010, 37–38). Pierre Berland, a journalist for *Le Temps*, one of the leading daily newspapers in France, wrote on May 31, 1932: "The catastrophe, *the coming of which was obvious even to the blindest* [emphasis added], and which we predicted a year ago, has gripped the country.... The food situation is surrounded by a kind of conspiracy of silence, but the catastrophic situation, nevertheless, is the secret of Polichinelle [an open secret]." William Henry Chamberlin, a Moscow correspondent for the *Christian Science Monitor* during the famine, wrote: "To anyone who lived in Russia in 1933 and *who kept his eyes and ears open* the historicity of the famine is simply not open to question" (Chamberlin 1935, 432; emphasis added).

Furthermore, given that Neurath divided his time between Moscow and Vienna (his primary place of residence), there is simply no way he could have missed the persistent public campaign of Theodor Innitzer, the archbishop of Vienna, for assistance to the starving population in the Soviet Union. As we learn from Menger (1994, 195), Innitzer was greatly admired by many members of the Vienna Circle, who met him when he was professor of theology at the University of Vienna (Menger 1982, 98). Innitzer's appeal for help received so much publicity that it reached the pages of the *New York Times*, which devoted an article on August 23, 1933, to his warning that millions of lives would be lost without foreign aid and that the situation was so desperate, cases of cannibalism had even been reported.

These facts all point to the conclusion that if Neurath was indeed unaware of the monstrosity of the regime he was serving, this must have been a case of willful blindness.[8]

In fact, Neurath and his IZOSTAT institute occasionally went beyond the call of duty and engaged in unabashed propaganda, as when they inserted in one of their graphs (see Figure 2.2, from IZOSTAT 1933, 51) a quotation from Stalin: "The period of the dictatorship of the proletariat and the building of socialism in the USSR is a period of flowering of national cultures, socialist in content and national in form."

The terrible irony is that this graph celebrating the treatment of ethnic minorities by the Soviet regime was made at the time of the Holodomor, which is regarded by mainstream historians as a genocide against the Ukrainian people.

Another book that illustrates the ideological uses of Neurath's institute is *Pictorial Statistics and the Vienna Method* which was published in Russian and was edited by one of Neurath's closest Russian

8 There is evidence that the scales finally fell from Neurath's eyes in 1939 when he became "completely depressed" after the Hitler-Stalin pact (Neider 1999, 330). But we should also remember that those who were completely depressed by Stalin's becoming Hitler's ally in 1939 were typically those who had placed blind faith in Stalin and the Soviet Union up until the signing of the pact.

FIGURE 2.2: The concern for minorities in the USSR

collaborators. The role of Neurath's method is explained there in the following way:

> Izostatistics should become a powerful weapon of mass agitation and propaganda in the hands of the party and the working class in the period of building socialism.... the socialist statistics (yes, the socialist statistics, and not statistics in general) helps the party and the administration.... the usefulness of Neurath's method for the purposes of our socialist class statistics (because statistics like any other science cannot be non-class)... the IZOSTAT diagrams acquire a special, extremely important agitation-propagandistic meaning (Ivanitsky 1932, 2, 4, 5, 33, 45).

It is hard to believe that the Austrian members of the IZOSTAT (particularly Neurath and Arntz) were unaware of what was said in such an important book that presented their work in the Soviet Union. And yet they gladly continued churning out new graphs and were apparently not bothered at all that IZOSTAT was explicitly and repeatedly described as producing propaganda for the Party.

Whitewashing IZOSTAT

A book coauthored by the distinguished philosopher of science Nancy Cartwright gives a curiously incoherent account of Neurath's Moscow episode (72–73). Here are its four key points, each followed by my comment:

(1) "Neurath's position in Moscow does not indicate full agreement with the political system he worked for."

All right, but the fact that Neurath didn't "fully" agree with Stalin certainly does not exonerate him from working for the Soviet government in the face of widely available information about its totalitarian nature and the massive crimes it perpetrated. Saying that Neurath did not support the Bolsheviks 100 percent sounds like a lame and desperate attempt to make him less culpable for his complicity.[9] Besides, although Neurath's support for Stalin's regime

9 Interestingly, Nancy Cartwright tried the same "Look, it's not all as bad as it could have been!" defense in another philosophico-political scandal in which she was also involved. When Saif Gaddafi (son of the Libyan satrap Muammar Gaddafi) applied to a PhD program at the London School of Economics in 2003, Cartwright urged the Department of Government to accept his application although she herself said at the time that Saif could do a PhD only if he "agreed to hiring a tutor again [!] and to having lessons to improve his English" (www.woolflse.com/dl/woolf-lse-report.pdf, 32). After the Department of Government rejected Saif's application, he was nevertheless accepted by the Philosophy Department and Cartwright agreed to be his main supervisor, although the topic of his dissertation was outside her academic competence. She insisted later, rather oddly, that "there is nothing objectionable about a situation where a main supervisor is an academic who confesses she is not an expert on the matters in the thesis" (ibid., 37). And when it turned out subsequently that parts of Saif's dissertation were plagiarized, Cartwright commented: "I can hardly be confident that nobody else helped him since there's evidence that he lifted bits, but I'm confident that it isn't in the sense done by anybody else start to finish" (www.independent.co.uk/news/education/education-news/lse-insider-claims-gaddafi-donation-was-lsquooopenly-joked-aboutrsquo-2240488.html). Again, is this easily detectable instance of academic dishonesty supposed to be somehow less worrying and embarrassing (especially for the principal supervisor) just because the plagiarism did not amount to 100 percent? It would be hard to deny that Cartwright and other philosophers

may have fallen short of 100 percent, it nevertheless remained quite high. For it was during his stay in Moscow that, despite some specific criticisms, he still described the *overall success* of Soviet policy as "colossal" (Sandner 2014, 232).

> (2) "At first it may seem that Neurath simply suspended judgment on the internal politics of the Soviet Union."

Why would this seem "at first"? Why would anyone think Neurath would sign a long-term contract to work for the regime while suspending judgment about its nature? Isn't it much more logical to presume that he committed himself to work for Stalin only after he formed a not-too-unfavorable opinion about his politics?

> (3) "But early on Neurath also evidenced enthusiasm for the Moscow job."

Indeed. He was initially "deeply impressed" with Soviet economic development. He wrote to Carnap that "it is a relief to be active [in Moscow]" and "not to be part of the decay." Contrast Neurath's Moscow excitement with his statement a year earlier that "the atmosphere in Vienna smells of putrefaction."

> (4) "It seems fair to conclude that once the nature of Stalin's reign became clear Neurath suspended his previous suspension of judgment about Soviet Communism."

This is a surprising leap. Recall that the hypothesis that when Neurath started to work for the Bolsheviks he suspended judgment about the Soviet Union was at the beginning introduced merely as something that "may seem to be true at first." But then, after strong

bear a large degree of responsibility for this whole affair and for the fact that LSE was later ridiculed and referred to as the "Libyan School of Economics" and "the London School of Useful Idiots" (Martins 2011, 287).

evidence to the contrary is presented, the hypothesized initial suspension of judgment is suddenly taken as an established fact.

It very much seems as if Cartwright and her coauthors are here trying to get Neurath off the hook, at least partially, for his collaboration with Stalin's government. But their attempt does not succeed.

• • •

It is ironic that a man who, like his fellow logical empiricists, always insisted on the supreme importance of empirical evidence was nevertheless unable to perceive, or properly take into account, some simple facts that were there in broad daylight for all to see. Also, it is grotesque that someone who thought the true task of a philosopher is to build a better and more humane world ended up providing mendacious propaganda in the service of one of the most evil and oppressive political systems in modern history.

And yet the Vienna Circle is still highly and unreservedly praised for its political stance even by scholars who surely must be acquainted with these embarrassing facts. An expert on the early history of analytic philosophy writes: "With regard to their politics, however, the logical positivists were always on the side of the angels, in that they rejected both Nazism and Stalinism" (Glock 2001, 211).

On the side of the angels? Rejected Stalinism? Always? One of the leading logical positivists, and the author of their manifesto, signed a formal contract to work for Stalin's agitprop operation! And for more than two years he discharged his obligations with due diligence. Moreover, I could find no record of any fellow logical positivist ever saying a single critical word about Neurath's happy arrangement with the Council of People's Commissars. In the article about Neurath in the Stanford Encyclopedia of Philosophy, the biographical section does not mention his collaboration with the Soviet government. There is no way this kind of information would have been omitted had he done the same work in Berlin, rather than Moscow.

To continue with the analogy, here is a rhetorical question: If a doyen of a philosophical movement worked for Joseph Goebbels's

State Ministry for Propaganda without any of his fellow philosophers ever batting an eye, can we imagine a historian of philosophy claiming that members of that philosophical movement were "always on the side of the angels" and that they rejected Nazism?

CHAPTER THREE

How Philosophers of Science Promoted Leftist Pseudoscience

"Everyone is a reactionary about subjects he understands."

—Robert Conquest

Otto Neurath was just one member of the Vienna Circle. What were the political views and activities of other logical positivists? It is well known that the majority clearly leaned to the left. As Rudolf Carnap stated: "All of us in the Circle were strongly interested in social and political progress. Most of us, myself included, were socialists" (Carnap 1963, 22). We should remember that declaring oneself to be a socialist in the 1920s and 1930s was often associated with either open or tacit support for the Soviet Union, or at least reluctance to criticize it harshly.

As a curiosity, the first-ever use of the term "logical positivism" is associated with the philosopher Albert Blumberg, who had an interesting philosophical–political career path (Blumberg & Feigl 1931). Blumberg was initially connected with the Vienna Circle in the 1920s, and in the early 1930s he became a professor in the department of philosophy at Johns Hopkins University. He was also on the editorial board of the journal *Philosophy of Science*, established in 1934. In 1933 he joined the American Communist Party and was appointed the chairman of its Agitprop Committee. His commitment grew so strong that he resigned from his university position and became the secretary of the Maryland/District of Columbia branch of the Communist Party of the United States.

When Blumberg was tried in 1956 for an attempt to overthrow the American government, a witness, who at one point had been interested in joining the Party, reported that Blumberg had scoffed at his suggestion that social change could be a peaceful process. The witness claimed that Blumberg insisted that bloodshed is inevitable in a revolution and then asked him: "Are you prepared to take a rifle and fight in the streets of Baltimore?" (Pedersen 2001, 114). Another witness testified as well that Blumberg advocated violence (Belfrage 1973, 250).

No Reactionaries, Please!

Let us briefly look at the journal *Philosophy of Science*, which was (and still is) published by the Philosophy of Science Association and in which many of the classic articles of logical positivists were published. The first editor-in-chief was William Malisoff, who steered the journal for thirteen years, until his death in 1947. The prominent philosopher Ian Hacking praises Malisoff's editorship and even compares it favorably to how the journal is run today: "William Malisoff welcomed all points of view and added many a spritely and nondoctrinaire touch of his own. The grim professionalism of today had not yet taken hold of the subject" (Hacking 1996, 456).

In fact, Malisoff (and others) did *not* "welcome all points of view." This was clearly signaled in the editorial he wrote for the first issue of the journal: "We have representatives of practically all the shades of opinion . . . radicals, progressives, a few tried veterans of established philosophic fashion, *but no reactionaries*" (Malisoff 1934, 3; emphasis added).

Who were these "reactionaries" who were so explicitly excluded from the journal? The term is notorious as a designation bestowed on the left's opponents. A possible hint about what type of thinker was meant to be covered by that label is to be found in a letter from Rudolf Carnap (one of the members of the original editorial board) to Karl Popper on February 9, 1946:

> I was somewhat surprised to see your acknowledgement of [Friedrich] von Hayek. I have not read his book [*The Road to*

> *Serfdom*] myself; it is much read and discussed in this country, but praised mostly by the protagonists of free enterprise and unrestricted capitalism, while all leftists regard him as a *reactionary* (quoted in Popper 2008, 98; emphasis added).

Were Hayek and other advocates of the free market supposed to be on the blacklist? We cannot tell. It is difficult to infer, or specify in more precise terms, which views exactly were supposed to be excluded from the journal by the use of the vague word *reactionary*.

Yet we know that many people on the left at the time actually used the term to refer to mainstream, right-of-center views in American politics. For instance, after the Republicans' victory in the mid-term elections in 1946, none other than Kurt Gödel wrote in a letter to his mother: "You have probably already read about the 'landslide' result of the election here fourteen days ago. So the Republicans (i.e., the reactionaries) are now again in power (Wang 1996, 52)."[1] In a similar vein, Carnap wrote to Popper in 1946: "The picture of the world is rather distressing, is it not? Especially since this country [the United States] moves more and more in a reactionary direction" (quoted in Popper 2008, 102).

Another path is worth exploring as well. Some people will immediately associate the label "reactionary" with Lenin's book *Materialism and Empirio-Criticism*, which has the subtitle *Critical Comments on a Reactionary Philosophy*. (The word *reactionary* occurs eighty-two times in the book.) Interestingly, in one of the first issues of *Philosophy of Science* the term *reactionary* was indeed used explicitly in Lenin's sense (Muller 1934, 13). Moreover, around the same time, Philipp Frank, a prominent member of the Vienna Circle, referred to Lenin's book as the "moving philosophical *chef d'oeuvre* of contemporary Communism" (Frank 1937, 46).

A "moving philosophical *chef d'oeuvre*"? In another place Frank mentions Lenin's book and points to similarities between "diamat" (dialectical materialism) and logical positivism. He says diamat contains "many elements which are closely related to the ideas that we represent" and that something in the Soviet dialectical thinking

1 For more about Gödel's views on politics, see Chapter 5.

"is quite in line with our own ideas": e.g., that the two approaches share the struggle against metaphysics, that diamat's conception of truth "is related to American pragmatism," and that one aspect of diamat's epistemology is "very close to the viewpoint that science is based on an intersubjective language, which Neurath and Carnap have designated more precisely as the physicalistic language" (Frank 1950, 200–202). Frank even claimed that this kind of dialectical thinking (promoted by Lenin) "is demanded also by logical empiricism" (ibid., 203).

It is amazing that Frank was not aware that this non-philosophy called "dialectical materialism" was merely state-imposed ideological drivel which was probably not taken seriously even by most of its public advocates. Besides, there is no sign whatsoever that *Materialism and Empirio-Criticism* ever had a smidgen of influence on philosophy proper.

It is also baffling that Frank, who belonged to the Ernst Mach Society and who was a great admirer of Mach, could shower Lenin's polemical piece with such praise when it was obvious from Lenin's book that he had waged an attack on Mach and "Machists" using political imputations and insults, rather than relying on philosophical arguments. Here are some typical examples of Lenin's invective: Mach uses "a reactionary philosophical trick" or "verbal trickery"; is "an egregious sophist," "a graduated lackey of fideism"; idealism "*seduces* Mach himself into drawing reactionary conclusions"; Machians "are reactionaries in philosophy," "are afraid to admit the truth," "are incapable of thinking," use "a cowardly and unprincipled method"; Mach's theory is "nothing but pitiful idealist nonsense" and an instrument of "reactionary bourgeois philosophy"; Mach's claim that religious opinion is a private affair "is *in itself* servility to fideism"; Mach's philosophy "is to science what the kiss of the Christian Judas was to Christ"; "Mach's renunciation of natural-scientific materialism is a reactionary phenomenon in every respect," and so forth.

It is hard to disagree with the statement that "anyone with any philosophical sensitivity would be appalled by the crudity of Lenin's thought" (Read 2013, 91). Even Lenin's own sister was so shocked by his strident tone and gratuitous personal attacks that she asked him to tone down the vituperative outbursts. Informed about Lenin's book, Mach himself wrote in a letter to Nikolai Valentinov (a Russian socialist and an advocate of empirio-criticism) that "he found it incomprehensible and quite remarkable (*unverständlich, ganz sonderbar*) that in Russia criticism of his [Mach's] scientific views had been transferred to the political field, of which he knew nothing" (Valentinov 1968, 238). Valentinov also made the following, striking observation about Lenin's *Materialism and Empirio-Criticism*: "From this book the road goes straight, well smoothed by bulldozers, to a state philosophy, resting on the GPU-NKVD-MGB" (these abbreviations refer to successive incarnations of the apparatus of Soviet repression).

All in all, there is little doubt that, contrary to Hacking's claim, when *Philosophy of Science* was founded it did *not* "welcome all points of view." Some points of view were excluded by the ominous "No reactionaries" message, which must have been approved by the editorial board, given that it was included in the programmatic editorial in the first issue. Presumably some potential contributors to *Philosophy of Science* were thereby rebuffed.

On the other hand, the journal opened its doors to discussion of topics that one would not have expected to take up the scarce space supposedly reserved for the best work in philosophy of science. In the first issue of *Philosophy of Science* one of the two books reviewed was Friedrich Engels's *Dialectics of Nature*, published nine years earlier by the Marx-Engels Institute in Moscow. The reviewer called the book "an important contribution" and did not raise a single criticism, not even the obvious one about Engels's extremely naive and hackneyed attempts to find many examples of three laws of dialectics at work in various areas of science.

Also, the reviewer oddly distorted Einstein's famously negative opinion about the value of *Dialectics of Nature*, making it sound like Einstein's praise of that work. Einstein's comment about Engels's book was first reported in a letter the reformist socialist Eduard Bernstein wrote to the Marx-Engels Institute on November 12, 1924. Bernstein had basically asked Einstein for the "second opinion," because another prominent scholar, Leo Arons, had already given a consistently negative assessment of the value of Engels's manuscript, advising against its publication. In a move of dubious intellectual honesty the *Philosophy of Science* reviewer gave a positive spin to Einstein's comments, omitting to mention that, closely echoing Arons, Einstein said the content of the book "*was of no special interest* either from the standpoint of physics or history of physics" and that "*he could not recommend publishing* if the manuscript did not come from a historically intriguing personality" (Hecker 2000, 167; emphasis added). Far from "advising in favor of publication" (as the reviewer put it), Einstein in fact agreed with Arons and said that Engels's work, being devoid of scientific merit, could be published merely out of biographical interest.

Let me end this section by pointing to an interesting contrast. On one hand, when I was growing up in Yugoslavia, which was a one-party Communist state, most people there (including many members of the Communist Party!) used their basic common sense to dismiss the scientific illustrations of the three laws of dialectics defended in the *Dialectics of Nature* as simply ridiculous and laughable. On the other hand, just a couple of decades earlier the journal *Philosophy of Science,* with all its sophisticated experts in methodology of science, had published an unreservedly positive review of Engels's book, which contains a lot of dialectical mumbo-jumbo but has virtually zero scientific or philosophical value.[2]

The Argument from *Pravda*

If "reactionaries" were excluded from the pages of *Philosophy of Science*, were contributors at least permitted to be politically neutral? Malisoff argued against this kind of tolerance:

---

2 For instance: "Ordinary incommensurability, for instance of the circle and the straight line, is also a dialectical qualitative difference; but here it is the difference in *quantity* of *similar* magnitudes that increases the difference of *quality* to the point of incommensurability." "*Identity and difference*—the dialectical relation is already seen in the differential calculus, where dx is infinitely small, but yet is effective and does everything." "A pretty good example of the dialectics of nature is the way in which according to present-day theory the *repulsion of like* magnetic poles is explained by the attraction *of like* electric currents." (*Dialectics of Nature*, according to www.marxists.org/archive/marx/works/1883/don)

> On the whole those who are "isolationists" with regard to science, tend to reactionary political views. In specific cases of some well-meaning individuals this is very unfortunate. They mean to be "neutral," but neutrality invariably turns out in practice to be a tolerance of the supremacy of evil over the good. And that is itself evil (Malisoff 1939, 128).

This is a warning to "some well-meaning individuals": If you try to be neutral and refuse to join in condemning reactionaries, your neutrality amounts in practice to a tolerance of the supremacy of evil over the good, and consequently your conduct is also evil. Ergo, if you want to avoid being evil, you must denounce reactionaries.

Turning science into a battleground between good and evil made it inevitable that ordinary scientific standards would be corrupted by politics. And indeed, history provides a striking example of an evidently pseudoscientific view being associated with "progressive" politics and therefore being defended in what was the only philosophy of science journal at the time.

I have in mind the infamous Lysenko controversy in the Soviet Union, which Andrei Sakharov with good reason called "probably the ugliest episode in the history of contemporary science" (quoted in Popovsky 1984, viii). Trofim Lysenko was a crackpot, uneducated plant breeder, but a skillful manipulator. He couched pseudoscientific ideas about biology and agriculture in the language of the official dogma of dialectical materialism and managed to get support from the Communist Party.[3] Soon after his ascent began in the mid-1930s, some scientists who opposed his views were arrested and shot. As an illustration of his modus operandi, here is how Lysenko injected politics into scientific "discussion" in his speech at a conference in Moscow in 1935: "You know, comrades, wreckers and kulaks are located not only in your collective farms.... They are just as dangerous, just as resolute in science.... And whether he is in the academic world or not in the academic world, a class enemy is always a class enemy" (quoted in Graham 1993, 128).

---

3 "It was obvious from the debate that Lysenko's supporters did not understand the views they were criticizing" (Maynard Smith 1992, 49).

It happened that Stalin himself attended this event. At one point he interrupted Lysenko's speech, exclaiming "Bravo, comrade Lysenko, bravo!" (ibid.).

Lysenko got the full official endorsement of the Communist Party in 1948. By that time, a number of distinguished geneticists had been killed "either with or without pretreatment in a concentration camp" (Fisher 1948). Lysenko's reign in Soviet biology lasted until the fall of Khrushchev in 1964. There is strong evidence that at least eighty-three experts in biology were repressed (Joravsky 1970, 320–28).[4] The true number is probably much larger because there must have been cases of authentic repression for which no sufficiently strong evidence could be found and also because, as Joravsky explains, "I do not pretend to have searched the public record exhaustively. I searched the record until my patience was exhausted" (ibid., 317).

Looking at reactions of Western scientists to the plight of their colleagues in the USSR, 1948 was a watershed year. Even before 1948 most scholars in the West were already extremely worried about the rise of Lysenko, the support of the Communist Party for his strange ideas, and the massive persecution of biologists. But after any opposition to Lysenko was eliminated in 1948, it became impossible to deny that the Marxist ideology had destroyed any remnants of freedom of scientific investigation in biology in the USSR.

It is interesting to observe how *Philosophy of Science* reacted to this affair up to the crucial year of 1948, when the scales finally fell from almost everyone's eyes. In 1945 the journal published an article, "Soviet Science and Dialectical Materialism," by philosopher John Somerville, in which he mentioned the case of Nikolai Vavilov, the best-known Soviet biologist at the time and an opponent of Lysenko. Somerville cited stories about the persecution and even imprisonment of Vavilov, as well as many other examples of political interference in science, but he assured the

4 Notice that David Joravsky used the term *repression* in such a way that a mere dismissal from a job did not count as repression. It had to include arrest plus at least one of the following: execution, internment (in jail or concentration camp), or some kind of internal exile.

reader that "you cannot believe all that you read in the newspapers" (Somerville 1945, 27).

Amazingly, in order to dispel these fears about the fate of Vavilov and other scientists that were expressed in many Western newspapers, Somerville referred to an article from ... *Pravda*! The article, published on December 7, 1939, was authored by the philosopher M. B. Mitin, director of the Marx-Engels-Lenin Institute of the Central Committee of the Communist Party of the Soviet Union.[5] Needless to say, the article claimed that scientists in the USSR were completely free in pursuing their research and were never subject to any political pressure.

According to Somerville, the "actual facts" reported by Mitin (in 1939) "bear upon the very problems we are discussing today" (in 1945). In other words, there was no reason at all to be concerned about Vavilov's whereabouts or well-being.

When Somerville's article was published, however, Vavilov had already been dead two years. He was arrested in 1940 and sentenced to death, which was commuted to twenty years' imprisonment. He died in prison of starvation in January 1943.

Somerville could not have known all the details of Vavilov's fate in 1945, but he must have known that most well-informed scientists were extremely alarmed about what might have happened to their missing colleague and that many of them suspected he was no longer alive.[6] At the very same time, the great geneticist Theodosius Dobzhansky wrote in a letter to his colleague L. C. Dunn: "Oh, Dunn, what an indescribable tragedy has overtaken almost every one of my old colleagues and friends [in the Soviet Union]! So many of them dead, and maybe after all this is the best for them" (quoted in DeJong-Lambert 2012, 62).

To have published Somerville's article brushing off these worries and painting a rosy picture of Soviet science in the midst of one of the worst abuses of scientific freedom in history—and citing *Pravda* as one's source—was certainly a low point for *Philosophy of Science.*

---

5 Mitin will be discussed further on pp. 96–98.

6 "In fact, reliable news of Vavilov's arrest and fate had long since reached the West, as early as 1944" (Harman 2003, 323).

Even worse, not only did no one challenge Somerville's strange claims, not a single critical comment on the Lysenko affair appeared in the pages of the journal until 1949, when the ugly truth could no longer be covered up. The pro-Soviet line was pushed by the editor Malisoff in 1947, in a short note he wrote about the book *Science and the Planned State*, by the Oxford biologist John R. Baker. In one chapter Baker raised the widely shared concerns about the destruction of Soviet science by Lysenko and his Party backers. Malisoff would have none of it. Here is what he said about Baker's book:

> A vicious and intellectually dishonest work, made all the more unpalatable by its tone of outraged virtue. The author makes much of the case of the genetics controversy, taken out of the huge context of Soviet investigations, to read any number of non-sequiturs. The fantastic word "totalitarianism" leads a long list of invectives (Malisoff 1947a, 171–72).

It is unclear how taking the "huge context" into account could have possibly changed the grim picture that Baker and many other Western scholars painted, drawing on many reliable reports.

While dismissing Baker's truthful account as "a vicious and intellectually dishonest work," Malisoff profusely praised John Somerville's book *Soviet Philosophy*, which was an apology for Stalinism and which insisted that all was well with Soviet biology. Malisoff called Somerville's book "scholarly, extraordinarily clear and leaning backward to be fair" and ended the note with the call, "Hurry, get this book!" (Malisoff 1947b).

Contrast this panegyric with another review in a non-philosophy journal that described the same book as "a *defense* of the Stalinist conception of dialectical materialism" lacking "an honest, objective exposition of Soviet philosophy" because it hides from the reader "that those who remained obdurate in their convictions lost their jobs, were exiled to Siberia or a Labor camp, or even executed" (Gotesky 1947, 115).

The Silence of the Darwinists

Why didn't any other member of the *Philosophy of Science* editorial board ever raise his voice to try to counter Somerville's and Malisoff's pro-Lysenko stance with a more realistic view? After all, at that point the journal's board of editorial associates and advisors included, among others, leading biologists such as J. B. S. Haldane and H. J. Muller.

We do not know, of course, whether Haldane and Muller paid attention to what was being published in the philosophy journal on whose board they served. But if they did, or if someone drew their attention to the fact that sporadic defenses of Lysenko appeared there without a word of opposition, there are reasons to think that neither of them would have been inclined to make too much fuss about it.

Haldane had joined the Communist Party of Great Britain in 1942 and he publicly defended Lysenko at least until the end of 1949 (Harman 2003, 324). In a BBC broadcast at the end of 1948, Haldane was still unwilling to concede that Vavilov had died in prison, although he apparently knew the truth by that time (Paul 1983, 13).

Four years after Stalin's public "Bravo" to Lysenko, Haldane wrote: "In view of the decreasing support given to this branch of biology in England, it is probable that, in spite of the dismissal of several Russian workers during the last year [1939], *the prospects for genetical research are considerably better in the Soviet Union than in the British Empire*" (Paul 1983, 10; emphasis added).

Moreover, Haldane said in a "self-obituary" recorded for the BBC in 1964 a few months before his death that "in my opinion, Lysenko is a very fine biologist and some of his ideas are right."

The American geneticist H. J. Muller (who received the Nobel Prize in Physiology or Medicine in 1946) also started as a Soviet sympathizer and even moved his lab to Leningrad and later to Moscow, conducting research there from 1934 till 1937. Disillusioned after Stalin ordered attacks on his work, he returned to the West. Muller knew very well how dire the situation of Soviet scientists was but he refused to talk about these matters in public. He explained the reasons for his reluctance in a letter to Julian Huxley in 1937. It is worth quoting at length:

> I have been asked to write private letters to my geneticist friends abroad, telling them that things are going well again for genetics in U.S.S.R. & asking them to use their influence with the international committee, to have the congress held there.... While I will not do that, *neither will I do the opposite—tell the truth to the world about the situation there.* It would be too damaging to the opinion of scientists about the U.S.S.R.
>
> *I do not want to become an agent of anti-Soviet propaganda.* While what I have told you are only facts, they cannot be appraised without taking them in connection with favorable facts concerning the U.S.S.R. and its system. I know you are familiar with these, & so I can tell you the above facts, *but the mass of people can hardly see two facts at a time & so these facts might have a dangerous effect on them.* When they are finally given out it must be in just the right setting (quoted in Paul 1983; emphasis added).

Given that many other members of the editorial board also had strong leftist leanings, it may well be that some of them reasoned the same way and concluded that the noble cause of socialism was a good reason to postpone telling the uncomfortable truth about the purge of Soviet scientists until some "appropriate" time in the indefinite future.

The final result is that the preeminent journal of the philosophy of science, which was supposed to explain the intricacies of the scientific method and advance good science, ended up with a major blemish on its record. During the entire critical period up to Lysenko's total victory in 1948, while scientists in the Soviet Union were under attack by Stalinist pseudoscience and were literally fighting for their lives, the only views published in the pages of *Philosophy of Science* on this topic were formulated to whitewash the ongoing persecution and spread the message "Move on; nothing to see here."

Around the same time, another top journal also opened its space to a paean to Stalinist assaults on academic freedom. In a rare case of a major philosophy journal publishing a piece devoted exclusively to the situation in Soviet philosophy, the *Philosophical Review* published a paper by John Somerville in which he praised Stalin's "famous speech" that "played such a large role in the philosophical discussion." Then he informed his American readers that, as far as he could judge, "the inner feelings of Soviet philosophers ... are probably considerably different from what is frequently and hastily assumed from a distance." He explained: "It does not seem to them that recommendations by the party constitute an inappropriate intervention or an unwelcome intrusion" (Somerville 1946, 262).

It is easy to imagine the "inner feelings" of those scholars in the Soviet Union who retained a genuine interest in philosophy if they read in Somerville's article that they regarded the Party diktats as appropriate interventions and welcome intrusions in their discussions. And to think that this nonsense was published in a premier philosophy journal in the West!

Some logical positivists continued praising the Soviet approach to biology until so late that they could no longer claim they were uninformed about what was going on. Philipp Frank, a leading philosopher of the Vienna Circle and a member of the editorial board of *Philosophy of Science*, wrote that "the creative scientific work, particularly in chemistry, physics *and biology* ... enjoys favorable conditions for development in the USSR" (Frank 1950, 205; emphasis added). Favorable conditions in the USSR for the creative scientific work, particularly in biology? Frank's book containing that statement was published in 1950, at a time when it was public knowledge that Lysenkoism was imposed on all biologists by the state and that many of its opponents were fired, arrested, sent to labor camps, or executed. The publisher of the book was Harvard University Press.

Similarly, in his well-known biography of Einstein Frank writes: "By studying events in Russia since the seizure of power by Lenin, we can see that *no attempt was ever made to exert political influences on physical theories proper*" (Frank 1947, 257; emphasis added). It is hard to understand how Frank could have made this statement in good faith. He must have known how bad the situation was, as he had contacts both with physicists and philosophers in the Soviet Union.

Here is the flavor of these typical ideological outbursts against "incorrect" physical theories:

> One of Einstein's Soviet critics responded that deism was logically inherent in the concept of a four-dimensional space-time continuum and that therefore relativity must be rejected. He noted Hessen's defence of relativity theory, a doctrine which he condemned as "a rotten swamp" (Graham 1985, 712).

Calling the theory of relativity "a rotten swamp" surely sounds like a crude political attack, especially since this characterization appeared in a widely read publication, tightly controlled by the Party. And of course being exposed to this kind of onslaught was usually just the ominous beginning. For example, the physicist attacked in the above quotation, Boris Hessen, was soon afterward dismissed from his post as deputy director of the Physics Institute in Moscow, then arrested, and finally, after being tried for "terrorism" by a military tribunal, condemned to death and executed the same day in December 1936.

This was the usual procedure: It started with physical theories' coming under political attack, after which harsh measures were taken against the physicists themselves. Those whose understanding of physical theories was colored by their scientific specialization in the West were often treated as ideologically suspect just on that basis. The downfall of some of these top physicists began with political denunciations and ended with their losing their jobs and in some cases their lives as well (Kojevnikov 2004, 117–18). (For a partial list of physicists and philosophers of physics persecuted in the 1930s, see Joravsky 1970, 318–19.)

Judging by what Philipp Frank wrote, it would seem that no such episodes had occurred. From what he said it would follow, absurdly, that even during the worst period of Stalinist terror (the so-called Yezhovshchina), scientists were completely safe in their work as long as they steered away from putting a non-Marxist philosophical spin on their scientific opinions. Would that it were so easy!

Frank was asked to write two articles for the first edition of the *Great Soviet Encyclopedia*, which indicates he must have been regarded as very trustworthy by Soviet authorities, especially since we learn from the website of the Russian Presidential Library that "all fundamental decisions relating to work on the Encyclopedia ... had always been taken at the highest state and party level" (prlib.ru/en-us/History/Pages/Item.aspx?itemid=812). Let us not forget that the inclusion of Frank's articles in that work was already very surprising given that he had been attacked by name in the Bolshevik sacred book, *Materialism and Empirio-Criticism*.[7]

Tinker, Tailor, Philosopher ... Spy

The story of *Philosophy of Science* would not be complete without a few more words about its first editor-in-chief, William Malisoff. The Venona documents (deciphered cables between Soviet spies in the U.S. and their superiors in Moscow) reveal that Malisoff was actually a KGB agent. He had two code names: "Henry" and "Talent." The sad fact is that he spied for the Soviets not because of ideological blindness or pure loyalty to socialism but largely for a quite banal reason: money. From the KGB files we learn that when Talent was informed that a large-scale payment (which he expected) would not be forthcoming, he "took this announcement exceptionally morbidly" (Haynes & Klehr 2000, 291). He complained that the materials he had provided to the KGB yielded the Soviet Union millions of dollars while the amount he requested (but did not

7 Gerald Holton recounts an amusing episode in which Frank cleverly put Lenin's attack on him to good use. Once when Frank was visited by FBI agents who were suspicious about his leftist orientation and possible Soviet connections, "he went to his bookcase, fished out the copy of Lenin's book, and opened it to the passage where Lenin attacked him personally. As Frank ended this story, the two FBI men practically saluted him, and left speedily and satisfied" (Stadler 1993, 70). No one can blame Frank for omitting to disclose on that occasion that he had actually conceded much to Lenin's criticism and even said he wished he had formulated his view differently so as to avoid Lenin's objection (Frank 1997, 232; originally published in German in 1932).

get) was "trifling." When he threatened to withhold information from the Soviets in response to not receiving an adequate financial reward, the KGB officer Kvasnikov informed his superiors and "recommended being patient and continuing contact until Malisoff . . . calmed down."

The whole thing had a humorous side too. We are told Malisoff "had been financially able to bear the burden of the journal's occasional losses" (Churchman 1984, 21), so it follows that some of the money he received from the KGB may have been channeled into paying the costs of running the journal. And given the way *Philosophy of Science* reacted to the Lysenko affair, it appears the money was not squandered.

CHAPTER FOUR

Rudolf Carnap: Blaming the West for the Iron Curtain

> "Since the first World War Carnap stood politically very far to the left. His reaction to the Marxist critique of philosophical empiricism is worth noting: whereas he criticized traditional metaphysical philosophers very sharply, he did not attack or criticize the Marxists."
>
> —Wolfgang Stegmüller

In discussing the political opinions and actions of logical positivists, our attention inevitably turns to the indisputably most important member of that movement, Rudolf Carnap. What were his views? Where did he stand compared to the notoriously radical Neurath?

The surprising answer is that, in terms of politics, there is some evidence that in the interwar period there was no difference at all between these two philosophers. According to a credible source, Carnap once said to the philosopher Robert S. Cohen: "If you want to find out what my political views were in the twenties and thirties, read Otto Neurath's books and articles of that time; *his views were also mine*" (from Marie Neurath's preface in Neurath 1973, xiii; emphasis added).

The huge difference between the two positivists was, of course, that Carnap devoted most of his energies to scholarship and did not have the time or interest for the kind of political activism Neurath was involved in. Carnap's political engagement was restricted to being a sponsor for various leftist causes and signing political petitions. But this still tells us a lot about the man.

Carnap wrote in his diary that he once expressed "an inclination to Communism" (Nemeth & Stadler 1996, 31). This was in 1934, at the time when Stalin had already consolidated his power and immediately after the horror of the Holodomor had been reported in all media.

He never joined the Communist Party, although he supported many of its actions. Political scientist Alan Gilbert gives an interesting explanation why Carnap never became a Communist:

> Carnap rightly felt that the only decent response to McCarthyism was to join the Communist Party[!]. He tried to look it up in the Los Angeles phone book, but the Party, under attack, had gone underground and was no longer listed. So he couldn't join (Gilbert 2016).

This hilarious story is probably true because Gilbert got it from Hilary Putnam, who had worked closely with Carnap in the early fifties.

Carnap publicly supported many progressive causes and signed many petitions that appeared in the *Daily Worker*, the newspaper of the Communist Party of the United States. So what, some will say. The Communist Party was a completely legal organization. As long as the views he defended were reasonable, it should not matter much where they were published. Doesn't objecting to someone's association with Communists smack of McCarthy-era witch hunting?

Not really.[1] Consider the following analogous situation. If a person's name regularly appeared in a bulletin of the Ku Klux Klan, usually we would not regard this as acceptable for an educator at a

1 Being wary of the Communist threat by no means entailed supporting Senator Joseph McCarthy's way of fighting it. Nor, for that matter, was the opposition to McCarthyism a good reason to join the Communist Party. The journalist Steve Usdin put it very well: "Enough time has passed, I hope, for students of American history to hold two notions in their heads at the same time: Joseph McCarthy was a demagogic bully who did great damage to his country; the Communist Party of the United States was a subsidiary of the Communist Party of the Soviet Union that actively engaged in and supported espionage" (Usdin 2005, xiii).

major American university, even if there were nothing particularly problematic about specific views he advocated there (say, support for family values). The association matters.

Many people during the Cold War were suspicious of Communist Party members, as well as of fellow-travelers, because they believed that, rather than being an autonomous political organization, the Party was controlled from abroad by the totalitarian and unfriendly government of the Soviet Union. These suspicions were later conclusively confirmed by a number of historical documents. One detail that speaks volumes is that the whole archive of the Communist Party of the United States up to 1943 (when the Communist International was dissolved) is still not in America, but in Moscow.

Also, the search for Communist spies in the United States in the late 1940s and early 1950s, which was at the time often dismissed as a "witch hunt," was later shown to have been based on justified fears. In light of the declassified Venona documents and data from the Russian archives that became (briefly) accessible to Western scholars after the fall of Communism, it is no longer possible to deny that "witches" actually did exist and that, moreover, some of them were placed in very high positions of the American government.

So Carnap's frequent association with the Communist newspaper gives us at least some reason to question his judgment. But what about his stand on particular issues? This is worse.

Henry Wallace, Clueless in Kolyma (and Elsewhere)

In 1948 Carnap supported the presidential bid of Henry Wallace. Wallace had served as Roosevelt's vice president from 1941 till 1945, but he was dropped from the ticket for Roosevelt's 1944 presidential run. He served later as Secretary of Commerce in the Truman administration but was soon fired for making public statements that were regarded as too pro-Soviet. In the 1948 election Wallace ran as a candidate of the newly founded Progressive Party, garnering around 2 percent of the vote.

One reason for the lackluster response to Wallace's candidacy was that many people were troubled by what they saw as undue influence by the Communist Party on his campaign. Indeed, it was later confirmed that a number of undercover Communists had infiltrated the campaign headquarters and in some cases went so far as to insert into Wallace's speeches specific comments that were directly lifted from articles published in the *Daily Worker.* Later, in 1953, Wallace himself admitted that allowing the penetration of his party by Communists was his major mistake and that this was why many potential voters were justifiably turned off:

> There were millions of liberals who wanted to be associated with what we stood for in the Progressive Party but who did not want to be in the same Party with certain very loud-mouthed people who preached a doctrine utterly in line with the Communist Party at all times. While I did not realize it fully during the campaign, I began to realize it more and more after the campaign ended that it is impossible to have anything in the nature of a common front with the Communist Party.... My only regret is that I did not hit harder in this direction. Because I did not, the liberals felt justified in leaving us. In retrospect I cannot criticize them for so doing (quoted in Devine 2013, 288).

In a harsh retrospective judgment, Wallace later went so far as to confirm the suspicion voiced by many during the campaign that his Progressive Party had in fact turned out to be "a division of Stalin's foreign legion" (Wechsler 1953, 218). But these worries apparently never tormented Carnap nor, for that matter, Einstein or Gödel, who both also supported Wallace. Gödel wrote in a letter to Einstein on June 9, 1948: "You have perhaps heard about the great success that Henry Wallace, a close colleague of Roosevelt's, had on his campaign tour. This seems to prove yet at least that the country is not as reactionary as the present regime" (quoted in Wang 1996, 52).

Notice again the term *reactionary*. It is only from a far-left perspective that the politics of the Democrat Harry Truman could be seen as reactionary.

Anyway, the cornerstone of Wallace's campaign was his radical criticism of American foreign policy—which appealed to Carnap.

One of the most shocking events in 1948 was the Communist coup in Czechoslovakia. It was seen by a huge majority in the United States (and in the West generally) as the frightening advance of Soviet totalitarianism into Eastern Europe and the enslavement of a country that had a long tradition of democracy and civil liberties. Surprisingly, Wallace begged to differ. He actually saw this development as a justified reaction of the Soviet Union. According to the *New York Times* (March 17, 1948), Wallace claimed in a press conference that "the Communists had seized power in Czechoslovakia to protect themselves against a rightist coup started in Prague by the United States Ambassador." When it turned out that the ambassador was on leave and was not even in Prague at the time, Wallace did not back down but declared that the ambassador's expression of hope that Czechoslovakia would be able to take part in the Marshall Plan was "a clearly provocative statement and a contributing factor to the Czech crisis."[2] The ambassador's mere offer of economic assistance was a "provocative statement" that somehow justifies the Communist takeover and abolition of democracy?

This was just too much for many people who may have agreed with Wallace on some other issues. For example, Walter Mondale, a well-known Democratic Party politician and the vice president of the U.S. in the Carter administration, says that after hearing Wallace's bizarre justification of the Communist coup, he thought to himself, "I'm not going to be a part of this" (Devine 2013, 116). Many Progressive Party sympathizers were perplexed as well and withdrew their support for Wallace.

In fact, even Wallace himself soon acknowledged that his reaction to this episode had been mistaken:

> I was deeply moved by reports of friends who had visited Czechoslovakia shortly after the Communists took control. In the summer of 1949, a member of the Progressive Party visited

2 The Marshall Plan was an American initiative meant to help the recovery of European countries in the aftermath of World War II.

> Czechoslovakia and reported the dispossession of relatives whose only crime was to own a small business. No one, I was told, could amount to anything who was not an outspoken critic of the U.S. and capitalism. Only Moscow-trained Communists were allowed in positions of authority.
>
> As I look back over the past 10 years, I now feel that *my greatest mistake was in not denouncing the Communist take-over of Czechoslovakia of 1948* (Wallace 1952; emphasis added).

So Wallace realized his momentous mistake and regretted it bitterly. But not Carnap. Strange as it may sound, Carnap also blamed the West for the situation in Eastern Europe, writing to the philosopher and pronounced anti-communist Sidney Hook on March 24, 1949:

> Since our government is persistently refusing to extend good will and cooperation to the other side, I welcome the getting together of scientists and artists in an attempt to lift the Iron Curtain (*which is chiefly caused by our military threats*) and to show each other respect and good will (quoted in Reisch 2005, 282; emphasis added).

The Iron Curtain—*chiefly* caused by American military threats? That seems off the wall, to put it mildly. The suggestion is that the division of Europe, with Russian tanks protecting the puppet regimes of Poland, Czechoslovakia, East Germany, Romania, Hungary, and Bulgaria, was mainly the result of American saber-rattling. Did Carnap really believe this?

It seems he did. For his letter defending that strange hypothesis was a part of a very unfriendly exchange with Hook in which he was presumably trying to express only those views he firmly believed to be both true and rationally defensible.

Carnap had lived and taught in Prague from 1931 till 1935, but a decade or so later he showed a poor understanding of the plight of the country that had once given him hospitality. At a time when the only glimmer of hope for people in Eastern

Europe was the possibility that Western pressure would somehow ease the stranglehold of Soviet tyranny, Carnap argued that the West should stop "provoking" the USSR. Not only that, he attributed responsibility for the predicament of countries with "people's democracies" more to Truman than to Stalin. People living behind the Iron Curtain would have regarded Carnap's opinion as nothing but a bad joke.

Against the Imaginary Gulag—but Not the Real One

Another issue that created a lot of negative publicity for Wallace was his opposition to the Marshall Plan. Among other things, he said that the Marshall Plan (which he was wont to spell "Martial Plan") was a "blueprint for war" introduced by militarists and Wall Street monopolists, intended "to suppress the democratic movements in Europe" and to "leave the recipient countries fully as bankrupt as they are today," that the plan "will not fight hunger but perpetuate it … not promote recovery but indefinitely postpone it," and, last but not least, that it "would convert western Europe into a vast military camp, with freedom extinguished" (Devine 2013, 96). He also said the Berlin Airlift, which started in June 1948 was simply a smokescreen whose real purpose was to hide the attempts of monopolists to rebuild and rearm Nazi Germany. As for the Secretary of State, George Marshall, he was allegedly trying to destroy the United Nations, "using it as a forum for reckless attacks on Russia—a forum for incitement to war" (ibid., 279). And the United States was descending into fascism: "We recognize Hitlerite methods when we see them in our own land."

In contrast to this rather paranoid attitude toward the Marshall Plan and the politics of the American government, Wallace was willing to give the benefit of the doubt to Communists, once going so far as to claim "I doubt if any Marxists today [apparently including Stalin!] are as violent as Lincoln and Jefferson were in their day" (ibid., 197). This kind of cluelessness about Communism was already on display when Wallace visited Russia as vice president in 1944. After the visit he gave reports about the excellent conditions enjoyed by workers in the gold mines of Kolyma (Wallace & Steiger 1946), without realizing at all that the Potemkin villages shown to him were in fact the infamous Kolyma camps, the most dreaded part of the Soviet gulag.[3]

It was painful and hugely embarrassing for Wallace when a few years later he had to confess that at the time of his visit to Kolyma he "had not the slightest idea that there were many slave-labor camps in Siberia in 1944" and that it was Elinor Lipper, a Belgian woman who had spent eleven years as a slave-laborer in the gulag, who had to explain to him later "the great effort put forth by the Soviet authorities to pull the wool over our eyes and make Magadan into a Potemkin village for my inspection."

Wallace's public statements raised a lot of questions among political commentators about his competence as a politician and even worries about his ability to perceive some basic facts about the world. Here are some selected illustrations, all taken from major newspapers like the *Washington Post, Los Angeles Times,* and *Minneapolis Tribune* (quoted in Devine 2013): "It was somehow painful and embarrassing to see the press conference of a former Vice President of the United States turned into something hardly more edifying than the baiting of a village idiot" (131). "If Mr. Wallace had suddenly dropped from another planet, he could scarcely have spoken with more naïveté as to what is happening in the world today.... [He] does not recognize the policy of violence and the adherence to Moscow when the evidence is plainly before his eyes.... In order to justify the course he has taken, he is insulating himself in a dream world" (197). The candidate was the portrait of a man "wandering in a pink fog, a man who gropes his confused and uncertain way through a cloudlike mass of unrealities."... "These outgivings do not necessarily prove that Wallace is nutty. They may merely prove that he has been chased out on a limb by

3 Wallace claimed that miners in Kolyma received salaries four times higher than those of their counterparts in European Russia, and that this was "the evident incentive" that had brought the miners into the Far East on their three-year contracts. In reality, of course, these "contracts" were much longer than three years and they were often terminated with death.

the facts ... and does not know how to get back, except by denying that the facts exist" (280).

These widely expressed concerns about Wallace's frightening inability to grasp political realities did not bother many of his supporters, simply because they shared even those of his views that most others regarded as downright preposterous.[4] It seems that Carnap belonged to that group of uncritical supporters of Wallace, probably along with Einstein and Gödel.

In a letter to Sidney Hook in 1949, Carnap wrote: "The maintenance of peace seems to me the main problem and task today, more important even than civil liberties" (quoted in Reisch 2005, 363). In response, Hook made the obvious point that the war against Hitler had been waged on the exactly opposite principle, i.e., that when freedom was under the threat of totalitarianism, preserving civil liberties was indeed more important than peace. So why should the Western world announce a reversal of these priorities (and put peace before liberty) precisely at the time when it was confronted again with a totalitarian state, which not only had killed millions of its own people and enslaved the rest for thirty years but was also busy using its military force to subjugate other countries? An even better response to Carnap is what Albert Camus said in Stockholm in 1957 after receiving the Nobel Prize in Literature: "I think that peace is the greatest possession, but not worth entering servitude to protect" (quoted in Todd 1997, 377).

But even in those situations when Carnap did fight for civil liberties, he again had strange priorities. For example, while he blew out of all proportion fears about dangers to basic freedoms from the McCarran Internal Security Act of 1950 (about which more in a moment), he showed no evidence of being much bothered by the very real and massive oppression that was at that very time occurring in the Soviet Union and was characterized by extra-judicial

---

4 Again, Wallace should be given credit for changing his views soon after the campaign and acknowledging that his position on many issues was untenable. In an odd anticipation of President Ronald Reagan's famous "evil empire" speech of 1983, Wallace wrote in 1949 that he became more and more convinced that Russian Communism is "something utterly evil."

executions, arrests by secret police, and millions of completely innocent people starving or being imprisoned for years in labor camps.

In connection with the McCarran Act, a number of academics and other prominent people, including Carnap, wrote an open letter to President Truman on January 27, 1952, urging him to "direct the Department of Justice to cease immediately steps recently announced to establish concentration camps in the United States." The very next day the *Daily Worker* published an article under a strident headline, reproduced in Figure 4.1.

A few months later Carnap signed a similar letter addressed to congressional candidates that claimed the McCarran Act

> has already led to serious infringements of the Bill of Rights [and] is responsible for the intolerable situation in which Government agencies, *in a manner all too reminiscent of Nazi Germany,* are already preparing *concentration camps,* are holding *thought-control hearings,* are denying passports to citizens, and are deporting and refusing admission to aliens (quoted in Reisch 2005, 263; emphasis added).

Of course there were strong disagreements at the time about the wisdom of the McCarran Act. After all, President Truman (who was a "reactionary," according to Gödel) vetoed it, but his veto was overruled by a huge majority who voted in favor of it, both in the House and in the Senate, and on a bipartisan basis. So, reasonable people could indeed have different opinions about it, but they could hardly share Carnap's view that the American government was preparing "concentration camps" "in a manner all too reminiscent of Nazi Germany." Or so I will argue.

What was the McCarran Act actually? One of its most controversial provisions was the "Emergency Detention Act of 1950," which allowed, *in a time of internal security emergency*, the detention of people who there was reasonable ground to believe would commit espionage or sabotage. This is the source of the "concentration camps" scare.

Daily Worker, New York, Monday, January 28, 1952 Page 3

NOTABLES ASK TRUMAN CALL HALT TO BUILDING OF CONCENTRATION CAMPS

Officers and initiators of the National Committee to Repeal the McCarran Act in an open letter yesterday urged President Truman "to direct the Department of Justice to cease immediately steps recently announced to establish concentration camps in the United States."

The open letter, signed by among others, Nobel Prize winner Emily Greene Balch, Dr. Frank Aydelotte of the Institute for Advanced Study, Princeton, New Jersey, Dr. Linus Pauling, California Institute of Techonology, Prof. Ralph Barton Perry, Professor of Philosophy, Harvard University, and Rabbi Leo Jung, Rabbinical Council of America, said that "the McCarran Act which condemns to detention camps citizens whose only crime a state of emergency in order that the McCarran Act detention camp provisions can go into effect at once, "the need for action is imperative.

Other signers of the open letter were:

Prof. Frederick K. Boutol, University of Nebraska, Prof. G. A. Borghose, University of Chicago; Rev. John W. Bradbury, Editor of the "WatchmanExaminer"; Prof. Edgar S. Brightman, Boston University; Prof. Harold Buschman, University of Kansas City.

Also, Witter Bynner, Santa Fe, New Mexico; Dr. A. J. Carlson, University of Chicago; Prof. Rudolf Carnap University of Chicago; Rabbi Jack J. Cohen, New York City; George Cosson, Esq., former Attorney-General of Iowa.

Also: Prof. Mabel L. Cummings, Also, Rev. John Scott Everton, Dean of Chapel, Kalamazoo College, Kalmazoo, Michigan; Thomas K. Farley, director California-Arizona Conference of Methodist Youth Fellowship, Los Angeles; Rev. R. Farley Fisher, general-secretary A.M.E. Zion Church, Washington, D. C.; Hannah L. Goldberg, New York City; Prof. S. Ralph Harlow, Smith College.

Also, Prof. Fowler Harper, Yale University Law School; Rev. John Paul Jones, Union Church of Bay Ridge, Brooklyn; Dr. Erich Kahler, Princeton University; Alice Croeney, Princeton, New Jersey; Robert Morss Lovett, former Secretary Virgin Islands.

Also, Prof. Robert S. Lynd, Columbia University;Prof. Kirtley F. Mather, President of the American Association for the Advance-

FIGURE 4.1: Carnap protests against the imaginary Gulag

But it was specified that the president was authorized to proclaim the existence of an "internal security emergency" only if at least one of the following three situations occurred: (1) invasion of the territory of the United States or its possessions, (2) declaration of war by Congress, or (3) insurrection within the United States in aid of a foreign enemy. So it was not as if the law described the conditions for detention very vaguely, thereby making it easy for the president to detain his opponents at will. It clearly said: *only* in cases of invasion, declared war, or insurrection in aid of a foreign enemy.

Also, the Act ended with the following sentence: "Nothing contained in this title shall be construed to suspend or to authorize the suspension of the privilege of the writ of habeas corpus." Therefore, arbitrary detention continued to be prohibited under this law.

Let me stress again that I am not defending the passing of the McCarran Act. I am only trying to show that, given its content, the suggestion that it opened the door to Nazi-like concentration camps in the United States was ludicrous.

Many people were against this law because they thought that giving such additional powers to the executive branch could lead to encroachments on civil liberties, and that Communism was not really so great a threat to the United States as to require such legislative measures. Others reluctantly supported the Act, believing its provisions were necessary to deal with a very serious danger. Interestingly, even the liberal senator Hubert Humphrey supported the McCarran Act, saying: "We are not living in a perfect world, and... when there is a real menace to our internal security, we must be able to act with speed and certainty" (quoted in Ritchie 2011, 134). Surely Humphrey was not preparing the ground for an American Hitler!

I do not want to start a debate here about who had the better argument, opponents of the McCarran Act or its advocates. Of course, no invasion, declaration of war, or insurrection ever occurred during the Cold War, so it might seem that critics who said the Act was an overreaction to the Soviet threat were in some respects vindicated. But a precaution introduced against a certain possible threat is not shown to have been unreasonable just because the threat eventually did not materialize. We often have to make decisions under the conditions of imperfect knowledge and prepare for meeting dangers that have different degrees of probability.

Let me just mention one "close-call counterfactual" that undermines the widespread belief that the fear of Communism was hysterical and completely unreasonable. Had Roosevelt died just a few months earlier than he did, he would have been succeeded by his then vice president, Henry Wallace, who, according to his own later statement, would have chosen Laurence Duggan as his Secretary of State and Harry Dexter White as his Secretary of the Treasury. There is strong evidence that both of these men worked for the Soviets. As Christopher Andrew, professor of history at the University of Cambridge, notes:

> The fact that Roosevelt survived three months into an unprecedented fourth term in the White House, and replaced Wallace with Harry Truman as vice-president in January 1945, deprived

Soviet intelligence of what would have been its most spectacular success in penetrating a major Western government (Andrew & Mitrokhin 2000, 109–10).

The story of the letter in which Carnap and others warned about American concentration camps does not end here. It surfaced soon afterward in a much larger context. First, on July 6, 1952, the American representative to the United Nations, Walter Kotschnig, submitted to the UN Commission on Forced Labor massive documentary evidence, which the *New York Times* called "conclusive," about the large-scale slave labor in the Soviet Union. According to the report, Soviet slavery existed "on a scope unknown in the history of man" and "for the most part these slaves are not ordinary criminals but political prisoners, men and women sentenced to living death for real or suspected opposition to the Soviet regime."

Just ten days later the Soviets responded to Kotschnig's report. The interesting part in the Soviet delegate's speech is how he attempted to neutralize the accusation. He did this not by disputing the evidence of slave labor but by trying to establish some kind of moral equivalence between the two blocs and accusing the Americans of building "concentration camps" for persons arrested merely because of their "progressive" views. Obviously the letter published in the *Daily Worker* several months earlier that made the same claim and was signed by many intellectuals (including Carnap) was quite helpful in lending credibility to Soviet propaganda and deflecting world attention from the slave labor issue.

What is additionally objectionable about Carnap's political activity is that many of the protests and petitions he signed were published in the *Daily Worker*, the newspaper of the Communist Party of the United States. So it is not just that some of his criticisms of the American politics were clearly over the top, but they appeared in a publication of a party that notoriously toed the Kremlin line and glorified Stalin's rule, turning a completely blind eye to the plight of tens of millions. There was something grotesque in the behavior of those Western intellectuals who raised the alarm about the imagined American "concentration camps" for political dissidents—and who did this in a Communist newspaper that treated the issue of very real Soviet labor camps as a forbidden topic.[5]

The Rosenberg Case: Will the Real Rudolf Carnap Please Stand Up?

Carnap sometimes allowed the distinction between his own political views and the platform of the Communist Party to be blurred almost to the point of their complete fusion. This is best seen in their respective reactions to the notorious case of Julius Rosenberg and his wife Ethel, Americans who were charged with being Russian spies, sentenced to death, and executed in June 1953.

Those who at the time campaigned against the death penalty for the Rosenbergs differed among themselves in how strongly they disputed the justification of the court decision. Roughly they had to choose between the following four possible positions, listed in increasing order of strength:

1. Don't dispute the Rosenbergs' guilt; only claim that the death penalty is too harsh for what they were convicted of.
2. Claim the Rosenbergs' guilt was not proved beyond reasonable doubt.
3. Claim the Rosenbergs are innocent.
4. Claim the Rosenbergs are innocent *and* that they were framed by the government.

Obviously there is a world of difference between (1) and (4). While (1) only questions the severity of the sentence (which in the case of death penalty often makes at least some sense), (4) is

5 For anyone curious about labor camps in the USSR, it was very easy at the time to find sources revealing the grim truth. An important book was *Forced Labor in Soviet Russia* (1948) by David J. Dallin and Boris I. Nicolaevsky, which provided a great deal of specific information, including the non-comprehensive list of more than one hundred existing camps (for details, see 49–84), the organizational structure of the gulag (209), as well as extensive literature on the topic (309–19). Furthermore, even socialists criticized the Soviet Union for its widespread use of forced labor, which they also called "slavery" (e.g., Howe 1947).

committed not merely to the innocence of the convicted couple but includes also a far-fetched conspiracy theory (i.e., the claim that the government contrived the evidence against two innocent people so that a verdict of guilty was assured).

Normally anyone who was ready to go only so far as (1) would never allow his name to be used in a public campaign for (4). But it seems that Carnap did exactly this.

Here is Carnap's opinion about the Rosenberg case, which clearly amounts to no more than (1):

> The court has greatly overstated the importance of the scientific information contained in the sketches of implosion lenses by [Ethel Rosenberg's brother] David Greenglass, or by any accompanying details which a man with his very limited theoretical background was able to furnish. For this reason I feel that the severity of the sentence is out of proportion to the actual damage that could have possibly been done ("The People Speak Out—On the Rosenberg Case," FBI Archive, NY file 100-107111).

In contrast, see Figure 4.2, the short report about the campaign for the Rosenbergs published in the *Daily Worker* January 14, 1953, stating they were "innocent" and "framed," which amounts to claim (4).

Notice that Carnap's name (among others) is appended below the text, which many a reader probably took to mean that Carnap stood behind the very strong statement. (It is worth pointing out that other people on the list include Einstein and another well-known philosopher, Charles Morris.)[6]

We have two good reasons to believe that in all likelihood Carnap was not committed to (4). First, if he was, why would he then defend *only* a much weaker claim, (1)? And second, no convincing evidence existed at the time (nor later, for that matter) for

6 For some reason Einstein also allowed his name to be used for a public campaign that went much beyond what he was ready to say himself. He never claimed the Rosenbergs were innocent (Isaacson 2007, 525), let alone that they were framed.

Cry of 'Save Rosenbergs' Sweeps World Art, Science, Literary Circles

The cry 'Save The Rosenbergs' is sweeping the world and the writers, artists, musicians, scientists and educators of every country are among those urging Presidential clemency for the young couple charged with "conspiracy to commit espionage" but actually framed as "atom spies." Following is a partial list of the notables who have raised their voices against the death penalty for the innocent pair:

ACADEMICIANS:

Dr. Robert Morss Lovett
H. Hubert Wilson
Malcolm Sharp
Prof. William C. Houk
Rudolf Carnap
Paul L. Whitely
Anatol Rapoport
Roland H. Bainton
Frank W. Weymouth
Charles Morris
Harry Kelven
Stephen Love
C. Murray Branch
Mary Van Kleeck
Francis R. Walton
Dr. Katherine Dodd
Bernard M. Loomer
George Sarton
N. Coburn

FIGURE 4.2: Daily Worker: Save Rosenbergs!

a minimally responsible person to claim confidently and publicly that the Rosenbergs were both innocent *and* framed.

And yet, for all we know, Carnap never explained why he allowed his name to be used in support of a view that he probably did not fully endorse.[7] A possible (and in my opinion plausible) answer is that he had such close ties with the *Daily Worker* as well as with many Communists and fellow-travelers that he just didn't think this false attribution was an important matter. Against the background of the views Carnap shared with the extreme left (see above), this kind of misinterpretation may have been something he found easy to accept. But if this was indeed the way Carnap operated in his political activities, then he has only himself to blame if

7 It is possible, of course, that someone will eventually dig up a document in Carnap's unpublished files showing that he tried to set the record straight about this. But color me skeptical.

many people came to the conclusion that he was ideologically much closer to the Communist Party than he actually was.

• • •

At the beginning of the Cold War, Carnap was investigated by the FBI for potential subversive activities. It is easy to condemn these suspicions and find it ridiculous that the FBI had a file on a harmless professor of philosophy. I agree that there is no evidence that Carnap was involved in anything illegal, let alone that he was a spy or Soviet agent. The question might be raised, though, whether this was all so evident at the time, but I obviously cannot go deeper into this. After all, my interest is in Carnap, not the FBI.

The main point is this: Even if we conclude that the behavior of the FBI was silly, we are still left with the separate question of what we should think about Carnap's excursions into politics. I maintain that when he entered the political arena, Carnap largely abandoned those characteristics that graced his philosophical work: careful thinking, consistency, and objectivity.

CHAPTER FIVE

Einstein and Gödel: Great Minds Err Alike

"Every day, the two of them, Einstein and Gödel, would walk home together from the Institute, deep in conversation, and others watched them and wondered."

—REBECCA GOLDSTEIN

Einstein is an interesting case in the context of this book's focus on the political irrationality of philosophers. Although he was of course not strictly a philosopher, he was hugely admired by all logical positivists and philosophers of science, who thought some of his work (primarily the theory of relativity) should be also classified as an outstanding contribution to philosophy, not just to physics. He was often treated as a fellow philosopher, which is reflected in the fact that one of the early volumes of the prestigious Library of Living Philosophers was devoted to him: *Albert Einstein: Philosopher–Scientist*, published in 1949. I am not alone in pointing to this book as a signal of Einstein's standing as a philosopher (cf. Friedman 2001, 3). For one of the many articles that try to demonstrate Einstein's philosophical relevance, see Norton 2010, which analyzes some of Einstein's most important scientific contributions and argues that he "quite consciously integrated philosophical analysis into his physical theorizing."

We saw in the previous chapter that, like Carnap, Einstein supported Henry Wallace's bid for the presidency. Given Wallace's pro-Soviet views expressed during the campaign, one might wonder whether this kind of attitude is also detectable in Einstein's thinking. The answer is yes.

It is true that Einstein was often critical of the Soviet Union. Nevertheless, it cannot be denied that on certain occasions he either tried to justify, or refused to condemn, some of the darkest actions of Russian Communists (including Stalin). This is incompatible with Einstein's standard image as a humane and kindhearted sage.

A Soft Spot for Lenin . . .

This is what Einstein had to say in 1929, on the fifth anniversary of Lenin's death: "In Lenin I admire a man who has thrown all his energy into making social justice real, at the sacrifice of his own person. I do not consider his method practicable. But one thing is sure: Men like him are the guardians and reformers of the conscience of mankind" (quoted in Grundmann 2005, 253).

Notice the only thing Einstein says about the Leninist method is that he does not consider it "practicable." The German word Einstein used is *zweckmässig*, literally "conducive to the goal." So his only criticism of Lenin's method is that it would not achieve its goal. There was no condemnation or moral disapprobation of the method itself, nor even any hint that it was widely criticized as highly unethical. (If one knows that a politician killed thousands of innocent people in order to achieve his goal, usually one would not object merely that the politician's method was "impractical" or "not conducive to his goal.")

Indeed, why did Einstein praise Lenin so profusely as a "guardian and reformer of the conscience of mankind" despite evidence, easily accessible at the time, that massive atrocities had been perpetrated under his leadership during the first years of the Soviet Union? For reasons of space I will mention only two well-known sources from the 1920s that pointed to dark aspects of Lenin's politics.

In 1924 a book titled *The Red Terror in Russia, 1918–1923* appeared in Berlin (in German). The author, Sergei Melgunov, was sentenced to death by the Bolsheviks in 1919 and later, after his sentence was commuted to imprisonment, was forced into exile. The book contains a wealth of information about proclamations and actions of the Soviet government under Lenin.

An illustration is a statement by Martin Latsis, a high official of Cheka (the Soviet secret police), which was issued and widely disseminated in 1918:

> *We are eradicating bourgeoisy as a class.* Do not seek evidence during the investigation that the accused acted or spoke against [the] soviet government. The first question that you must ask would be—what class do you belong to, what is your background, upbringing, education or trade. *These questions must seal the fate of the accused* (Melgunov 1924, 45; emphasis added)

A particularly relevant section of Melgunov's book is chapter 6, "Bloody Statistics," which documents the horrors of Communist rule in detail, year by year.

I am not suggesting that Einstein had to take Melgunov's accusations at face value. My point is, rather, that in light of such and many other similar troubling reports about the Bolsheviks, a reasonable person should have been at the very least reluctant to call Lenin a "guardian and reformer of the conscience of mankind." This is especially true of Einstein, who knew he had a considerable influence on world opinion.

Another source that should have dampened Einstein's enthusiasm for Lenin was the book *Letters from Russian Prisons*, published in New York in 1925, which presented letters from many of those who had spent years under horrible conditions in labor camps just because they had expressed disagreement with the politics of the Soviet government (Berkman 1925).

The book has a section with comments from "celebrated intellectuals" from the West, including Einstein. Here is the full version of Einstein's reaction to the letters from the political prisoners:

> If you study these accounts as a reader in a peaceful, well-regulated system of government, *don't imagine that those around*

> *you are different and better than those who conduct a regime of terror in Russia.* Shudder to view this tragedy of human history where one murders out of fear that one will be murdered. It is the best, the most altruistic who are tortured and killed because their political influence is feared—*but not just in Russia.*
>
> All serious men owe a debt of gratitude to the editor of these documents. He will help to reverse this dreadful fate. After the publication of these documents the rulers of Russia will have to change their methods if they wish to continue their effort to gain moral credibility with civilized nations. They will lose all sympathy if they cannot show through a great and courageous act of liberation that they do not need to rely on bloody terror to lend support to their political ideals (in Rowe & Schulmann 2013, 412–13; emphasis added).

Two comments. First, like anyone else, Einstein obviously wanted to condemn the labor camps, but he nevertheless tried to downplay the natural revolt against those who were responsible for them. He said to people in the West who abhorred the treatment of the detainees of the early gulag: "Don't imagine that those around you are different and better than those who conduct a regime of terror in Russia!" This somehow "normalizes" the terror, suggesting, oddly, that those perpetrating it are in no way different from, nor worse than, ordinary people one meets every day. (But later, Einstein would never dream of similarly "normalizing" the behavior of the Nazi leaders, nor of the Germans as a whole for that matter.)[1]

Also, his decision when talking about torture and killings to add "but [this did] not [happen] only in Russia" again has the effect of

1 On the contrary, according to Einstein the Germans are not just different; they are actually *worse* than others. "I have not changed my attitude to the Germans, which, by the way, *dates not just from the Nazi period.* All human beings are more or less the same from birth. The Germans, however, have a far more dangerous tradition than any of the other so-called civilized nations" (Einstein's letter to Max Born, September 15, 1950; emphasis added). In a similar vein: "The Germans can be killed or constrained, but they cannot be reeducated to a democratic way of thinking or acting within a foreseeable period of time" (Einstein 1944).

normalizing the terror and neutralizing the outrage it generates.[2] This is like saying "Yes, it's terrible, but this happens elsewhere too, so there is no reason to focus too much on the Bolsheviks really."

Second, Einstein says the rulers of Russia "will lose all sympathy" if they do not renounce the terror, but this was not true of his own reaction to them. Lenin never renounced the terror, yet Einstein called him a "guardian and reformer of the conscience of mankind."

. . . and for Stalin too

In Einstein's correspondence with the physicist Max Born, the issue of the Moscow trials of the thirties came up. In an undated letter written some time in 1937 or 1938, Einstein gives his opinion:

> By the way, there are increasing signs that the Russian trials are not faked, but that there is a plot among those who look upon Stalin as a stupid reactionary who has betrayed the ideas of the revolution. Though we find it difficult to imagine this kind of internal thing, those who know Russia best are all more or less of the same opinion. I was firmly convinced to begin with that it was a case of a dictator's despotic acts, based on lies and deception, but this was a delusion (quoted in Born 1971, 126).

The amazing thing is that Einstein managed to swallow the Stalinist story *after* he had already been "firmly convinced" it was

---

2 Bertrand Russell's reaction was similar. After expressing willingness to sign letters of protest to the Soviet government, he added: "But I am not prepared to advocate any alternative government in Russia: I am persuaded that the cruelties would be at least as great under any other party" (Russell's letter of February 14, 1925, cited in Griffin 2002, 251). How on earth could Russell reach this conclusion? And, more importantly, was he aware of what he was thereby saying? If "the cruelties would be at least as great under any other party," this would mean that under the circumstances any opposition to the horrors of the Red Terror was irrational. A better political system was impossible and any change would be for the worse. Therefore, Russell's message was in fact that, despite the secret police, arbitrary executions, concentration camps, and famine, the people should have realized that, according to the principle of the lesser evil, they should actually have been grateful for having the Bolshevik rule.

"based on lies and deceptions." What kind of evidence could have convinced him to change his mind and give full credence to accusations of the infamous Stalinist prosecutor Andrey Vyshinsky?[3] It is hard to see how this conversion could have been based on rational considerations, especially since Einstein had such easy access to many credible sources of information that pointed to the weakness of the prosecution case. Speaking about the Moscow trials, it is difficult to disagree with Tony Judt's statement that "the steady stream of absurd admissions of guilt...convinced only the most nakedly servile of Communist intellectuals" (Judt 1992, 102).

And this was not the first time Einstein had reversed himself and withdrawn his support for the victims of political persecution in the Soviet Union. He did something even worse in 1931 when he used his huge fame in support of a terrible miscarriage of justice, and that time he did it *publicly*. Initially he joined a group of European intellectuals in a campaign against the prosecution of forty-eight "wreckers" in the USSR because the accusations against them seemed to him to be based on flimsy evidence and probably politically motivated. Soon, however, the Berlin journal *Das Neue Rußland* (published by the Society of Friends of the New Russia,[4] of which Einstein was a founding member) issued the following explanation by Einstein about why he had changed his mind:

> I gave my signature at the time after some hesitation because I trusted in the competency and honesty of the persons who had approached me about this signature, and also because I considered it psychologically impossible that people bearing the full responsibility for implementing technical tasks of utmost importance could purposefully harm the cause they are

---

3 The trials were public and already the way the accused were referred to was enough to indicate that it was all just a legal travesty. Among other things they were called "white guard insects," "typhus ridden lice," "accursed reptiles," "bloodthirsty monkeys," "damnable cross of fox and swine," "vermin," "useless rubbish," "stinking carrion," "foul-smelling heap of human garbage," "despicable pygmies," and "those who were once people" (Hirschfeld 2009, 20–21).

4 All these Societies of Friends of the New Russia popping up in different countries were controlled both by the Comintern and VOKS (for more about VOKS, see p. 26, footnote 4).

> supposed to be serving. Today I regret most profoundly that I gave this signature, because I have since lost confidence in the correctness of my views at that time. I was not sufficiently aware then that under the special conditions of the Soviet Union things were possible that are totally unthinkable to me under conditions familiar to me (Grundmann 2005, 254).[5]

Notice how little sense Einstein's explanation makes: He was "not sufficiently aware" that in the Soviet Union things can happen that are elsewhere "psychologically impossible" and "totally unthinkable." Yes, the USSR—a land of wonders!

Seriously, the very way that Einstein accounted for his conversion raises a grave suspicion that it was caused by something other than a rational assessment of evidence. The view he started with—and later renounced—that the insinuated sabotage did not make any psychological sense—was eminently plausible. Why was the "unthinkability" of the accusations not sufficient to counteract any of the "proofs" provided to Einstein by his pro-Soviet sources? And why didn't he mention any alleged evidence that ultimately convinced him of the wreckers' guilt?

The saddest part of Einstein's involvement is that in this particular case no evidence had been presented that could have changed his mind for the simple reason that there was no real court case at all, not even a sham Stalinist show trial. This is how the whole thing started:

> In the past September of 1930, there was an ominous rumbling across the land: forty-eight people—"wreckers in the food supply chain"—were sentenced to be shot. "Responses from workers" appeared in the newspapers: "Wreckers must be wiped from the face of the earth!" The front page of Izvestia proclaimed: "Crush the serpent beneath your heel!" and the

5 The readers of the journal were also informed that "Einstein is keeping close track of the successful advances made toward the socialist construction of the Soviet Union," and that he had declared: "Western Europe will soon be envying you." As far as I could check, Einstein never denied he said this.

> proletariat demanded that the OGPU [the early name for the security and political police of the Soviet Union] be awarded the Order of Lenin (Solzhenitsyn 2011, 68).

The first news about the arrest of forty-eight "counter-revolutionaries," mostly scientists, was published on September 22, 1930. Only three days later it was announced that all of them had been shot. Many reacted by circulating the following macabre joke: "Now the Kremlin has acted to solve the meat shortage by slaughtering forty-eight professors" (Böhler et al. 2014, 303).

Vladimir Tchernavin was associated with the "wreckers," but he was not executed. He ended up in the gulag but later managed to escape to England and write a book that is a good source of information about the whole case. He comments on the execution of his colleagues: "Such a monstrous slaughter was beyond belief: forty-eight of Russia's foremost scientists had been shot without trial. The most pessimistically inclined could not have imagined anything so horrible" (Tchernavin 1935, 80).

What would Tchernavin have thought if he had been aware that Einstein, with his public change of heart, had actually made it easier to spread the lie that the accused were criminals rather than victims of "such a monstrous slaughter"?[6] And, more interestingly, how long was the period during which Einstein occasionally expressed the belief, against his better judgment, that the accused in the Stalinist parodies of justice were guilty? The answer: at least six years (it is documented for the period between 1931 and 1937), probably longer.

Einstein revealed his soft spot for the Soviet Union on other occasions as well. For instance, the journalist and writer Isaac Don Levine, who was on good terms with Einstein for years, contacted him after the assassination of Party official Sergei Kirov in 1934

6 Intriguingly, in March 1936 Einstein and Tchernavin (together with Erwin Schrödinger) published a note in the London *Times* expressing gratitude to the Academic Assistance Council for its aid to displaced scholars. It is unlikely Tchernavin knew anything about Einstein's disgraceful role in the case of his Russian colleagues who perished just a few years earlier.

and asked him to join protests against Stalin's "retaliations" that involved the execution of many people without any investigation or trial. In his response on December 10, 1934, Einstein explained he could not join the protest because, in his opinion, its only probable effect would be in countries that were not friendly to Russia. Then he added: "Under the circumstances I regret your action and suggest you abandon it altogether."

We see that Einstein's protectiveness toward the Soviet Union went so far that he not only refused to take part in Levine's protest, he actively tried to dissuade him from organizing any public condemnation of Stalin's bloodbath.

And then came a statement from Einstein that is even more difficult to comprehend: "Consider further that the Russians have proved that their only aim is really the improvement of the lot of the Russian people, and that they can in this regard already show important achievements" (quoted in Levine 1973, 172).

Levine's response to Einstein contains a pointed retort: "I was grieved to read your statement that the only aim of the Soviet rulers is the improvement of the people's condition. How can one reconcile that belief with the fact that in 1933 from three to five million peasants were deliberately starved to death by the Stalin regime?" (ibid., 173).

How did Einstein answer that question? He did not. As Levine reports, "the letter remained unanswered, and to my grief terminated a relationship which had lasted over ten years."

The same thing happened in 1948 in a better-known debate on the same topic, between Einstein and Sidney Hook. In one letter Einstein again made a similar point about the "great merits" of the Soviet system of government:

> I am not blind to the serious weaknesses of the Russian system of government and I would not like to live under such government. But it has, on the other side, great merits and it is difficult to decide whether it would have been possible for the Russians to survive by following softer methods (quoted in Hook 1987, 471).

Predictably, Hook responded vehemently:

> Precisely what methods have you in mind? I am puzzled on what evidence anyone can assert that cultural purges and terror in astronomy, biology, art, music, literature, the social sciences, helped the Russians to survive, or how the millions of victims in concentration camps of the Soviet Union, not to speak of the wholesale executions, contributed in any way to the Russian victory over Hitler (ibid., 473).

Again, there was no reply from Einstein.

Recruitment by Remote Control

Given that Einstein was obviously not a Communist, why was he (as shown above) reluctant to criticize Stalin's rule, sometimes even urging others to keep their mouths shut about it? And why did he and some other prominent intellectuals often take part in Communist-infiltrated initiatives like, say, agreeing to be sponsors of the notorious Waldorf Peace Conference in 1949 in New York?

Even in its preparatory stages, the Waldorf Peace Conference carried the clear signature of heavy Communist involvement, and many knowledgeable political commentators suspected the primary purpose of the conference was to serve as propaganda for the USSR, presenting it as the main force for peace in the contemporary world. Even if one were not immediately convinced by warnings that participants would turn out to be useful idiots, many observers questioned the judgment of people like Einstein and Carnap (as well as others like Thomas Mann, Arthur Miller, Charlie Chaplin, Linus Pauling, and Leonard Bernstein) who agreed to be associated with a conference widely suspected of having been organized (and/or dominated) by Stalinists. It did not matter either that the State Department warned that the conference would be manipulated by the Communists and that "none of the cultural leaders of Eastern Europe would be free to express any view other than that dictated by the political authorities in Moscow."

Indeed, this is exactly what happened. Soon after the conference started, the "sponsors" had good reason to have second thoughts about their involvement. What they might have found especially troubling was the speech of the famous Russian composer Dmitri Shostakovich. His speech (if it really was his) was read by an interpreter, while Shostakovich sat next to him and "appeared nervous and uneasy" (Fay 2000, 172). The speech contained the composer's response to the recent criticism of his music by the Central Committee of the Communist Party: "The criticism brings me much good. It helps me bring my music forward." About Stravinsky, whose work had been condemned in the Soviet Union, Shostakovich concurred with the Party's opinion, saying "Stravinsky betrayed his native land and severed himself from his people by joining the camp of reactionary modern musicians."

Later it transpired that Shostakovich had tried hard to avoid participating in the conference, giving various excuses to the Soviet authorities (his health situation, criticisms of his music in editorials in *Pravda*, etc.). Then one day he was informed that he would receive "an important phone call." When the phone rang, it was Stalin on the line, politely requesting that Shostakovich join the delegation and travel to New York. Of course, this was an invitation he couldn't refuse.

But in contrast to Shostakovich, who attended the conference because otherwise his life would be in grave danger, Einstein and others did not have that excuse for their sponsorship. They had not received a phone call from Stalin and no one was in a position to threaten them. They became involved of their own free will and were even proud of it. The literary critic Morris Dickstein, in a review of a biography of Arthur Miller, neatly summarizes this phenomenon, in connection with Miller's participation in the Waldorf event:

> It was one thing... to be a radical in the 1930s. [But] to remain a fellow traveller throughout the 1940s, culminating in the notorious Stalinist-inspired Waldorf peace conference in New York in 1949, long after the crimes, purges, and repressions of

> Stalin had been exposed to the world, demanded a special kind of obtuseness (Dickstein 2009).

In fairness to Einstein, it should be noted that immediately after the Waldorf conference he realized he had made a mistake. In a letter to the mathematician Jacques Hadamard on April 7, 1949, he wrote:

> In answer to your cable I must frankly confess that, in view of my experience with the first congress of this kind in Wroclaw last August, and from what I have observed concerning the recent congress in New York, I have the strong impression that this kind of procedure does not really serve the cause of international understanding. *The reason is simply that it is more or less a Soviet enterprise and everything is managed accordingly* (in Rowe & Schulmann 2013, 481–82; emphasis added).

Still, as far as I know, Einstein never publicly acknowledged that he had changed his mind about the Waldorf conference nor divulged that he had been basically duped by the crudest Stalinist propaganda.[7]

Why *did* he change his mind, though? It is hard to tell, but it is interesting to note that only three days before Einstein wrote that letter to Hadamard, *Life* magazine published a long article headlined "Red Visitors Cause Rumpus" that ridiculed the naïveté of those who supported the conference, describing them as "ranging from hard-working fellow travelers to soft-headed do-gooders." The article ended with the following sentence: "The Communist-front organizations have been exposed often enough, however, so that by now the perennial joiner whose friends try to excuse him because he is 'just a dupe,' is clearly a superdupe."

---

7 Even the author of a recent book that documents the excesses of anti-Communism during the Cold War had to acknowledge that "the weight of evidence suggests that Waldorf was a Communist Party 'front' initiative with the blessing of the Communist Information Bureau (Cominform)" (Deery 2013, 114–15).

In contrast to Einstein, Rudolf Carnap never budged later, even in private correspondence. Twenty years after the event he was "still proud that he gave his name as a sponsor for the peace conference" (Reisch 2005, 281). One year after Waldorf, Carnap supported the 1950 Stockholm peace appeal, another initiative that was also widely regarded as a Communist front and for this reason strongly condemned even by people with impeccable leftist credentials. For example, Tage Erlander, prime minister of Sweden (and the leader of the Social Democratic Party), didn't mince words:

> We have noticed lately that communists, both in Sweden and abroad, have intensified their propaganda for the so-called Stockholm peace appeal. I must confess that it is with feelings of considerable disgust that we here in Sweden witness the brandishing of the name of our capital in this way in the international communist propaganda... The overwhelming majority of the Swedish people have no sympathy to spare for the attempts of the communists to exploit for their own ends, mankind's love for peace and abhorrence of war ("'Stockholm' Appeal Stirs Swedish Leader's Wrath," *The Milwaukee Journal*, September 9, 1950).

The German left-of-center weekly *Die Zeit* published a short article on August 3, 1950, warning about the Stockholm Peace Appeal being a Communist machination. It said at the beginning: "The white dove is a symbol of peace. No one can object to that. But if the dove suddenly appears in red plumage, there is reason to be suspicious." Carnap, however, found nothing to be suspicious about.[8]

Getting back to our question about how Einstein, Carnap, and others ended up getting involved with organizations and activities widely thought to be forums for Soviet propaganda, an obvious

8 In the same year there was a plan for another Soviet-organized peace initiative that was supposed to take place in Sheffield, but the British government refused visas to many participants. The Labour Prime Minister Clement Attlee described the event as "a bogus forum of peace with the real aim of sabotaging national defense."

suggestion would be that they, and possibly many others, had been wooed by acquaintances with moderate-sounding views who insisted that their politics were primarily progressive, resolutely anti-fascist and peace-oriented, and who carefully avoided any directly Soviet-style, crude rhetoric that could upset the people they were trying to recruit.[9]

Louis Budenz, an American former Communist turned informer, reports that this is exactly how these celebrated intellectuals were induced to associate themselves with Soviet-backed activities, and that the method even had a name—"remote control":

> The relationships with [Thomas] Mann and Einstein were established by what the Communists called "remote control," while I was still part of the Red leadership. The chain of communication with Mann ran through associates of his daughter Erika; while with Einstein, means of reaching him were set up at Princeton. In both instances, these men were persuaded to their pro-Communist stands by playing upon their hatred of Nazism. This I know from what I heard said in Politburo meetings. No more striking illustration could be found of the way well-known men and women of unquestionable integrity are deceived and exploited by the Communists (Budenz 1950, 211).

Although some may wonder whether Budenz should be regarded as a trustworthy source, in this particular case his account seems to be the most plausible as well as the most charitable explanation of how Einstein was politically manipulated into actions that served Soviet interests.

Some of Einstein's Soviet connections, however, raise more troubling questions. In a brief but richly documented article, Frederick S. Litten describes the case of Hilaire Noulens, an official of the Communist International (Comintern), who was arrested in China in 1931 because of his political activities against the regime.

---

9 "[Einstein] was an innocent man, and sometimes, I should think, taken in by fools and knaves" (Berlin 1998, 73).

Einstein repeatedly intervened on Noulens's behalf, and even sent telegrams to three U.S. senators asking for their help in this affair. Litten argues, on one hand, that it is unlikely Einstein did not know Noulens worked for the Comintern—and that, if he did not, it must have been willful ignorance on his part. On the other hand, if Einstein did know, why did he intervene, given that the man was a Soviet agent working on behalf of Stalin? Litten comments: "If one keeps in mind that communism at that time was already quite murderous, in the Soviet Union as well as in China, we are back again to the question of how much Einstein did want to know about the causes he supported" (Litten 1991).

An additional fact that might have justifiably raised suspicions about Einstein's involvement is that the address he used in correspondence about the case was c/o *Internationale Arbeiter Hilfe* (Workers International Relief), an organization founded under the auspices of the Comintern by the notorious Communist propagandist Willi Münzenberg. It seems this episode might have been one of the reasons for the FBI's later investigation of Einstein. Litten concludes: "I believe that, *temporibus illis*, Einstein had laid himself open to the possibility of being used as a relay by the Comintern and Soviet intelligence, although I don't know to what extent he had been aware of it" (ibid.).

The Nazification of America?

It should be added here that the reluctance of people who were used as instruments of Communist propaganda to criticize the totalitarian system of the Soviet Union was only one side of the coin. The other side was their tendency to picture the political situation in the United States in excessively negative terms, sometimes ridiculously so.

Some examples of such statements from Einstein: "We have come a long way toward the establishment of a Fascist regime. The similarity of general conditions here [in the United States] to those in the Germany of 1932 is quite obvious" (letter to W. Stern, January 14, 1954, quoted in Isaacson 2007, 533). "The separation [between Jews and Gentiles] is even more pronounced [in America] than it *ever* was anywhere in Western Europe, *including Germany*" (letter to Hans Mühsam, March 24, 1948, Einstein Archives 38-371; emphasis added).

Similar views were expressed by Einstein's friend, the logician Kurt Gödel, whose fame knows no bounds among philosophers, logicians, and mathematicians. John von Neumann, one of the greatest geniuses of the twentieth century, called Gödel "the greatest philosopher since Aristotle" and said about him: "Kurt Gödel's achievement in modern logic is singular and monumental—indeed it is more than a monument, it is a landmark which will remain visible far in space and time" (quoted in Dawson 1997, 195).

Here is how Gödel saw the political situation in the United States in 1951, four years after he became a U.S. citizen:

> The political situation developed wonderfully here during the holidays, and you only hear of defense of the homeland, compulsory military service, increase of taxes, increase of prices, etc. *I think, even in the blackest (or brownest) Hitler Germany, things were not that bad* (letter to his mother, January 8, 1951, quoted in Dawson 1997, 191; emphasis added).

One might think this opinion could perhaps be explained by Gödel's otherworldliness and possibly his unwillingness or lack of time to follow current events very closely. But this hypothesis is dubious. Around the same time, he wrote: "For the last two months I have been so much occupied with politics, that I had almost no time for anything else" (quoted in Wang 1990, 118).

There is evidence that Gödel was already leaning strongly to the left as a young man. For instance, Rudolf Carnap noted in his diary on October 10, 1931: "Gödel reads Lenin and Trotsky, is for planned society and socialism, and interested in the mechanism of influences in society, e.g., that of finance capital on politics" (ibid., 91).

Amazingly, just a few weeks after the erection of the Berlin Wall in 1953, Gödel's only reaction to that event (in a letter to his mother) was an attempt to *justify* the closing of the only remaining possibility for people in East Germany to flee the police state: "The wall that was erected in Berlin, this is really a culmination. But the Russians are probably right that spies and saboteurs were coming there from the West" (Gödel 2002, 203).

In a letter of July 7, 1965, he likens Charles de Gaulle to Hitler: "Why do you ask me whether I like de Gaulle? His foreign policy has a lot of similarity with Hitler" (ibid.).

And earlier, he described John F. Kennedy as encouraging the Nazis and fascists:

> With regard to the new president [Kennedy], one sees quite clearly already where his politics is leading: war in Vietnam, war in Cuba, *the belligerent Nazis or fascists* (in the form of "anticommunist" organizations) beginning to bloom, more rearmament, less press freedom, no negotiations with Khrushchev, etc. (April 30, 1961, quoted in Wang 1996, 53; emphasis added).

Notice how glibly anti-Communists are equated with "belligerent Nazis or fascists."

It is odd for several reasons that someone like Gödel would be throwing Nazi accusations at these two world leaders, each of whom in his own way showed great courage in fighting fascism during the Second World War.

First, in 1935 Gödel *himself* officially joined a fascist movement, the Fatherland Front, when membership became a condition for keeping a university position (see Figure 5.1).

Notice point no. 6, according to which a member of the Fatherland Front is "bound by his honor to show unconditional loyalty and obedience to the Führer."[10] It should be stressed that Gödel's livelihood at the time did not depend on his keeping that job in Vienna. The fame of his proof of the incompleteness theorem meant he could count on receiving invitations and job offers

10 Here *Führer* did not refer to Hitler but to the leader of the Fatherland Front, an "Austrofascist" political organization that suspended democracy and introduced a one-party state.

080146

Die V. F. ist berufen, die Trägerin des österreichischen Staatsgedankens zu sein. Ihr Ziel ist die politische Zusammenfassung aller Staatsangehörigen, die auf dem Boden eines **selbständigen, christlichen, deutschen, berufsständisch** gegliederten Bundesstaates Österreich stehen und sich dem Führer der V. F. oder dem von diesem bestimmten Nachfolger unterstellen. Jeder, der der V. F. beitritt, bekennt sich damit zu ihren politischen Zielen, erklärt, diese jederzeit vertreten zu wollen und verpflichtet sich bei seiner Ehre im besonderen:

1. Für Freiheit, Ehre und Ansehen Österreichs einzutreten;
2. der Volksgemeinschaft zu dienen;
3. Heimattreue und Heimatliebe selbst zu pflegen und bei anderen zu fördern;
4. Uneinigkeit und Hader beiseitezustellen;
5. keiner Vereinigung anzugehören, die den Klassen- oder Kulturkampf will oder deren Ziele sonst den Zielen der V. F. widersprechen;
6. dem Führer unbedingte Treue und Gehorsam zu leisten;
7. in Auftreten und Lebensführung der Würde der vaterländischen Bewegung zu entsprechen;
8. Das Abzeichen der V. F. zu tragen und zu schützen.

23

VATERLÄNDISCHE FRONT

Mitgliedskarte

C-Nr. 228456

für

Herrn Dr. Kurt Gödel

Beruf: Priv. Dozent Geburtsjahr: 1906

Wohnort: WIEN

VIII. Josefstädterstr. 43

Bezirk: Josefstadt

Beigetreten am: 15. IX. 1935.

FIGURE 5.1: Gödel's membership card

in many countries, especially in the United States. (He already had a visiting position at the Institute for Advanced Study at Princeton in 1934.) In fact, it was as late as 1941, well into the ninth year of Hitler's rule and in the middle of the war, that Gödel was still inquiring at the German consulate in New York about whether he could get a salaried position in Nazi Germany in case his application for the extension of his leave of absence was rejected by German authorities (Sigmund et al. 2006, 84).

Another potentially relevant fact is that Gödel's wife apparently applied for membership in the Nazi Party in 1938, after the Anschluss (ibid., 60). Although presumably he must have known about this, there is no record of his reaction. Nor do we know what he thought about the annexation of Austria:

> Of Gödel's letter to [American mathematician Oswald] Veblen only a burnt fragment has survived; it is dated 26 March [1938], just thirteen days after Hitler's Anschluß [309]. It would be interesting to know what, if anything, Gödel had to

say about that event, or what immediate effect it had on his life or work, but, incredibly, there is no mention of the Nazi takeover in any of Gödel's correspondence (ibid., 127).

At the beginning of World War II, Gödel was asked by the Austrian physicist Hans Thirring to warn Einstein that Nazi Germany might develop a nuclear weapon—but Gödel never transmitted the message.[11] So we see that when he was in a position to do something to support the anti-Nazi coalition, he failed to act. (For the awkward reasons he gave later to explain his passivity, see Sigmund et al. 2006, 143.)

To the dismay of many of his friends, Gödel traveled from the safety of Princeton to post-Anschluss Austria in 1939 with the aim of convincing the Nazi authorities there to renew his university lectureship. He must have been aware that the condition for taking up the lectureship was signing an oath of loyalty and obedience to Adolf Hitler.

It is hard to fathom why Gödel wanted to go back to the city from which all other members of the Vienna Circle had escaped in any way they could and where even the university came to be almost completely Nazified.[12] According to Karl Menger's report about the situation in Vienna a year or two before Gödel's visit, the percentage of Nazis among mathematicians he was in contact with (apart from some of his pupils) was not far from 100 percent (quoted in Goldstein 2005, 226). During that visit Gödel had no qualms about adapting to the "new order" and occasionally even ending a note with "Heil Hitler!" (see Figure 5.2, from Dawson et al. 2006, 66).[13]

---

11 Thirring did not know that Einstein had already been warned about that possibility by the Hungarian physicist Leo Szilard, who had moved to the United States in 1938.

12 "Even after World War II began in September 1939, he apparently still wanted to remain in Vienna. In November 1939 he and [his wife] Adele bought an apartment there and spent a good deal of money improving it.... He even considered obtaining a position in industrial research in the autumn of 1939" (Wang 1996, 29).

13 Tellingly, in response to Gödel's application for a *Dozentur neuer Ordnung* that was filed on September 25, 1939 (after the start of the war and when Austria was firmly a part of the Third Reich), the *Dozentenbundsführer* reported that Gödel "was not known ever to have uttered a single word... against the National Socialist movement although he himself moved in Jewish-liberal circles" (Kreisel 1980, 156).

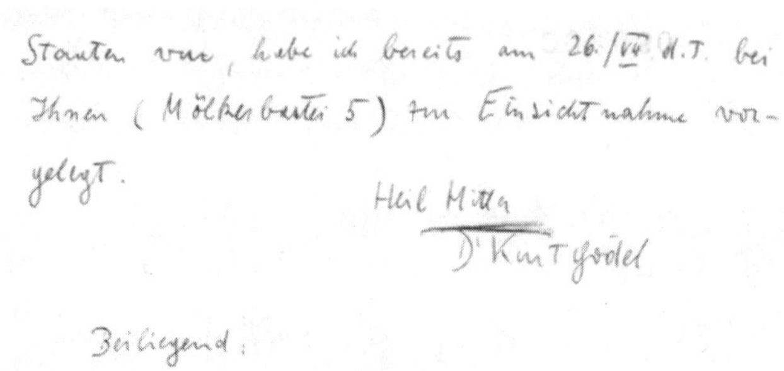

Staaten vor, habe ich bereits am 26./VII. d.T. bei Ihnen (Mölkerbastei 5) zur Einsichtnahme vorgelegt.

Heil Hitler

Dr Kurt Gödel

Beiliegend:

FIGURE 5.2: Gödel goes with the flow

In the end, it appears that Gödel left Vienna mainly because he was worried about his personal safety. He was once attacked in the street because he was mistaken for a Jew and he was also in danger of being drafted into the German army after he was unexpectedly declared to be fit for military service.

Months after Gödel was back at Princeton his application was finally approved. In the document issued on June 28, 1940, "in the name of the Führer," he was officially declared to be a lecturer "of the new order." He was also assured that he would enjoy the special protection of the Führer (Sigmund 2015, 311). And this time *Führer* did refer to Hitler.

• • •

Einstein and Gödel became friends at the Institute for Advanced Study at Princeton and they had similar opinions about the postwar political situation. When it came to their critical attitudes toward the United States, their views were "nearly indistinguishable" (Kennedy 2007, 74).

Now it is easy to understand that reasonable people could find some aspects of American politics in the late forties and early fifties worrying or deserving condemnation. Many would especially single out the methods of Senator Joseph McCarthy in his clumsy and counterproductive attempts to deal with the dangers of Communist infiltration.[14] But to suggest that things in America were at that time

14 In an interesting twist, the historian Fred Siegel argues that McCarthy actually did a huge service to the American left: "McCarthy was a great and long-lasting gift to the

worse than in the "blackest (or brownest) Hitler Germany" or that the separation of Jews and non-Jews was "even more pronounced" in America than in the Third Reich—this borders on insanity. No, this actually crosses the border.

And yet these opinions come from two of the greatest minds of the twentieth century.

American left. He allowed apologists for Stalin's murderous regime to present themselves as innocent victims of Main Street's prejudices. Even more important in the long run, McCarthyism meant that America's Communists were never required to explain themselves. This would become a matter of considerable import when a so-called New Left emerged in the 1960s" (Siegel 2013, 96).

CHAPTER SIX

Ludwig Wittgenstein: To Russia with Love

"Never stay up on the barren heights of cleverness but come down into the green valleys of silliness."

—Ludwig Wittgenstein

Ludwig Wittgenstein is widely regarded as the twentieth-century genius par excellence. What about his politics? As with many aspects of his philosophy, his political views are also hard to pin down. Almost the only evidence we have consists of casual remarks he made to his friends, which have been passed down to us with varying degrees of reliability.

Nevertheless, I will try to show that it is reasonable to infer that Wittgenstein had strong sympathies for the Soviet political regime of the thirties. Several pieces of evidence, which individually may be difficult to interpret with certainty, converge to support this conclusion. But there is also one specific, verifiable fact (to be introduced last) which has a lot of probative force on its own and which strengthens the argument considerably.

Language Games at the Soviet Embassy

Wittgenstein was born in Vienna in 1889. After the publication of his *Tractatus Logico-Philosophicus* in 1921 he achieved something of a cult status, in philosophy and beyond. When Wittgenstein returned to Cambridge in 1929, John Maynard Keynes wrote to his wife: "Well, God has arrived. I met him on the 5:15 train." Soon Wittgenstein became a philosophy lecturer at Cambridge University.

An important event for our purposes is his visit to the Soviet Union in 1935. At that time he was even seriously considering the possibility of moving there permanently. Ray Monk in his excellent biography of Wittgenstein sets the stage for us:

> The summer of 1935 was the time when Marxism became, for the undergraduates at Cambridge, the most important intellectual force in the university, and when many students and dons visited the Soviet Union in the spirit of pilgrimage.... Despite the fact that Wittgenstein was never at any time a Marxist, he was perceived as a sympathetic figure by the students who formed the core of the Cambridge Communist Party, many of whom...attended his lectures (Monk 1990, 348).

Monk suggests that "Wittgenstein's reasons for wanting to visit Russia were very different" from those of his Communist acquaintances at Cambridge. I am not so sure, for reasons I will explain in a moment.

Wittgenstein's initial efforts to get a Soviet visa were unsuccessful. So on July 6, 1935, he wrote a letter to his friend Keynes to ask for help:

> [I]t might be useful for me to get an introduction from you to [Ivan] Maisky [the Soviet ambassador in the United Kingdom]. ...You would have to say in your introduction that I am your personal friend and that you are sure that I am in no way politically dangerous (that is, if this is your opinion).

Keynes wrote a letter of introduction to Maisky on July 10 and sent a copy to Wittgenstein. The key part: "[Wittgenstein] is not a member of the Communist Party, but has strong sympathies with the way of life which he believes the new régime in Russia stands for."

Since it is well known how sensitive Wittgenstein was about personal honesty and how much he hated duplicity and dissembling, the fact that he accepted Keynes's statement without a murmur tells us he probably thought it was a good description of himself.

Notice that the statement does not say anything about Wittgenstein's love of, say, Tolstoy, Russian culture, the "Slavic soul," or anything like that. No, it cites his strong sympathies for the way of life he believes *the new régime in Russia stands for.* This is hard to interpret in any other way than meaning Wittgenstein had strong sympathies for Russian Communism. And if Wittgenstein did not mind Keynes's describing him this way to the Soviet ambassador, then perhaps neither should we. As I said, it is possible this was a false statement that Wittgenstein let pass just to obtain a visa, but it seems to me that resorting to such a crass maneuver would be very much out of character for him.

Also, in asking Keynes to let Maisky know he was "in no way politically dangerous," Wittgenstein's message was clear: Please explain to Maisky that, if I am allowed to go to the Soviet Union, the authorities there can rest assured I will never be a troublemaker and will refrain from criticizing their policies or causing problems for them in other ways.

But why would Wittgenstein promise such a thing? Remember, this request of his was being made after millions had died from the government-caused famine in Ukraine and other parts of the USSR, when a large number of kulaks were being arrested and liquidated, when many people were executed without trial or after kangaroo court proceedings. Why would he want to profess his political innocuousness when approaching a high official of a government with such a monstrous record? Moreover, why would he wish to go to a country where such massive brutalities were being committed by the government on a daily basis, especially if it was not a tourist visit but a plan to settle there and start a new life?[1]

---

1 When the American sociologist Lewis Feuer told his mother he was planning a very short visit to the Soviet Union (and this was ten years after Stalin's death!), she asked: "Why do you want to go there? People would do anything just to get out of it" (Feuer 1988, 52–53).

Wittgenstein must have been aware that only a few months before he wrote the letter to Keynes, a huge uproar had erupted in England over large-scale summary executions in the Soviet Union after the Kirov murder. Given Wittgenstein's intense interest in Russia, he probably also knew that when representatives of trade unions and the Labor Party in England publicly protested at the Soviet Embassy against these atrocities, it was Maisky, of all people, who defended those killings, arguing that under the circumstances the Soviet authorities found it imperative to "expedite" the investigation of the Kirov murder.[2] But if Wittgenstein knew about this episode—and given his interest it would be strange if the news didn't reach him in one way or another—it seems it did not bother him enough to give him qualms about trying to establish a contact.

Speaking of Maisky, I cannot resist making a short digression to report an incident that looks very much like a high-profile tit-for-tat exchange and that has so far escaped the attention of philosophers (and others). As noted, in 1935 Maisky was asked by Keynes to do a favor for his philosopher colleague, Wittgenstein. But it appears that in 1944 it was payback time: Now Keynes was asked by Maisky to do a favor for Maisky's philosopher comrade, Mark Borisovich Mitin.

Briefly, Keynes was asked to use his influence to help Mitin publish a paper glorifying the Stalinist philosophy of dialectical materialism in *Philosophy*, one of the leading philosophy journals in England. Keynes complied, and the editor of *Philosophy*, for reasons unknown, also agreed to cooperate (see editor's note in Mitin 1944).

The reader may remember Mitin (see p. 45) as the author of a *Pravda* article claiming that Soviet biologists were subject to no political pressure, and he made that statement at the very time Lysenko's opponents were being arrested, sent to labor camps, and murdered. Here is how Mitin explained, in 1936, the core of his philosophical method: "I was guided [in 1931] by a single idea: how better to understand every word and thought of our beloved

2 See the report "Labour and Soviet Executions" in the *Times* of London, January 3, 1935.

and wise teacher, Comrade Stalin, and how to... apply them to the solution of philosophical problems" (quoted in Kline 2012, 305).

No doubt this was the best way to become a Marxist-Leninist in good standing. And indeed, Mitin soon became a top philosopher in the USSR, helped Stalin write sections of *A Brief History of the All-Union Communist Party of Bolsheviks,* successfully accused other philosophers of sabotage and counterrevolutionary activity (which was of course accompanied by repressive measures against them), became a member of the Central Committee of the Communist Party, and so on.[3]

What was Mitin's article in *Philosophy* about? Titled "Twenty-Five Years of Philosophy in the USSR," it claimed, among other things, that "philosophy has been raised to an unparalleled level in the Soviet Union" and that "many problems in philosophy which are being argued by outstanding philosophers abroad have been solved here on the basis of dialectical materialism." The reader is also informed that "from 1917 to 1938 in the Soviet Union 327,200,000 copies of the works of Marx, Engels, Lenin and Stalin have been issued." And yes, there are several paragraphs praising Lysenko's theories as well.

To sum up, my hypothesis is that the tit-for-tat exchange of services (involving philosophers) was conducted in two separate stages. First, Keynes incurred a debt to Maisky via the following causal sequence: Wittgenstein's request → Keynes' mediation → Maisky's intervention → Wittgenstein goes to Russia. In the second round the debt is repaid along the path: Maisky's request →Keynes' mediation → Editor's decision → Mitin publishes an article in *Philosophy*. Wouldn't it be grotesquely ironic if my guess is correct and if the price of Wittgenstein's visit to the Soviet Union consisted

---

3 One of the philosophers who perished in the purges was Jan Sten, whom Stalin had asked in the mid-1920s to teach him about Hegelian dialectics. They met twice a week for some time, but later the teacher was rewarded for his efforts by being killed in Lefortovo prison on June 19, 1937. Sten's fall from grace created a problem, as his long article "Dialectical Materialism" was scheduled to appear in a forthcoming volume of the *Great Soviet Encyclopedia.* The problem was solved simply by keeping the body of the article unchanged and replacing Sten's name with that of another author: M. B. Mitin (Medvedev 1989, 439).

in a major Western philosophical journal agreeing to publish the Marxist drivel of one of Stalin's henchmen?

Needless to say, even knowledgeable philosophers at the time were perfectly aware that dialectical materialism was gibberish. For instance, had the editors of *Philosophy* consulted Isaiah Berlin (indisputably an expert on Marxism and Russian thought) there is no way he would have recommended publishing Mitin's piece. This is what he thought about this kind of "philosophy":

> Communists of first-class intellectual ability had nothing to do with Marxist philosophy or dialectical materialism or anything of that kind. Russia? Well, I've read Russian and I can testify to the fact that nothing poured out except bureaucratic gibberish, absolutely mechanical stuff, which wasn't up to any kind of intellectual standard at all (Hampshire & Berlin 1972, from 7:19). [A]s I think Professor Ayer would corroborate, the formal pronouncements of Soviet philosophers... are quite worthless. They do not express anything that their authors may in fact be thinking, but are plainly written for or by them by mechanical expounders of the official doctrine (Berlin 2011, 627).

The Attractions of Stalinism

What was Wittgenstein's impression of the Soviet Union? In his well-known *Biographical Sketch*, Georg Henrik von Wright, who was Wittgenstein's successor at Cambridge, his friend, and one of his literary executors, writes: "He visited Moscow and Leningrad in September [1935] and apparently was pleased with the visit" (Malcolm 2001, 15). That Wittgenstein's reaction to what he saw was not unfavorable is confirmed by the fact that two years later he considered going to Russia again (Engelmann 1967, 59). Ray Monk has a puzzling view of Wittgenstein's relation to the Soviet Union. Monk first says: "[E]ven after the show trials of 1936, the worsening of relations between Russia and the West and the Nazi-Soviet Pact of 1939, Wittgenstein continued to express his sympathy with the Soviet regime—so much so that he was taken by some of his students at Cambridge to be a 'Stalinist'" and then continues: "This label is, of course, nonsense" (Monk 1990, 354).

But why would it be nonsense? Monk does not say. In fact, the opposite seems to be true. It is disputing the label "Stalinist" that is nonsensical, under the circumstances. Remaining sympathetic to the Soviet regime after the show trials of 1936 and the Nazi–Soviet Pact of 1939 implies—in the absence of countervailing evidence—being a Stalinist. (And Monk does not provide any countervailing evidence.)

According to A. C. Jackson,[4] an Australian philosopher and Wittgenstein's former student and follower, Wittgenstein was regarded as a Stalinist "by those who knew him well" (Moran 1972, 92). In a later conversation Jackson went further and assured his interviewer that "Wittgenstein's politics were ultra-left wing and... he had strong sympathy for Stalin and the Soviet Union" (Cornish 1998, 49).

Interestingly, when Elizabeth Anscombe, one of Wittgenstein's most trusted friends and collaborators, was directly asked whether those in his close circle saw him as a Stalinist, she actually did not deny it at all but resorted to equivocation (Moran 1972, 92). This is telling because as one of Wittgenstein's greatest admirers and defenders of his legacy,[5] in all likelihood she would have reacted vigorously had she thought the label was "nonsense." Therefore the best comment on Anscombe's reply is to say: The lady doth protest too little, methinks.

It is worth stressing that many of Wittgenstein's friends were Communists or fellow-travelers, so it would not be surprising if some of them had infected him with the Stalinist bug. Take Piero Sraffa, an Italian economist Wittgenstein met with once a week for discussion over several years during the time they were both at

---

4 Jackson is probably best known for being the father of a much more prominent (contemporary) philosopher, Frank Jackson. Another curiosity about Jackson *père* is that Wittgenstein is reported to have once said to him: "We sweat blood to make progress in philosophy and what is the result? It is people like you, Jackson!" (quoted in Dilman 1984, 206).

5 "[Anscombe] was [Wittgenstein's] translator, his interpreter and his *leading disciple and spokesman* in Oxford at the time" (Searle 2015, 184; emphasis added).

Cambridge. Wittgenstein acknowledged his indebtedness to Sraffa in the preface to *Philosophical Investigations*, stating that Sraffa gave a stimulus for the most consequential ideas of that book.

Sraffa visited the Soviet Union a few years before Wittgenstein and came back "enthusiastic and very confident about the future of the Soviet system" (Potier 1991, 26). Might this enthusiasm have rubbed off on Wittgenstein? After all, Sraffa had a huge influence on him. Wittgenstein once said that "his discussions with Sraffa made him feel like a tree from which all branches had been cut" (Malcolm 2001, 14–15).

It speaks volumes about Sraffa's political views that, according to former president of Italy (and former Communist) Giorgio Napolitano, Sraffa maintained regular contacts with the Italian Communist Party: "whenever he came to Rome, he never missed meeting with Togliatti and other [Communist] leaders" (Napolitano 2007, 411). As we know now on the basis of documents from Russian archives that became accessible after the collapse of the Soviet Union, Palmiro Togliatti was a hardline Stalinist. For example, he secretly asked the authorities in Moscow whether the Italian Communist Party should plan for an armed resurrection in case the Popular Front won the election in 1948 and their victory were challenged by "reactionaries" (Agarossi & Zaslavsky 2011, 255–56). Also, he sided with Stalinists after Khrushchev's 1956 speech in which the cult of Stalin was denounced and advocated Soviet intervention in Hungary even before the Kremlin had made the decision about it.[6] When his Italian comrades deviated from the Party line in private conversations with him, Togliatti reported them to the Russian ambassador.

The fact that Sraffa kept such close contacts with the Italian Communist Party, which "received more Soviet financing and for a longer time than any other European or American Communist Party in the twentieth century" (ibid., 287) and that he regularly

6 "Inside the Soviet Union, Soviet propaganda employed Togliatti's telegram to justify military intervention in Hungary" (Agarossi & Zaslavsky 2011, 314). "Insofar as Togliatti influenced the Soviet leadership during the Hungarian crisis, through his secret telegram of 30th October 1956 to the CPSU, it was in the direction of a harsher and more ruthless approach to Nagy and the insurgents" (Flett 2007, 126).

met its leaders who had such impeccable Stalinist credentials certainly tells us something about the man himself and the extent of his leftist loyalties. And yet this was the person "whose opinion Wittgenstein valued above all others on questions of politics" (Monk 1990, 343) and who informed Wittgenstein about current affairs, because Wittgenstein disliked reading newspapers (Kanterian 2007, 120).

Let us look at some reminiscences from people who knew Wittgenstein. It should be stressed that these were all his personal friends, so any bias would be expected to be in his favor.

> The atmosphere of Stalinism contained something that attracted him: a total destruction of early twentieth-century social forms was required (he thought) if there was to be any improvement. "*Die Leidenschaft verspricht etwas,*" he said to [Austrian philosopher Friedrich] Waismann: the passion that infused society there meant that some good could come from it (McGuinness 2002, 45).
>
> Fania Pascal had the impression that the *sufferings of so many* in the Russia of the 1920s and 1930s were accepted by Wittgenstein as *an accompaniment, relatively unimportant, of the affirmation of a new society.* Misery there would have been anyway: now at least it was for a purpose (ibid.; emphasis added).
>
> These attitudes did not dispose him to think well of the British government or of its attitude towards the European situation. He looked at a picture of them—'a lot of wealthy old men'—and contrasted them (God forgive him!) with Stalin (ibid., 46).
>
> On political questions, from 1939 onwards anyway, Wittgenstein was generally sympathetic with the Russian communists. . . . I loathed Stalinism from 1937 onwards (or earlier) and I used to disagree with Wittgenstein's judgments on Russia on this account (Rush Rhees, quoted in Moran 1972, 95).
>
> If you spoke of regimentation of Russian workers, of workers not being free to leave or change their jobs, or perhaps of *labor camps,* Wittgenstein was *not impressed.* It would be terrible if the mass of the people there—or in any society—had no regular

> work. He also thought it would be terrible if the society were ridden by "class distinctions," although he said less about this. "On the other hand, *tyranny...?*"—with a questioning gesture, shrugging his shoulders—"*doesn't make me feel indignant*" (Rhees 1984, 205; emphasis added).

If the existence of labor camps did not impress Wittgenstein, nor did tyranny make him indignant, he probably did not share that high regard for human liberty that usually makes people outraged at totalitarian oppression. Likewise, if the "sufferings of so many" are regarded as just "an accompaniment," and "relatively unimportant" at that, then it becomes easier to justify rougher methods of building "a new society." And it appears that this is precisely what Wittgenstein did.

His friend Maurice Drury says Wittgenstein once told him: "People have accused Stalin of having betrayed the Russian Revolution. But they have no idea about the problems that Stalin had to deal with; and the dangers he saw threatening Russia" (quoted in Rhees 1984, 144).

Two comments should suffice. First, Wittgenstein's excuse is exactly how Stalinists themselves typically tried to justify Stalin's actions when it was no longer possible to deny the grim truth. And second, it is ludicrous to suggest that it was necessary to kill millions and send millions of others to the gulag in order to achieve any legitimate political goal.[7]

Here is another recollection of Wittgenstein, from his student Theodore Redpath:

> One evening I saw an English film in which Ralph Richardson took the part of a landowner, who seemed to me a thoroughly decent sort of chap, but who was morally condemned by the

---

7 When Clark Glymour (2011) claims that Pol Pot was in a way a product of irresponsible continental philosophers and their "remoteness from analytic thought," he gives as an example Merleau-Ponty, to whom he attributes the belief that "Stalin's mass murders were regrettable, but necessary to the advance of socialism." But we see in the above quotation that Wittgenstein, who was at the very center of "analytic thought," defended Stalin in a very similar way.

> film, apparently simply for being a landowner. This struck me as grossly unfair, and not long afterwards I happened to tell Wittgenstein what I thought. His reply struck me, as so much of what he said used to do. *He said that simply being a landowner could have been quite bad enough* (1990, 36–37; emphasis added).

Now, if one believes that *merely* being a landowner can be "quite bad enough," hasn't one thereby made a giant step toward condemning kulaks? And isn't one then already on the path of finding at least some justification for Stalin's policy of dekulakization ("liquidation of kulaks as a class")?

Philosophical Genius Opposes the War against Hitler

In an article in the *New York Review of Books*, the physicist Freeman Dyson writes that Wittgenstein returned to Cambridge in 1946 after "six years of duty at the hospital" (2012). Dyson is wrong: Wittgenstein did indeed volunteer to work at Guy's Hospital in London—his contribution to the war effort against the Nazis—but his service was considerably shorter than six years. And his noninvolvement with the war for a couple of years is crucial for inferring his political views.

The distinguished English philosopher and one of Wittgenstein's literary executors, Anthony Kenny, gets temporal facts wrong too: "In 1939 [Wittgenstein] was appointed Professor of Philosophy at Cambridge in succession to G. E. Moore, but before he could take up his chair war broke out. He served as a medical orderly during the war" (2006, 9).

In fact, it was *more than two years after the war broke out* that Wittgenstein applied for a leave of absence from Cambridge, informing the vice-chancellor that he "decided to take on some war-work" at Guy's Hospital (McGuinness 2012, 345).

In fact, Wittgenstein's attitude toward the war changed sometime during the summer of 1941. We know this because in November 1940 he signed a letter in support of the so-called People's Convention, an anti-war event organized by the Communist

Party of Great Britain that was about to take place in London on January 12, 1941.

The People's Convention was a result of the Nazi–Soviet Pact in 1939, which forced the British Communists to make a volte-face overnight: They switched from all-out support for the war against Hitler to a strident condemnation of both sides (the Nazis and the allies) for waging an unjust, imperialist war. In that spirit, they organized the People's Convention to gain wider support for their freshly adopted appeasement stance. Douglas Hyde, a former British Communist who had served as a member of the Central Committee of the Party, described later how at the beginning of the war the leadership was given new instructions from the Comintern. The Central Committee was in the middle of a meeting, preparing a passionate manifesto in support of the anti-fascist war, when the message from Moscow arrived:

> Then, unexpectedly, in walked the British representative to the Communist International whom everyone had thought was still in Moscow. He took one look at the manifesto, and told the leaders they would have to scrap it. It was, he said, an imperialist war. The Comintern had said so, and that meant opposing it in the classical Marxist way (Hyde 1950, 70).

After a short discussion, as expected, the leadership made a U-turn and issued a manifesto that now condemned the war against Hitler as "imperialist" and "unjust":

> This war is a fight between imperialist powers over profits, colonies and world domination.... The leaders of the Labour Party and Trades Union movement have sided fully with the Government of Chamberlain and Churchill and are attempting to get the working-class movement to support their imperialist war aims. This policy, if not challenged...will hand over enormous numbers of young people to become cannon fodder in an unjust war (Childs 1977, 240).

Although the People's Convention was organized by Communists, they used it to attract much broader-based opposition to Churchill's government, including many of those who did not support the official Party line about the "imperialist war." For this reason the anti-war tenor could not be as openly expressed as in the Party's documents. Nevertheless, some of the six "main points" of the People's Convention—a complaint about low living standards, a request for "bomb-proof shelters," and a plea for "people's peace"—have widely been seen as undermining the nation's morale and encouraging defeatism. And this was all happening at a critical historical moment when the British were in a desperate fight for survival, with very uncertain prospects. Needless to say, the six main points made no mention of Hitler or, God forbid, the war against Hitler.

One of the remaining main points added an air of absurdity to the People's Convention: friendship with the Soviet Union. Why on earth would a country that was in the midst of a mortal battle against Hitler single out for special friendship the country that had just recently signed a pact with him?

If there remains any doubt about how much the Communist Party was involved in the People's Convention, here is Douglas Hyde again, with the insider's perspective:

> [I]t was not surprising that Dunkirk, when it came, troubled us not at all and served only to make what we regarded as being the almost inevitable defeat of Britain appear as a magnificent opportunity…
>
> Taking this to heart we administered all the blows we could, through the tactics of the People's Convention, through trying to create war-weariness, through industrial disputes, through the spread of disaffection among the members of the armed forces and through exploiting every possible grievance, political, social, economic or industrial, upon which we could seize . . .
>
> Whilst the Party had perforce publicly to pretend that it had no intention of sabotaging the war effort or of turning the war

> into civil war, our members could at the same time be discussing in their classes every conceivable detail of how best to achieve the defeat of one's own government in war (1950, 75).

Of course, everything changed on June 22, 1941. After Hitler's attack on the Soviet Union, the Communists radically changed their minds about the war. As did Wittgenstein (McGuinness 2012, 309, 345).[8]

The enormous sophistication and hypercritical spirit that Wittgenstein displayed in his philosophical work disappeared when his thoughts turned to politics. In that context, to use his famous simile, he was like a fly that could not find a way out of the fly bottle.

In a letter to Norman Malcolm in 1944, Wittgenstein lamented that the clear thinking nurtured in philosophy is often abandoned when philosophers address practical issues of great importance: "What is the use of studying philosophy if all that it does for you is to enable you to talk with some plausibility about some abstruse questions of logic, etc., and if it does not improve your thinking about the important questions of everyday life?" (quoted in Malcolm 2001, 93).

Wittgenstein was obviously unaware that his lament about the uselessness of philosophy for everyday thinking also applied to his own case, and with a vengeance.

---

8 One of the rare philosophers who concedes that "Wittgenstein was sympathetic to Soviet communism" is Peter S. Hacker (2014–15), a leading Wittgenstein scholar. But his attempt to explain Wittgenstein's pro-Bolshevik attitude largely by his fear of the rise of Nazism is not very convincing in light of Wittgenstein's support for the People's Convention. Anyone whose attitude to Hitler changed depending on what was an injunction from Moscow showed that he was much more driven by pro-Sovietism than by anti-Nazism.

CHAPTER SEVEN

Imre Lakatos: Eulogized in England, Unforgiven in Hungary

> "You can still advertise that the Devil is coming, for the Devil chooses strange shapes to confound the innocent. For example, he may choose the shape of a rationalist from London with a Hungarian accent."
>
> —PAUL FEYERABEND

Imre Lakatos is one of the most important philosophers of science of the twentieth century. His approach to scientific methodology was very influential, and the contribution he made to the philosophy of mathematics is, according to Ian Hacking, "to put it simply, definitive: the subject will never be the same again" (Hacking 2000, 28). It took Lakatos only eight years after receiving his Ph.D. at Cambridge to ascend to the prestigious philosophy chair at the London School of Economics in 1969, after Karl Popper's retirement. Currently, the greatest recognition in the philosophy of science bears his name: the Lakatos Award.

LSE: Economical with the Truth?

On the Lakatos Award page on the London School of Economics' website, one could until recently click on a link and get access to Lakatos's short biography. The link is still there but the file is no longer accessible. If you click on "Lakatos biography" on the LSE Lakatos webpage (www.lse.ac.uk/philosophy/lakatos), you are now redirected to the webpage of the LSE philosophy department. See

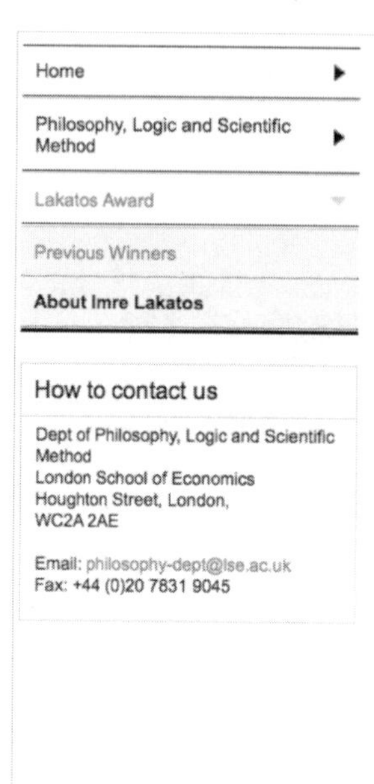

Home

Philosophy, Logic and Scientific Method

Lakatos Award

Previous Winners

About Imre Lakatos

How to contact us

Dept of Philosophy, Logic and Scientific Method
London School of Economics
Houghton Street, London,
WC2A 2AE

Email: philosophy-dept@lse.ac.uk
Fax: +44 (0)20 7831 9045

About Imre Lakatos

Imre Lakatos in 1961 on the occasion of his Cambridge University doctoral award ceremony

Imre Lakatos, who died in 1974, aged 51, had been Professor of Logic with special reference to the Philosophy of Mathematics at LSE since 1969. He joined the Department of Philosophy, Logic and Scientific Method in 1960 on Popper's invitation. Born in Debrecen in eastern Hungary in 1922, he graduated (in Physics, Mathematics and Philosophy) from Debrecen University in 1944. He then joined the underground resistance against the Nazi invasion of Hungary. (His mother, grandmother and uncle perished in Auschwitz.) After the War he was active in the Communist Party and played a highly influential role in the Ministry of Education in Hungary's key period of radical educational reform for universal access to Higher Education on the basis of merit. He also completed a doctoral dissertation at Debrecen University in 1947 on concept formation in science. But in 1950 he was arrested and spent the next three years as a political prisoner in Recsk labour camp without legal trial.

After his release, shortly after the death of Stalin, he was given a position as librarian and then translator and researcher in the Hungarian Academy of Science by the head of its Institute of Mathematical Research, the internationally renowned mathematician Alfred Renyi. There Lakatos translated English language works in science and mathematics into Hungarian. These included George Polya's renowned work on mathematical heuristics, *How to Solve It*.

After the suppression of the 1956 Hungarian uprising, Lakatos left Hungary and went immediately to Vienna, and from there to Kings College, Cambridge (on a Rockefeller Fellowship won with the help of Victor Kraft). There Lakatos prepared his 1961 doctoral thesis on the logic of mathematical discovery, out of which grew his famous BJPS articles, collected after his death into the book *Proofs and Refutations* (CUP, 1976). Two volumes of Lakatos's *Philosophical Papers*, edited by John Worrall & Gregory Currie, appeared in 1978, also with CUP.

FIGURE 7.1: Lakatos biography (recently disappeared from the LSE website)

Figure 7.1 for a screen shot of the now missing LSE version of the Lakatos biography.

Here are the key parts:

> Born in Debrecen in eastern Hungary in 1922, he graduated ...from Debrecen University in 1944. He then joined the underground resistance against the Nazi invasion of Hungary. ...After the War he was active in the Communist Party and played a highly influential role in the Ministry of Education in Hungary's key period of radical educational reform for universal access to Higher Education on the basis of merit.... [I]n 1950 he was arrested and spent the next three years as a political prisoner in Recsk labour camp without legal trial.

Although there is some truth in these passages, they are mixed with distortions and misleading implications to such a degree that the reader is bound to be led astray. I will mention three points.

First, the claim that Lakatos "joined the underground resistance against the Nazi invasion of Hungary" sounds as if he was engaged in fighting against the German occupation. But this is simply not true. As we can read in one of the main sources about Lakatos's life in Hungary, he in fact *firmly rejected* a suggestion that members of his secret seminars should engage in anti-fascist resistance (Long 2002, 265).

The preprint of Jancis Long's article "The Unforgiven: Imre Lakatos' Life in Hungary" was circulating among philosophers when I was at Kings College London in 1999–2000 and it was widely discussed then. It is odd that now, almost fifteen years after the article was published, the myth about Lakatos's brave (armed?) resistance against the Nazis is still being propagated. See the most widely used introduction to the philosophy of science, Peter Godfrey-Smith's *Theory and Reality* (2009, 103); an article by Ian Hacking (2000); and recent announcements about Lakatos Award recipients: e.g., www.philsci.org/announcements/archive-of-announcement/24-announcements/archived-announcements/139-lakatos-award-2012.

Second, it sounds as if Lakatos must have done something praiseworthy if he took part in "radical educational reform for universal access to Higher Education on the basis of merit." But wait, this was all happening immediately after the Communist takeover in Hungary, right? And isn't it well known that such "radical educational reforms" in postwar Eastern Europe never involved meritocracy but that rather, without exception, they ended with ideological indoctrination, censorship, and persecution of remaining "bourgeois elements" and other "enemies of the people"? So perhaps there is nothing to celebrate about Lakatos's "playing a highly influential role" in actions of the Ministry of Education?

Indeed, there is evidence that Lakatos should be condemned, not celebrated, for his "role" in the Ministry of Education:

> Lakatos worked for the Ministry of Education between 1945 and 1948, and was an active writer supporting the hard Party line against the liberal factions to be demolished by [Hungarian Prime Minister Matyas] Rakosi. During the

> 1947–1948 academic year, Lakatos dedicated himself to helping destroy the distinguished Eötvös College, targeted by the Communists because of its resistance to transforming itself into an indoctrination tool like the recently established Györffy College.... In articles and speeches, Lakatos polemicized against the Eötvös curriculum, intimating that the college provided no significant resistance against the fascists and was unsympathetic to the aims of a people's democracy. The college's goals, argued the young Lakatos, were fundamentally elitist, and thus, unsupportive of the great social transformation taking place.... [A]nd in 1950, [the Minister of Culture József] Révai disbanded Eötvös College.... As a reward, Lakatos was sent to study in Moscow (Kadvany 2001, 288–89).

Apparently, the real goal was not to implement universal access to higher education but rather to destroy an institution of higher learning with a long tradition and excellent academic reputation, and through *Gleichschaltung* turn it into yet another gray Party-controlled school. Moreover, Lakatos's getting a reward for his effort indicates that his actions were probably regarded as a key part of the successfully accomplished mission.

Before his destructive actions at Eötvös College, Lakatos was one of the leaders of a student group, Debrecen University Circle, which not only demanded the dismissal of "reactionary" professors but also established a "screening committee" aiming to "cleanse the student body of fascists and reactionaries who had wormed their way into the ranks" (Bandy 2009, 59–61).

Ralf Dahrendorf, former director of the London School of Economics, says Lakatos was "reared by" the Marxist philosopher György Lukács (Dahrendorf 1995, 425). In reality, Lakatos's association with Lukács included digging up compromising quotes from Lukács and providing other information to the Party ideologue László Rudas when he attacked Lukács for "right deviation" in 1949. (As a consequence of Rudas's accusations, Lukács was forced out of public life for years.) A secret police document kept in the Historical Archives of the State Security Services says that

Gábor Kovács (Lakatos's codename as an informer) "gave us valuable information about [György Lukács' circle]" (Bandy undated, 5). According to the philosopher Agnes Heller, Lukács was aware that Lakatos was helping the Party build an ideological case against him and once said resignedly: "So much for disciples."

And third, the information on LSE's website and elsewhere (Godfrey-Smith 2009, 103) that Lakatos ended up as a *political* prisoner in Stalinist Hungary will naturally be interpreted as suggesting this happened because he opposed, or was perceived to oppose, Stalinist policies. In all likelihood, hardly anyone would consider the possibility that he was a political prisoner simply because he was *more* Stalinist than many of the leaders of the Hungarian Communist Party. But there is evidence that this was exactly the case. It seems, furthermore, that Lakatos actually remained a Stalinist even after leaving prison:

> Lakatos was expelled from the Party and taken into custody by the ávh [Hungarian secret police], possibly because of a plan to denounce Révai [a Communist politician and the Minister of Culture at the time] as an imperialist agent based on Lakatos's research: Révai, for Lakatos, *was not Stalinist enough*. . . . Lakatos nonetheless may still have been cooperating at Recsk with the ávh. Lakatos maintained the Party line after his release, arguing that Rákosi must have had good reasons for his actions. *He continued, as he had for years, to spy and inform on others, including his mentor Árpád Szabó*. Recall that after the prisoners' release, the writers and others were opposed in two camps supporting Nagy [reformist Communist] and Rákosi [Stalinist]. *Lakatos was still a staunch Rákosi backer* (Kadvany 2001, 290; emphasis added).

Speaking of Árpád Szabó (who was one of his closest friends and a witness at his wedding): Lakatos went so far as to search Szabó's wastebasket in the hope of finding something incriminating (Congdon 1997, 281).

Now, it is surely appalling that Lakatos was forced to spend three years in a labor camp without being tried for any crime. Yet it is unclear why the LSE website would describe this unfortunate episode evasively and misleadingly so as to insinuate an act of anti-totalitarian resistance that in fact did not happen.

Murder by Suicide

Another key event in Lakatos's life (left out in his LSE biography) that casts an even darker shadow over his character has to do with his role in the suicide in 1944 of a young woman named Éva Izsák. I will present the basic facts of this case by relying on a number of sources, including a transcription of the hearings conducted at the Political Department of the State Police in Nagyvárad (the city's Romanian name is Oradea) on June 18 and 19, 1945. This document is appended to a moving essay written by Izsák's sister, Mária Zimán, in which at the beginning she says something striking (that will make more sense in a moment): "Éva was the victim of a cruel age, the age of Hitlerism. But her execution outdid even the most devious methods of execution of the time" (Zimán 1989).

During World War II Lakatos joined the Communist Party and became the unofficial leader of a small underground cell in Nagyvárad. One of the cell members was a nineteen-year-old Jewish woman, Éva Izsák. She, like many other members, was in hiding and had false papers. It was feared she was a particular security risk for the whole group—that she was more likely to be arrested and that she might be forced to disclose information about her comrades. This problem had to be addressed and there was no doubt about who should be in charge: Imre Lipsitz (Lakatos's original surname), the cell's undisputed leader as well as the authority on Marxism, political issues, strategy questions, and basically everything else. He didn't disappoint, coming up with a totally unexpected idea, or what one later commentator called an "insane proposal" (Kadvany 2012, 277): The best way out was for Éva Izsák to commit suicide.

The proposal was supported by an argument couched by the future LSE professor in terms of Marxist dialectics which the other members found so compelling that they all immediately voted

FIGURE 7.2: Éva Izsák (1925–1944)

for it—including Éva's own boyfriend! In that fateful meeting, Lakatos's girlfriend requested that she get Éva's winter coat after her death, which was approved.

After poor Éva learned about the decision, she only asked whether there was some other way. As a witness later recounted to the police, Lakatos explained that "there was no other solution and that what we prove theoretically . . . we must also realize in practice, so she had to do it." And she did. She first had to travel to a remote place where her dead body would not be recognized by anyone. She was accompanied by another trusted Communist, Nyuszi Levente, whose duty was to prepare things and make sure there was no change of heart at the last minute:

> Nyuszi told us that when he and Éva went to Nagyerdő, they looked for a deserted place where no one ever goes. He had the water with him and then Éva took the poison when it was growing dark already. Nyuszi told Éva that it would be over in a few moments. After Éva drank it, Éva was so strong and brave that she even asked Nyuszi when would it be over, but she couldn't finish the sentence, because she collapsed, made a rattling sound, and Nyuszi, allegedly, closed her mouth which was foaming (report of Alfonz Weisz, a member of Lakatos's Communist cell: police interrogation in 1945).

When Elie Wiesel read about the death of Éva Izsák, his comment was: "Jews killing Jews! In the midst of the Holocaust! I have never heard of anything like that!" (quoted in Bandy 2009, 49).

The sad thing is that in reality there was no reason whatsoever for Éva Izsák to die. Before her suicide, her sister (also a Communist) was doing everything she could to get in touch with her and bring her to a safe place. However, she was unable to make any contact because all communication with Éva had to go through the cell leaders (who even opened her mail). They inexplicably refused to respond in any way to her sister's letters and inquiries. When a good friend of Éva's came to Nagyvárad to pick her up and take her to a safe house in another city, this friend was informed that Éva had already left, although she was in fact still there, while the group, under the influence of their forceful leader, was strangely unwilling to consider any alternative to the suicide "solution."

Furthermore, this way of dealing with comrades who were regarded as a security risk was simply unheard of at the time. Imre Tóth, a philosopher of mathematics who was at the end of the war involved in the same kind of underground activity in Hungary as Lakatos, later said:

> [The death sentence] by a perverse suicide as imposed by Imre Lakatos was even at this time and in its referential system in flagrant contradiction with all the tactical, political and moral standards of the underground movement. It was certainly an absolutely subjective invention of Imre Lakatos. And taking into account the Jewish background of Imre Lakatos, it remains a horrible singularity (quoted in Bandy 2009, 49).

Lakatos was such a dominating influence on the minds of other group members that they were ready to obey all his instructions unconditionally. In some respects the atmosphere resembled that of a sect like Jim Jones's infamous People's Temple community in Jonestown. Apparently even the idea of a collective suicide was mentioned at one point, which shows that in the case of Éva Izsák too this kind of proposal may have been Lakatos's way of testing whether there were any limits to his subordinates' obedience. "And when Imre Lipsitz told us on the banks of the Körös [River] that we must also commit suicide, we would have obeyed just as Éva did, but then he laughed to show that it was just a 'test' to see whether or not we would submit" (transcript of the police interrogation in 1945).

LSE philosopher John Worrall once said Lakatos was "an exceptional human being" (1976, 1). Information from many sources (some of which has been cited here) confirms this statement, but not in the way Worrall intended. Lakatos's extreme manipulativeness, unscrupulousness, lack of concern for other people, and rigid loyalty to a totalitarian ideology make a combination that is, if not unique, certainly quite rare.

Worrall, who is also the convener of the Lakatos Award committee at LSE, appears to be particularly ill-disposed toward negative personal characterizations of his former teacher. So when on the basis of the aforementioned facts one scholar described Lakatos as "a dangerous thug with something like a criminal record, and who consistently displayed a pattern of dissemblance and cunning across the decades" (Kadvany 2001, 314), Worrall called this "an appalling, perhaps even libelous remark" (Worrall 2003, 83). Worrall's indignation is misplaced. This allegedly "appalling" remark seems to be tracking the known facts about Lakatos pretty well. It is the reality that is appalling, not the words describing it. According to Kadvany, it was actually Bernard Williams, the preeminent British moral philosopher, who once described Lakatos as "a kind of a thug."

Someone might say that, in terms of the main theme of this book, in Lakatos's case it was more the heart, rather than reason, that went on holiday. There is some truth to this. Yes, a certain coldheartedness, to put it very mildly, is evident in some of the episodes described above. This is additionally corroborated in judgments from acquaintances and commentators who said, among other things, that he was "evil" (Joseph Agassi, philosopher and colleague), that he was "an impossible infantile monster, completely unable to understand other people" (a former girlfriend), that he was "not fully human," that "his drives and his mind are in place, but the rest missing" (a mathematician colleague), that "people did not matter to him," that he was "a truly Satanic figure" and that "it was scary to see him in action" (a historian colleague), that he was "diabolic" (philosopher Agnes Heller), that he was seen as "an evil spirit" and "demonic" (Endre Ságvári a Communist activist), that he was "diabolic" in his "total disregard for people" (István Márkus, a journal editor), that he was "like the devil...absolutely inhuman...that he had no human feelings for anyone...and that he would trample on anyone to get ahead" (András Nagy, professor of economics), that he was "a Satanic figure" (an editor Zoltán Zsámboki), that he was "unbelievably unscrupulous" (Péter Németh, a literary historian), that he "met the criteria for Antisocial Personality Disorder in the current DSM IV" (Long 2002, 294). All in all, a lot of the evidence points to the possibility that Lakatos was a psychopath, which is indeed how he was described by Dr. Klára Majerszky, who worked at the National Psychiatric and Neurological Institute in Budapest and who knew Lakatos personally before the war[1] (Bandy 2009, 123).

On the other hand, though, such a radical deficit of empathy would certainly not be incompatible with a cognitive failure. And there is some evidence for that too.

Sticking with the Superego

Needless to say, there was nothing inherently irrational about adopting the Marxist ideology and becoming a member of the Communist Party during World War II in Hungary, especially for someone like Lakatos whose closest family members were persecuted and eventually perished in the Holocaust. But the fact that he kept the true Stalinist faith until 1956 (as he apparently did) is much harder to understand, particularly given his indisputable

1 Interestingly, although the authors of the 2016 article about Lakatos in the Stanford Encyclopedia of Philosophy seem to be aware of the severely negative comments about Lakatos's character from many of his friends and close acquaintances, all this is inexplicably disregarded and the biographical part of the article begins with the blithe statement that "Imre Lakatos was a warm and witty friend."

intellectual brilliance as well as his easy access to information that was unavailable to others. (From 1953 until his departure from Hungary in 1956 Lakatos worked in a library where he could freely read a lot of sources that were strictly forbidden to the public, including books of his later teacher and prominent anti-Marxist, Karl Popper.)

Yet in a 1971 letter to the psychologist Paul Meehl, Lakatos says that the Communist Party was his last superego and that *it was only in 1956* that he finally got rid of that superego. He is not more specific about the time when this happened, but one Lakatos scholar dates his break with the Party to the autumn of 1956 (Kadvany 2001, 290). This is embarrassingly late if we remember that the Soviet tanks rolled into Budapest on October 24, 1956.

Let us telegraphically review a sequence of excellent but strangely missed opportunities for Lakatos to recognize the monstrosity of the regime that he had so faithfully served for years. When in 1947 some leading members of a non-Communist party that had won the first election in postwar Hungary were accused by the Communist Minister of Internal Affairs, László Rajk, of plotting against the state and were then either executed or given long prison sentences, wasn't that very odd? Wasn't that a clear reason to have doubts about what one's "superego" was really up to? And when two years later that same László Rajk was officially tried (and soon executed) for being a Titoist spy, an agent of Western Imperialism, and for trying to restore capitalism and undermine Hungary's independence, didn't all this raise at least some suspicion about what was really going on? And if not, why not? Also, didn't Lakatos's terrible three-year experience of being illegally imprisoned in a labor camp and leaving that place of abuse with broken and missing teeth move him to start harboring some distrust toward the Party that obviously stood behind that experience?

Apparently not, because even after his release Lakatos defended his own internment, saying "the Party must have had some good reason for what it did" (Congdon 1997, 289). And if, as Solzhenitsyn said, Marxism in the Soviet Union "has fallen to such a low point that it has become a joke, an object of contempt...and that no serious person, not even university and high-school students, can talk about Marxism without a smile or a sneer" (1976, 47), how is it possible that a genius with a doctorate in philosophy[2] took seriously the official ideology that was drenched in the tired and ridiculous rote formulas of dialectical materialism?

Paradoxically, this was the man who had such a penetrating mind that in London in 1961 he wrote a thesis that would soon be universally regarded as a stunningly original and highly influential contribution to philosophy of mathematics. But just five years earlier this same man was still incapable of extricating himself from the clutches of a totally ludicrous philosophical doctrine or distancing himself from the manifestly inhumane political regime that was based on that ideology.

And to make matters worse, according to a letter from MI5 October 10, 1962, to the Home Office, Lakatos, who was then already a lecturer at the London School of Economics, was still collaborating with the Hungarian secret police (see Bandy 2009, 304). This is apparently why his application for British citizenship was refused. He tried again in 1967, this time garnering the support of luminaries like Sir Karl Popper, who assured the British authorities that Lakatos "had broken with his communist past before he left Hungary," and the LSE economist Lord Lionel Robbins, who called Lakatos "a man of outstanding qualities of intellect *and character*" (emphasis added). But the request was refused again; Home Secretary Roy Jenkins approached Lord Robbins and explained that the negative decision was made after "full and careful consideration." Clearly there must have been powerful evidence behind the refusal, but its nature was never as much as hinted at.

Another puzzling thing, touched on earlier, is the tendency of some of the most prominent Lakatos-related sources today to omit compromising information about him, or even sometimes to twist it so that it appears less unfavorable. In some sense this is understandable, for if one is receiving, and especially if one is bestowing,

2 Lakatos received his first Ph.D., from the University of Debrecen, in 1947, *summa cum laude.*

a coveted award named after X, one will naturally be reluctant to loudly announce to the world that X was in fact an ultra-Stalinist and a secret police informer or that X was assisting the Party apparatchiks in their ideological attacks on fellow philosophers and that he was directly responsible for the cruel and pointless death of an innocent and vulnerable young woman.[3]

Nevertheless, hushing up or de-emphasizing this kind of biographical information is surprising. Would philosophers be equally cagey about mentioning (or reacting to) such publicly accessible information about one of their own if it turned out he had done something similar to what Lakatos had—with the only difference being that he was in the service not of Stalin but, say, Franco, Pinochet, or Hitler? To ask that question is to answer it.

A striking contrast: Lakatos's real-life actions that caused loss of life and immense human suffering have barely produced a yawn among philosophers; meanwhile, in another case, top scholars in the profession have issued strident condemnations and repeatedly expressed disbelief and shock over what one old and disillusioned man had written in the last year of his life in his *private* diary, which was published seventy years after his death (see pp. 188–193).

Another pertinent example is the German philosopher Günter Figal, who recently stepped down as the chair of the Martin Heidegger Society after learning about the appalling extent of Heidegger's anti-Semitism, which has been revealed in the newly published *Black Notebooks* of Heidegger. In an interview in the *Badische Zeitung* Figal said this discovery was "a compelling reason for him to rethink his relation to Heidegger as a person" and added: "The ever more pressing question for me was the following: do I want, with my core beliefs, to be associated with this person? And the answer was a clear No" (Schulte 2015).

In a further development, these recent discoveries have caused so much embarrassment that the University of Freiburg

3 From the British file about the Lakatos citizenship interrogation: "At times he seemed to take a perverse pleasure in recounting the details of his more sordid activities, showing no shame or embarrassment, for instance, about his betrayal of his friends to the AVH [the secret police]" (Bandy 2009, 303).

has abolished Heidegger's former chair and, the ultimate insult, replaced it with a junior professorship in analytic philosophy! (Kaube 2015). Although this reaction is regarded by some philosophers as excessive, it shows that, as a matter of fact, many do feel an irresistible impulse to disassociate themselves from the name of anyone who plunged so deeply into political irrationality and totalitarian insanity. Again, I am not supporting this impulse but just registering its existence and its apparently wide appeal on some occasions, but notably not on others.

Although the cases of Heidegger and Lakatos are similar in an important way—each of them played an active, infamous role in an odious political regime of his own country—they are of course very different in many respects. So I am not suggesting that our reactions to their misdeeds should necessarily be the same. But something else is also worth stressing: Differences between the two cases are not always in Lakatos's favor. After all, Heidegger is not known to have been directly responsible for anyone's death.

CHAPTER EIGHT

Jerry Cohen: Don't Celebrate the Collapse of Soviet Communism!

> "The addiction to the Soviet myth is as tenacious and difficult to cure as any other addiction. After the Lost Weekend in Utopia the temptation is strong to have just one last drop, even if watered down and sold under a different label."
>
> —Arthur Koestler

Gerald Allan "Jerry" Cohen held the prestigious Chichele Chair in Social and Political Theory at Oxford from 1985 to 2008. He was one of the founders of analytical Marxism. The goal of that movement (whose members also called it "non-bullshit Marxism") was to use the tools of analytic philosophy, such as logic and rigorous conceptual analysis, to extract the salvageable core of Marxist doctrine from the various historical deposits of undisciplined speculation, obscurantism, and dubiously meaningful jargon. Some argue that this new approach has breathed new life into Marxist theorizing; others disagree. For instance, one former analytical Marxist concluded that the non-bullshit Marxist movement exposed the flaws of Marxism so thoroughly that in the end nothing of value was left and "non-bullshit Marxism was revealed to be an empty set" (Elster 2011, 163).

It is surprising that despite Cohen's undeniable philosophical sophistication and his declared interest in advancing human liberty, he always had a soft spot for the Soviet Union. This can partly be explained by his having been a red diaper baby growing up in an environment with strong Communist sympathies. Nevertheless, one would have expected that his years-long scholarly research, especially since it was devoted to *political* philosophy, should have done something to neutralize the effects of his hard-left indoctrination and that it should have led him later to join millions of others in celebrating the eventual demise of Soviet totalitarianism. But this did not happen.

A "Fascist Rebellion" in Hungary in 1956

Here is how Cohen describes his own reactions to two key historical events:

> [T]he Soviet action in Hungary in the autumn of October 1956 was regarded, at the time, by virtually everyone in the party, as an entirely justified suppression of a fascist rebellion. I myself so regarded it at least as late as 1968. I recall contrasting it, then, with the invasion of Czechoslovakia that year [1968], which thoroughly rid me of my pro-Sovietism (Cohen 2001, 188).

Notice an inconsistency in Cohen's report. He says that he regarded the 1956 Hungarian revolution as "a fascist rebellion" *at least as late as 1968*, whereby he obviously allows that he may have kept this view a bit longer—that is, after 1968. On the other hand, he claims he abandoned his pro-Sovietism thoroughly in 1968. Which is it?

Also, he says he remembers that in 1968 he contrasted the Soviet action in Hungary with the Soviet invasion of Czechoslovakia, which seems to imply that at the time (in 1968) he actually had a very different opinion of these two events. Yet anyone who got pro-Sovietism "thoroughly" out of his system would have basically the same attitude to these two historical episodes. He would regard both the Hungarian revolution and the Prague Spring as legitimate battles against Communist oppression that were crushed by brute military force.[1]

---

1 This is why Jon Elster's statement (2014–15) that Cohen "became disillusioned with communism in his early twenties" cannot be correct. According to Cohen himself, he supported the Soviet intervention in Hungary *at least* until his *late* twenties.

That Cohen did not terminate his loyalty to the Soviet Union in 1968 is also supported by what Michael Rosen, his former Oxford colleague and now Harvard professor of government, wrote after Cohen died: "But *even then* [after the invasion of Czechoslovakia], I think, he was *too much of a loyalist* to make the kind of noisy break with the Party that the historian E. P. Thompson (and many others) had done" (Rosen 2010; emphasis added).

But there is a more pressing issue here. Although Cohen's sincerity in reporting his past pro-Communist dogmatism may in some sense be admirable, the fact that he believed for years that what happened in Hungary in 1956 was *a fascist rebellion* is mind-boggling and defies easy explanation. How could such a thing be believed by someone who had studied at Oxford, who had taught philosophy for years at University College London, whose main research interest was politics, and who, after all (Cohen 2001, 26), had even visited Hungary himself in 1962? And what exactly could he have taught students about politics (or more specifically Communism, which obviously loomed large in his mind), if he could believe "at least until 1968" that the Russian tanks did a great favor to Hungary in 1956, saving it from fascism?[2]

Cohen also visited Czechoslovakia in 1964 and stayed there two weeks. He went out often, talking to many people about politics, and he says their response was always the same: "Going out and about the town, I found no one with a good word for the regime" (Cohen 2013, 17). And yet, even after witnessing the universal disillusionment with Communism in Czechoslovakia (and in all likelihood having seen something very similar in Hungary in 1962), Cohen still somehow managed, for four years, to keep his belief that people protesting in the streets of Budapest in 1956 were fascists and presumably that it is fortunate they were in the end defeated (and many of them killed) by the Red Army.

In a prepared address Cohen was scheduled to deliver in Prague in 2001, he wrote about his long allegiance to Soviet Communism:

---

2 While the Communist Party of Great Britain lost as much as two-thirds of its members after 1956 because of its leadership's support for the Soviet intervention in Hungary (Applebaum 2012, 481), the philosophy lecturer at University College London managed to keep his faith in the Kremlin intact until 1968, possibly longer.

> I know that what I had believed was paradise, or on the road to paradise, was for you and your forebears a form of hell. I don't think I can be *blamed* for not having realized that, for having thought the very opposite. My false belief was borne up by noble sentiments. But, rationally or otherwise, I nevertheless feel a need to apologize, and I hereby do (Cohen 2013, 17).

Translation: "I will succumb to a possibly irrational need to apologize; in fact I cannot be blamed for claiming that your hell was actually a paradise—nor for doing my part to support its continuation—for, you see, my sentiments were noble." There is no way these remarks would have been received well by people with a lot of recent unpleasant memories of Communist oppression, so Cohen was in a way lucky that he could not make it to the Czech Republic (due to visa problems).

But in his prepared remarks he went on:

> My Soviet allegiance came from an upbringing in which I was raised as a Marxist (and Stalinist communist) the way other people are raised Roman Catholic or Muslim. My parents and most of my relatives were working-class communists, and several of them had served years in Canadian jails for their convictions. One of those who had been jailed was my Uncle Norman: he was married to my father's sister Jenny, who, I can tell you, once danced with Joseph Stalin (ibid.).

What was the point here of mentioning that Cohen's Aunt Jenny danced with Stalin? Was the audience supposed to be impressed? Or was this just an interesting curiosity that the listeners were expected to find amusing?

Let's try to see how this would work in an analogous situation. A person comes to Israel and offers an insincere and half-hearted apology for continually denying the plight of Jews in the Third Reich. Then at one point he starts talking about his aunt "who, I can tell you, once danced with Adolf Hitler." The most likely reaction would be *Yimach shemo!*

When Cohen says his Uncle Norman was one of those who "served years in Canadian jails for their convictions," this sounds as if he went to jail merely because he had the courage to express unpopular political views. In reality, Norman Freed was interned (rather than jailed) at the time of the Nazi–Soviet Pact of 1939 simply because the Canadian government feared that a number of militant and hardline Stalinists like him could follow instructions from Moscow and try to undermine preparations for the much anticipated war against Hitler. In other words, Freed and others were detained *not* because of their Communist convictions but because it was believed they might subvert the upcoming battle against the evil of Nazism.

I am not saying the internment of Freed and his fellow Stalinists was justified. I am only arguing that Cohen withheld an important piece of information and thereby led the reader seriously astray. In addition, there is strong evidence that Uncle Norman was actually an agent of the NKVD! This is what we can read in secret documents on Soviet espionage that Igor Gouzenko, a clerk in the Soviet Embassy in Ottawa, stole from the embassy and gave to the Canadian authorities when he defected to the West in 1945 (see *The Report of the Royal Commission,* Ottawa, June 27, 1946, 23). The part of the report in which Norman Freed was mentioned by name as a Soviet agent was easily accessible public information already about twenty years before Cohen wrote the above text. It is hard to believe that he was unaware of it, especially given his strong interest in his family history and close emotional ties to his uncle and aunt.

The reason Cohen decided to share information about some of his family members was this was supposed to help explain the origins of his own commitment to Communism. One wonders, though, why he decided to disclose some things and not others. For example, if the purpose was to illustrate his Stalinist roots, was it not more important to mention that his uncle was probably an NKVD agent than the fact that his aunt once danced with Stalin?

Even up to his sixties Cohen could not come to terms with his past, and toward the end of his life his autobiographical remarks continued to be tendentious, disingenuous, and on occasion intentionally misleading.

Cohen's penchant for idealizing the Soviet system sometimes reached ludicrous proportions. For instance, in the book that made him famous, *Karl Marx's Theory of History: A Defence* (1978, 316), he says that in a conversation with Soviet academics he once remarked: "Whereas an American manager is motivated to conceal pollution caused by his plant, a Soviet manager can publicize it and request subventions to counteract it." A local sociologist schooled him: "You are naïve. If he [the Soviet manager] publicizes it, he will be replaced by someone who is more discreet."

Needless to say, Cohen's assumption that "a Soviet manager," basically a Party apparatchik, would be so environmentally conscious that, amid notoriously dire economic straits, he would request (and get!) subventions to counteract pollution was preposterous. This was clear to everyone at the time, except to those Western visitors to the Eastern Bloc whose wishful thinking and wide-eyed enthusiasm for all things Soviet made them lose contact with reality.

The Price of Dreaming about Socialism

At some point—it is unclear whether in 1968 or somewhat later—Cohen abandoned his long-held belief that the Soviet Union "amply merited every leftist's allegiance." But he still retained a certain affection for the Soviet Union until its inglorious end. At the time of its collapse, Sam Bowles, one of Cohen's analytical Marxist friends, told him "We're partying," but Cohen did not want to join the celebration:

> I thought that was a very superficial response to the collapse of the Soviet Union, because with the disappearance of the great rival to capitalism, it begins to appear axiomatic that there is no alternative to capitalism. Sam had a point, but his celebration was premature. It was only once capitalism got into serious difficulties, recently, that the demise of the Soviet Union proved to be a boon, because now our thinking about alternatives

> to capitalism can be freer and more imaginative. It can't be stigmatizing as favoring the Soviet system, because the Soviet system is no longer there as a vivid example (in Tormey 2009).

This is an odd argument, based on purely strategic reasoning. The point is simple: The socialist critics of capitalism do not need the Soviet Union when capitalism is in serious difficulties, but they do need its existence when capitalism is doing relatively well. Notice that in opposing the celebration of the breakdown of the Soviet Union, Cohen totally ignores one issue that almost everyone else would regard as being of paramount importance: the fate of all those millions of people who suffered so long under the yoke of Communist tyranny. Cohen, however, resolutely rejects the idea that the liberation of the populations of many countries from a half century of one-party dictatorship and terror of secret police is perhaps a decisive reason for celebration.

The same omission is strikingly present in another article Cohen wrote in 1989 in which his pro-Soviet sentimentality comes to the fore again:

> It is true that I was heavily critical of the Soviet Union, but the angry little boy who pummels his father's chest will not be glad if the old man collapses. As long as the Soviet Union seemed safe, it felt safe for me to be anti-Soviet. Now that it begins, disobligingly, to crumble, I feel impotently protective towards it.... Those of us on the left who were stern critics of the Soviet Union long before it collapsed needed it to be there to receive our blows. The Soviet Union needed to be there as a defective model so that, with one eye on it, we could construct a better one. It created a non-capitalist mental space in which to think about socialism (Cohen 1995, 250).

Again, one may understand that Cohen wanted the Soviet Union to continue to exist so that he and other leftist intellectuals in the West could keep thinking about socialism while maintaining a foothold in the real world. But should he not have given at least some thought to the costs of this temporal extension that would be incurred by those who would have to live through these additional grim years of the "really existing" socialism? Indeed, could it be so enjoyable to go on dreaming about socialism in Oxford if one were aware that the price for this in East Berlin would be the prolongation of the notoriously miserable existence that was universally known and that was depicted later in the movie *The Lives of Others*?

In his unbreakable attachment to the Soviet Union, Cohen resorted to a perverse logic similar to that of Jean-Paul Sartre half a century before:

> Should we call this bloody monster which lacerates itself socialism? I reply frankly: yes. It was even the *only* socialism in its primitive phase, there was no other, except perhaps in Plato's heaven, and it was necessary to will that, or not to will any socialism at all (quoted in Birchall 2004, 165).

In choosing between socialism with all its horrors and any other alternative, neither Sartre nor Cohen could wish the "bloody monster" to go away. This is a curious instance of a continental and analytic philosopher finding common ground—in the apology of totalitarianism.

In his last book, published posthumously (2009, 10), Cohen tried to illustrate the advantages of socialism by proposing an analogy with a camping trip, pointing out that the nonexistence of private property seems perfectly acceptable in that context. He then added, humorously, that there are limits to his outdoorsiness and that "he'd rather have his socialism in the warmth of All Souls College, Oxford, than in the wet of the Catskills." But Cohen either failed to realize, or was just not bothered by, something important: namely that, according to his own Faustian bargain, his having an opportunity to continue fantasizing about socialism in All Souls College would be possible only in exchange for many other people spending not a short camping trip in the wet of the Catskills, but many additional years in the cold of Siberia.

It is curious how people like Jerry Cohen and Hilary Putnam (see Chapter 10) never seriously considered the possibility of leaving the capitalist world they detested so much and moving to a Communist country which, despite all its imperfections, they saw as being on a road to Utopia. The prospect of taking part in building the radiant socialist future themselves did not appeal to them at all. They preferred to cheer from a safe distance. Nevertheless, they argued that for the sake of the great cause the Russians or Chinese should patiently endure every hardship, in order to keep the flame of the Revolution burning.

W. H. Auden had something interesting to say about such an attitude in 1955:

> [O]ur great error was not a false admiration for Russia but a snobbish feeling that nothing which happened in a semi-barbarous country which had experienced neither the Renaissance nor the Enlightenment could be of any importance: had any of the countries we knew personally, like France, Germany or Italy, the language of which we could speak and where we had personal friends, been the one to have a successful communist revolution with... the same phenomena of terror, purges, censorship, etc., we would have screamed our heads off (quoted in Davenport-Hines 1996, 157).

CHAPTER NINE

Michael Dummett: A Bumbling Anti-Racist

> "When they come downstairs from their Ivory Towers, idealists are very apt to walk straight into the gutter."
>
> —LOGAN PEARSALL SMITH

Michael Dummett was Wykeham Professor of Logic at Oxford and Fellow of All Souls College. He is one of the most celebrated philosophers of the twentieth century, with important contributions to the philosophy of language, the philosophy of mathematics, and the history of analytic philosophy. He received many prestigious awards, including the Lakatos Award in the philosophy of science in 1994, the Rolf Schock Prize in 1995, and the Lauener Prize for an Outstanding Oeuvre in Analytical Philosophy in 2010.

Paid by Oxford to Do Research, Does Politics Instead

Dummett was knighted in 1999 for "services to philosophy and racial justice," but his contributions to these two areas were not always in perfect harmony. The clash started very early in his career, in 1964:

> Back from Stanford in the autumn of 1964, Ann and I decided that the time had come for organized resistance to the swelling racism in England. From that moment, while keeping up with

> my heavy teaching load, I devoted every moment I could spare to the fight against racism. I abandoned my book on Frege; I gave no more time to thinking about philosophy. This condition lasted until the summer of 1968... (Dummett 2007, 18; similarly, Dummett 2001, ix).

This is a striking confession: An Oxford philosophy professor admits he "abandoned all attempt at creative work in philosophy" and "gave no more time to thinking about philosophy" for a full four years, although this was an important part of his job description and what he was actually paid to do. Instead of devoting his time to philosophical research, he engaged in political activity because he simply decided the latter was more pressing, entirely unconcerned with the fact that this constituted a breach of his contractual obligations with the university.[1] The only reason he did not neglect his philosophical work for longer than four years is that he became disappointed with the effects of his efforts against racism (Dummett 1973, xi).

In any case, Dummett's way of waging a battle against racism had itself many strange and illogical aspects. Here he describes how he became involved in helping asylum seekers upon their arrival in the UK:

> At that time [the mid-sixties], there were no entry clearance certificates: people simply arrived at the airport and were put back on the next plane if the immigration officer refused them. It was possible, however, to intervene and "make representations" on a refused immigrant's behalf if one could do so before he was put on the plane.... I of my own initiative... took up this work. I set up a network of informants at Heathrow, who would telephone me at any hour of the day or night to tell me of someone refused and with no one to speak for them. I would then have first to telephone the Chief Immigration

1 If Dummett considered the fight against racism so urgent and supremely important, surely he could have found another way to engage in it, without receiving a salary for a scholarly work that he intended to ignore, and did ignore completely, for years.

> Officer, which took a long time to get through, say I wished to make representations and then dash to the airport as quickly as possible. There I had to find out what I could about the case and say whatever I could on the refused person's behalf; he was then often admitted. This was the most exhausting period of my life (Dummett 2007, 21; a similar passage is found in Dummett 2001, x).

Notice the odd thing about the regular scenario: Upon receiving the information that someone has been refused by immigration officers, Dummett "dash[ed] to the airport as quickly as possible," and it is only then and there (at the airport) that he "had to find out what [he] could about the case and say whatever [he] could on the refused person's behalf." This means Dummett went to the airport with the intention of defending someone's right to stay in the United Kingdom *without knowing the background facts of this person's case at all.* We have to ask ourselves: Given this level of initial blind commitment, would it have been easy for him, upon reaching the airport, to recognize indications that, say, some of these people might have been coming to the UK to escape criminal charges in their homeland? Surely there must have been many cases of people who tried, for various reasons, to get into the UK by claiming, falsely, that they had been persecuted in their countries.

A Logician's Strange Route to Empirical Truth

Two years after becoming Wykeham Professor of Logic at Oxford, Dummett published a paper in which he claimed:

> [I]t should seem ... obvious that contemporary psychologists in the United States and Britain, advancing the thesis of the hereditary inferiority of Negro intelligence, are ... reflecting prejudices still widespread in these countries ... [and that hereditarianism about race differences in IQ,] so obviously conforming to a palpably powerful prejudice, can be set aside by any rational judge without further examination (Dummett 1981, 296, 298).

Dummett's reasoning is transparently fallacious. Clearly, even beliefs "conforming to a palpably powerful prejudice" may in fact be (strongly) supported by evidence. Moreover, they may well be correct. Exactly the opposite of what Dummett is saying is true: No opinion should be rejected merely because it conforms to a powerful prejudice.

The idea that it might be rational for a person lacking necessary expertise to dismiss a scientific hypothesis "without further examination" is alien to both the common sense and empiricism that have been a mark of British philosophy for centuries. It is regrettable that when it comes to psychological research about racial differences, Dummett did not heed the excellent general advice that "an ignorant but rational person can be no more than agnostic about questions that require a moderate degree of knowledge to answer." The name of the philosopher who gave that advice is Michael Dummett (2004, 29).

Later Dummett tried again, but in a different way, to show that the possibility of a significant genetically based IQ difference between racial groups can be dismissed *a priori*. Here is his argument:

> No one can rationally think that the great majority of members of any racial group are intellectually or artistically inferior to the great majority of members of some other group. It is obvious that within any racial group there is a great range of intelligence and of artistic talents. A belief in the inferiority of a whole racial group in either respect can be sustained with some show of rationality *only if* it is held that the group will *never* produce anyone of the highest achievements (ibid.; emphasis added).

Although Dummett insisted than no one can rationally think that the great majority of members of any racial group are intellectually inferior to the great majority of members of some other group, some scholars doing research on these issues have thought exactly this (and offered a rationale for their view). For example, citing the official data from the University of California at Berkeley, Arthur Jensen (1991, 182), a very prominent psychologist, stated that 90 percent of students belonging to the group consisting of blacks and Hispanics had a lower SAT score[2] than 90 percent of those belonging to the group consisting of whites and Asians, thereby producing precisely the kind of near bimodal distribution that Dummett so adamantly ruled out *a priori*. Let me stress that I am not claiming here that Jensen was necessarily right. My point is only that Dummett was clearly wrong in his resolute claim about what "no one can rationally think."

Dummett's only reason in support of his claim is the assertion that a belief in the inferiority of a certain group is sustainable "with some show of rationality" only if the group in question will never produce anyone of the highest achievement. But he is wrong about that too. Yes, if group A has a sufficiently higher mean IQ than group B, then under the assumption of normal distribution a great majority of As will indeed have a higher IQ than a great majority of Bs. But no, Dummett is wrong in saying that this situation entails that group B will *never* produce anyone of the highest achievement. Simply, the premises are statistical and for this reason alone they just cannot establish the conclusion that group B will never produce a very high achiever. On the contrary, rather than the probability of a very high achiever in group B being zero (as Dummett says), it will in reality always have a positive numerical value. Moreover, as the group size increases, the probability will rise steadily, becoming closer and closer to 1.

One does not expect this kind of misjudgment about elementary statistics from someone who received the prestigious Lakatos Award in the philosophy of science (which, as noted, Dummett did in 1994). Although his erroneous inference might perhaps be regarded as a well-meaning but clumsy attempt to advance racial justice, it certainly does not qualify as service to philosophy.

---

2 "[T]he SAT is an adequate measure of general intelligence" and it even appears to be "a better indicator of [general intelligence]... than are some of the more traditional intelligence tests" (Frey & Detterman 2004, 376–377).

A Pimp, a Criminal, and a Racist Invited to Talk at All Souls College

Another troubling feature of Dummett's political activism is the company he (occasionally) kept. Of course, when fighting for a social cause one often has to join forces with people who may be controversial in many respects. But here we are talking about something more drastic and sinister. Let me start with a passage from Christopher Hitchens's autobiography (2011, 261–62):

> A ludicrous but menacing local figure had named himself "Michael X" in the hope of attracting some cross-Atlantic street cred: as a Trinidadian pimp and hustler called Michael de Freitas he had won notoriety as an especially nasty enforcer of evictions for a rack-rent landlord named, in one of those Dickensian coincidences, Mr. Rachman. The soi-disant X had a group—actually a gang—called RAAS. The letters were supposed to stand for Racial Adjustment Action Society and some white liberal clergymen and similar dupes were induced to take it seriously, but in Caribbean patois, as one soon discovered, a "raas" was a used tampon.... At Oxford in my first term, a rather silly Catholic bleeding-heart don named Michael Dummett managed to use his privileges to get X to speak in the All Souls dining room.

Aside from the Hitchensian rhetorical flourishes, is his basic report trustworthy?

First of all, Michael X was indeed a shady character deeply immersed in a criminal milieu (Naipaul 1980), but this did not stop him from being active in the black power movement and founding RAAS. And second, Dummett was at the time heavily involved with another organization called the Campaign Against Racial Discrimination (CARD), whose goals largely overlapped with those of RAAS. So the two groups inevitably had mutual contacts and attempted to find a common platform in fighting for the same anti-racism cause.

Therefore, it seems prima facie very plausible that the two Michaels did meet on some occasion and that they knew each other. Hitchens places their joint appearance at All Souls at the time of his own first term as a student at Oxford, in the fall of 1967, just after Michael X had garnered a lot of press attention with a speech in Reading. This was the height of his political fame, the best moment for anyone to invite him to speak and expect that people would be interested. Another black activist, Stokely Carmichael, reports in his autobiography (2003, 574) that he met Michael X in London in the summer of 1967 and that his new acquaintance told him he had just attended a meeting with "some decent, very respectable people" and discussed with them solutions to "the growing racial problem in Britain." One of these respectable people was identified as "an Oxford don." As this was the time when Dummett had "abandoned all attempt at creative work in philosophy" and when he was devoting "every minute that [he] could spare" to battling racism, he must be the main candidate for being that Oxford don. It is virtually impossible that anyone else at Oxford at that time had this level of academically self-destructive devotion to the cause. In sum, we see the convergence of different lines of evidence that corroborates the story about Michael X speaking at All Souls at Dummett's invitation.

Some will say: So what? Even if it's true that Dummett was naive to get mixed up with a certain criminal who abused women for profit, what's the larger point here? Well, Michael X was not just a criminal but a vocal and notorious racist too. In the aforementioned Reading speech that put him in the public eye he said, among other things:

> If you ever see a white man laying hands on a black woman, kill him immediately.... Whitey is a vicious, nasty person. The fear of this white monkey is nothing—we will deal with him if necessary. The white man has no soul; you are dealing with a heartless sort of person if you are talking to a white man (reported in the *Times* of London, September 30, 1967).

For these statements he was later convicted of inciting racial hatred and spent eight months in jail.

If after Michael X's inflammatory statements came to public attention Dummett still decided to give such a person a platform at Oxford, he displayed a shocking lack of judgment, especially for someone professing to oppose racism *of any kind*. But did Michael X really give a talk at All Souls?

Indeed, this is conclusively confirmed by a short report published in the London *Times* on October 24, 1967, according to which Michael X did talk in front of two hundred people at All Souls College. He warned them about impending race riots in Britain and repeated his racist message by saying: "I get terrified of white people because I know they are vicious and nasty."

Obviously this kind of incendiary statement should not have surprised anyone, given what he had said in his widely publicized Reading speech. And this is precisely why a post-Reading talk at the London School of Economics was promptly canceled by the organizers. In contrast, his Oxford host, an arch-critic of racism, was neither alarmed nor had any second thoughts about inviting a person who was at that very time being tried in a court of law for stirring up race hatred.

Two weeks after his appearance at All Souls, Michael X was convicted for his previous statements inciting race hatred and went straight to jail. Soon after his release he was involved in another criminal-cum-racist incident and had to leave England in order to avoid a new trial and probable conviction. He moved back to Trinidad, where he was implicated in two murders; in one of them a young English woman was first badly injured in a botched murder attempt and then finished off by being buried alive. In the end, Michael X was sentenced to death in Trinidad and executed in 1975.

Someone will say these gruesome developments could not have been anticipated. But in fact, there were clear and ominous signs that Michael X was capable of committing horrible crimes, including murder. For example, he is quoted as having said at the Reading Magistrates' Court hearing: "Killing is a very strange thing.

The first time I ever killed a man I thought about it. A book I read said I would not be able to sleep at night. But that is not true. You can sleep at night."

Dummett was most probably aware of this because what transpired in the courtroom was extensively reported in the newspapers and also because the whole trial was closely monitored by a solicitor on behalf of the Campaign Against Racial Discrimination, in which (as noted) Dummett was very active.

A fact that bears emphasis: It was only some three weeks after Michael X's statements about killing came to public attention that All Souls College put out the welcome mat for him.

If despite all those red flags Dummett was still willing to lend support and respectability to a thug, pimp, and racist, this raises another worry about his judgment. Could it be that Dummett was sometimes similarly clueless when (as mentioned above) he rushed from Oxford to Heathrow to "represent" newly arrived asylum seekers and when he may have again occasionally swallowed tall tales of political persecution that were in some cases just a ruse of his protégés to enter the country with not necessarily the best intentions?

A Sham Engagement with Philosophy

Dummett was once asked whether he saw any connection between his philosophical ideas and his struggle against racism. He responded that he did see a connection in the following sense:

> In the situation we were then in in Britain, I saw a possibility for me to do something significant in a sector in which there were very few people taking any such action or even aware what the situation was. I do not think I could have respected myself *as a philosopher* if I had not undertaken that work: I should have felt that all my engagement with philosophy was a sham (1996, 194; emphasis added).

Dummett has got things backwards in his own case. He worried that had he not undertaken his "significant" political work, he could not have respected himself as a philosopher and that his engagement with philosophy would have been a sham. In reality, however, the worry about losing respect for himself as a philosopher should have been prompted *not* by what Dummett counterfactually might have failed to do but rather by what he actually did—i.e., waged an ill-considered battle against racism, made patently false and illogical statements in this context, and got duped into a shady world of reverse racism, ideological manipulation, and criminality. And yet for a full four years, Dummett was so enthusiastic about this kind of political engagement that for its sake he "gave no more time to thinking about philosophy." But he failed to see the obvious: Working as a philosopher for years while simultaneously abandoning thinking about philosophy comes as close as one can get to having "an engagement with philosophy that is a sham."

Could we imagine, by way of analogy, a surgeon who became upset about some social injustice and who, although continuing to work at the hospital, devoted every moment he could spare to his noble political cause and gave no more time to thinking about medicine for years? Hardly, because his lack of dedication to his profession would be soon detected by his patients, colleagues, and administrators, and he could not hope to keep his job with such an attitude.

It is a sad testimony to how irrelevant and dispensable philosophical activity has become (even in the eyes of philosophers themselves) that neither Dummett nor other philosophers apparently saw anything wrong in his open admission that over a long period of time he largely replaced his expected (and remunerated) philosophical work with political activism. Quite the opposite: His behavior has been regarded as admirable.

CHAPTER TEN

Hilary Putnam: A Follower of Chairman Mao

> "Mao demanded that university staff leave their lecture rooms and join with the peasants in the labor of the fields, a requirement that delighted many liberal academics on American and European campuses, though surprisingly few of them rushed to engage in these enriching activities themselves."
>
> —MICHAEL LYNCH

Hilary Putnam was indisputably a central figure in contemporary philosophy. When he died in March 2016 the *New York Times* published an obituary calling him "a giant of modern philosophy." Over a long career, he made a number of far-reaching contributions to the philosophy of mathematics, the philosophy of language, the philosophy of mind, the philosophy of science, and metaphysics. He received numerous professional recognitions, including the most prestigious ones like the Prometheus Prize of the American Philosophical Association, the Rolf Schock Prize, the Lauener Prize for an Outstanding Oeuvre in Analytical Philosophy, and the Nicholas Rescher Prize for Systematic Philosophy.

A Lover of Wisdom Joins a Cult

From 1968 to 1972, while he was in his forties, Putnam was a member of the Progressive Labor Party (PLP), which the historian Ronald Radosh called "a Marxist-Leninist sect that made the Communist Party look like a group of tame reformists" (2001,

12). Since some readers may regard Radosh as biased against the left, it should be noted that Martha Nussbaum, an academic with impeccable liberal credentials, described the PLP in a similar way, as a "cult":

> The Progressive Labor Party, the part of the SDS [Students for a Democratic Society] that was prominent at Harvard, always struck me as a corporatist and totalitarian movement, a cult in all but name. People I knew were ordered to marry (or, as the case may be, to leave their marriages) for the sake of correct political values. People would say, quite seriously, absurd things, such as, "We are getting married to emulate the lifestyle of the workers." Children were suddenly told not to talk to some adult they loved, because that person had the wrong view on some microsliver of revolutionary politics.... The PLP newspaper, called *Challenge*, quoted many people.... But all of them talked the same Maoist jargon, suggesting to me that either they were not quoted correctly or they had been brainwashed into a kind of group speak.... Hilary Putnam used to sell *Challenge* on the street corner in Harvard Square (2003, 95).

A former member of the party describes it thus:

> The "Progressive Labor" handle was the brainstorm of a couple of Buffalo, New York, steelworkers who had been booted out of the Communist Party USA for espousing the "Albanian Tendency" and, in the process, had embraced not only the glorious thoughts of Enver Hoxha but that of Mao as well. Progressive Labor talked tough, worked arduously at building a base for the coming revolution, and popularized Mao's Little Red Book before anyone else saw its commercial possibilities. Indeed, we lived by and for the Book. What is to be done? Here, read this. One step forward and two steps back.... Or is it two steps forward? I could never get it right.
>
> We studied Hegel and took target practice out at the Coyote Point police range right under the snouts of the pigs and held

> secret meetings at the International House of Pancakes where we wondered if it was time to go underground yet. Mostly we criticized ourselves and each other for not being revolutionary enough (Ross 2004, 43).

This is the group whose political program Putnam chose to identify with, as a card-carrying member, for four years of his life. One indication of the intensity of Putnam's activism is that he himself said that during that phase he was "never able to function as a philosopher" (quoted in Borradori 1994, 56). Indeed, he had a period of particularly low output precisely between 1968 and 1972 (as pointed out in De Gaynesford 2006, 3). Perhaps this should not be surprising: One cannot publish much if one believes that the most important truths are contained in a Little Red Book.

Three issues merit our attention here. First, the very fact of Putnam's long loyalty to the PLP. Second, his later comments on this episode. And third, the reactions of other philosophers.

In a 1970 article that starts with Marx's eleventh thesis on Feuerbach ("Philosophers have hitherto only *interpreted* the world in various ways; the point is to *change* it"), Putnam called on liberals to move further to the left and "participate in the radical task of remaking our world—the true task of philosophy" (1970, 74). There is nothing extraordinary about an Ivy League professor yearning to get out of his academic bubble and become "relevant." If he wanted to get involved in some kind of misty-eyed revolutionary activity, that's also unsurprising. There have been many such cases. But a highly intelligent[1], accomplished philosopher and exceptionally clear and rigorous thinker with some knowledge of politics—joining a party that glorifies Maoism? And staying in that party four years? In the middle of the Cultural Revolution?

Something is very wrong here. Of course, being wickedly smart in philosophy is compatible with having silly political views (as we have already seen), but it is hard to reconcile it with *that* level of protracted silliness.

---

1 Even among philosophers Putnam was famous for his "soaring IQ" (McGinn 2002, 166).

Could it be that Putnam somehow failed to be informed about what was going on in China at the time? This is extremely unlikely. The reports about the terrible events there could have been missed only by someone who had been living on another planet (Twin Earth, perhaps).

How did the ideology Putnam was extolling work in the real world? Among other things it included scenes of class enemies wearing dunce caps and others being forced on the stage bowing their heads in shame, with signs hung around their necks explaining their wrongdoings. Many of his colleagues in China were exposed to the same kind of public humiliation. Some of them were also brutally beaten up and killed.

Books were banned and burned, as shown in Figure 10.1, all in the frenzied attempt to destroy the so-called "Four Olds": old ideas, old customs, old culture, and old habits. Did Putnam, the Maoist, ever think about how much of the collection of, say, the Widener Library at Harvard would have to be burnt if old and "useless" books were discarded using similar ideological criteria? After all, on what grounds could he approve of what the Red Guards were doing in Beijing or Shanghai but oppose the same thing in Cambridge, Massachusetts? In fact, Putnam advertised the Cultural Revolution to his own students; he used to speak on a podium and advise them to read Mao's *Little Red Book* (O'Grady 2016).

Inside the Chinese Utopia

How much did Putnam know about the situation in China? Surely he must have at least been following the *New York Times*, which on January 2, 1970, published a long article headlined "The Making of a Red Guard." It was written by a former Red Guard who had managed to escape from mainland China to Taiwan and who gave a detailed and harrowing report about how he and his fellow students had horribly abused their own teachers, all in the name of Maoism. The essay was hard to overlook as it was splashed across seven pages of the newspaper.

Here is an excerpt:

FIGURE 10.1: Book burning during the Cultural Revolution

At 12 o'clock on June 12, as a few of us were on our way back from a swim, we heard screams and shouts as we approached the school gate and some schoolmates ran up to us shouting: "The struggle has begun! The struggle has begun!" I ran to the athletic field and saw rows of teachers, about 40 or 50 of them, all with black ink poured over their heads and faces to make them truly a "black gang," a term used from the beginning of the Cultural Revolution in condemnation of intellectuals. Hanging on their necks were placards with such words as "Reactionary academic authority So-and-So," "Class enemy So-and-So," "Corrupt ringleader So-and-So," "Capitalist roader So-and-So," all taken from the newspapers. On each placard was a red cross, making the teachers look like condemned prisoners awaiting execution. They all wore dunce caps painted with similar slogans and carried dirty brooms, shoes and dusters on their backs. Hanging around their necks were pails filled with

> rocks. They were barefoot, hitting broken gongs or pots as they walked around the field, shouting, "I am black gangster So-and-So." Finally, they all knelt down, burned incense and begged Mao Tse-tung to "pardon their crimes."
>
> I had never before seen the tortures I was to see here: eating night soil or insects, being subjected to electrical shocks, forced to kneel on broken glass, being hanged by the arms and legs.
>
> During this period, the worst shock to me was the fatal beating of my most respected and beloved teacher, Yang Hsin-yung. Teacher Yang, advanced in age and suffering from high blood pressure, was dragged out at 11:30, exposed to the summer sun for more than two hours, then paraded through the streets carrying a placard and hitting a gong. He was dragged up to the fourth floor of a building and down again, being savagely beaten along the way. Imagine, a man over 60 years of age! He passed out several times, but was brought back to consciousness each time with cold water splashed into his face. He could hardly move his body, his feet were cut by glass and thorns. But his spirit was unbroken. He shouted, "Why don't you kill me? Kill me!" This lasted for six hours, until at last he collapsed.
>
> Many outsiders did not realize that a lot of the "teachers of the people" whose sudden deaths during the Cultural Revolution were officially certified as natural and many Communist cadres who were later declared dead due to illness or declared missing by the Red Guards actually died under torture.

And yet even after this disturbing story disclosed some of the horrors of the Maoist Cultural Revolution, Putnam remained the member of the Maoist party for another three years. Why? Here is, to the best of my knowledge, the only place where he addresses that question:

> "Why didn't you know all this in 1968?" I will be asked, especially by my social democratic friends who were never tempted by the vision of Marxism-Leninism. Well, I did know about the Gulags. That is why I joined a group that supported no existing state. But I found within the group itself the same contempt for

> genuine discussion, the same manipulation, the same hysterical denunciation of anything that attempted to be principled opposition, that my father had found in the American communist party back in the forties. Perhaps I was dumb. Certainly I was depressed and desperate (1992, 190).

This explanation will not do. If Putnam's former party was Maoist, isn't it clear that, contrary to what he says, it did support the political system and ideology of "an existing state," namely China? Also, his complaints about all the bad things he found in the party may tell us why he eventually left it, but they are irrelevant for the much more interesting question: Why did he join the party in the first place and why did he stay in it so long?

In his intellectual autobiography as well, Putnam focuses exclusively on his reasons for leaving the PLP. He explains that in the end he realized that not only was the PLP's talk about democracy "a complete sham," the party leaders' favorite expression about other liberal politicians, "He should be shot," was not just an expression but a symptom of their fixation on "the fantasy of a violent revolution in which all rival political leaders and intellectuals would indeed be killed" (Putnam 2015, 81–82). So it took "one of the 20th century's true philosophic giants" a full four years of obedience to the PLP's leaders to figure out that they were actually dangerous people prepared to kill others over ideological disagreements.[2]

In a post on his blog "The Life of Hilary Putnam," Putnam stated that his involvement with the PLP "was ultimately wrong and on the extreme side," but he failed to say what exactly was wrong about it. Yet he was quite specific about what he saw as virtues of the PLP: "I did admire the PLP for their commitment to alliance building between nations, as well as their strong-willed attempts to

2 Immediately after Putnam left the PLP, his philosopher wife Ruth Anna Putnam joined the party. This sequence of events would hardly make sense if it was precisely at that time that Putnam recognized the murderous intentions of those running the organization. Another illustration of how politically radical the Putnams were is that, commenting on this "PIPO" episode (Putnam in, Putnam out) the *Harvard Crimson* reported in February 1973 that Ruth Anna "begins each term's classes by declaring herself a communist and telling her students that if they care to subscribe to the party newspaper, they should contact her."

organize within the armed forces throughout the country" (http://hilaryputnam-blog.tumblr.com/post/34263130128/activism).

Contrast this high praise of the PLP with Putnam's strident condemnation of American mainstream politics over the years. For instance, in an article first published in 1987 he mentioned with admiration the mathematician Norbert Wiener's announcement that he would no longer work for the U.S. Department of Defense. Wiener explained his decision by saying: "I don't give four-year-olds razor blades" (Putnam 1992, 207).

Putnam was not only impressed with Wiener's "deep" remark, he used it himself, pouring similar scorn on the Reagan administration's handling of the Cold War: "So we continue passing out razor blades to the children, and the children continue promising not to use them." He explained further:

> I do not believe that it can possibly be right to help make weapons—*any sort of weapons*—under *present* conditions, when we live under a government that does not—I believe—have the slightest desire for arms control at all, a government that refuses to move in the direction of reducing the danger of nuclear war. That much seems clear to me (ibid., 208).

A huge and obvious irony of the situation was completely lost on Putnam: The highest officials in the American government were being likened to little children by someone who just a few years earlier admired an unhinged and violence-prone sect for its attempts to infiltrate the American armed forces "throughout the country." Now, who exactly is more like the four-year-olds here?

In a long article, "Two Experts Explain China's Cultural Revolution: Trying to Comprehend the Incomprehensible" (published in the *New York Times* on November 17, 1968), readers were informed that Red Guards 10 to 18 years old were the masters of Beijing for months "while the police were forbidden to intervene." Hence another irony: Putnam condemned what he metaphorically described as giving razors to four-year-olds but earlier he himself glorified a leader who was reported by the main American newspaper to have let children, some of them literally ten-year-olds, terrorize a city of more than 7 million people.

In one interview Putnam comments very briefly on his involvement with the PLP: "I was connected with a Maoist group. I am no longer a Maoist" (Borradori 1994, 59). The first sentence is an understatement. Not merely "connected" with a Maoist group, he was in fact a full and very active member. The second sentence, however, needs some unpacking in order to appreciate its full implications. What the statement "I am no longer a Maoist" really says is "I am no longer a supporter of the biggest mass murderer in human history."

One would have expected here a follow-up question from the interviewer, because Putnam's terse remark screams out for further explanation. One would have also expected that at least some commentators or journalists would probe deeper and try to make some sense of the famous philosopher's descent into totalitarian madness. But there was no curiosity about this. And apparently there is none today either. It is almost as if this Maoist episode only spiced up Putnam's biography and in some people's eyes just made him look more "cool" and less boring than a typical academic.

Would university professors have reacted with similar indifference and mild amusement if, in the sixties, a leading Harvard scholar had praised, say, the authoritarian regime in Spain and campaigned passionately to introduce Franco's political system in the United States? Of course not. And yet there should be no question that Mao's regime was incomparably more inhumane than Franco's.

A troubling thought is that Putnam's evasiveness about his past may be a sign that he has never fully understood the enormity of Mao's crimes. Here is what he said in an interview many years after he abandoned his attempts to bring the Chinese Communist utopia to America: "Then we had two very atheist dictators, called Stalin and Hitler, who between them killed even more people than anyone had killed in the name of the sacred" (Borradori 1994, 65).

How can one talk about murderous atheist dictators without mentioning Mao? Especially if one had worshipped him for a long time and is now allegedly ready to recognize entirely the monstrous nature of Mao's rule.

At one point Putnam's party experienced a huge disappointment with the Chinese "road to socialism" and then took the Albanian turn: "The climax to this relentless sectarianism came after Nixon's visit to Peking when the PLP broke with China herself for seeking a rapprochement with the USA. *Only Albania remained, in all the world, wholly admirable*" (Caute 1988, 387; emphasis added).

In brief, as long as Mao maintained his strict isolation from the West, the PLP considered him great, although he was killing and terrorizing his own people. But as soon as he allowed his country to establish contact—horrors!—with the United States, his "path" had to be abandoned immediately. Now the PLP's utopia had to be built by dropping the old model and by emulating the political regime in Tirana. For almost a whole year, Putnam obediently followed this new party line that extolled Enver Hoxha as the only hope for the future of humanity.

But Putnam's militant activism was not restricted to party politics. It also spilled over into his views about academic issues and led to vicious attacks on his own colleagues at Harvard and attempts at character assassination. In a 1972 talk at Princeton he first gratuitously labeled the psychologist Richard Herrnstein as "racist" (see p. 166, footnote 2, for the explanation of why this accusation was wrong) and then publicly urged that Herrnstein be fired from the university (see the *Daily Princetonian*, March 13, 1972).

The fact that Putnam's intolerance for different opinions sometimes went so far that he was willing to denounce other scholars in a way that trampled basic principles of academic freedom shows that, after all, joining a Maoist party may have been an excellent fit for someone with his views on politics and scholarship.[3]

---

3 Apparently there were other card-carrying Maoists among the leading philosophers of the time but we don't know their names: "And many in the profession wince at the memory of a band of Harvard philosophers who went out and joined the Progressive Labor Party in the 1960's, possessed of an ideological fervor that moved them to chant and proselytize and do all manner of things they soon came to regret" (*New York Times*, August 14, 1977).

CHAPTER ELEVEN

Donald Davidson: A Dupe of the Communist Party

"In the end the Party would announce that two and two made five, and you would have to believe it."

—GEORGE ORWELL

Donald Davidson is one of the most important figures in contemporary philosophy. He made significant contributions to many fields, primarily to the philosophy of mind, the philosophy of action, and the theory of meaning. But in contrast to the high level of sophistication and careful argumentation characteristic of his philosophical work, his involvement with politics sometimes failed the minimal test of rationality.

An Unjust War Yesterday, a Just War Today

On a number of occasions Davidson described an interesting episode from the beginning of his academic career, when he was a graduate student of philosophy at Harvard in 1941. It is always basically the same story, with slight variations. For example:

> It suddenly became apparent [in the spring of 1941] that the United States was probably going to get into the war. . . . I thought I saw it coming. . . . And my politics were very left-wing. In fact, I certainly was the kind of person that was at the time

> called "fellow-traveler." At that time, if you were in those circles, you were against the United States getting into the war.... *That is what you were told to think*.... So [in order to stay out of armed services] I got into the Harvard Business School.... But meanwhile something else had happened. And that was of course that the Germans had invaded Russia, and we fellow-travelers at that point changed our minds about the nature of the war. I am not proud of this history, but it is a history that quite a number of people had at that time, certainly a lot of my friends (Fara, 1997; emphasis added).

And again, in a similar vein:

> My politics were like all my left-wing friends. I never joined the communist party, but I followed the party line.... When Germany invaded Russia we fellow travelers changed our minds about the nature of the war. *Now* there was a good and a bad side (Lepore, 2004, 241; emphasis added).

This is a fascinating psychological transformation. Davidson was consistently and strongly opposed to the war against Nazi Germany for a couple of years, and then suddenly on June 22, 1941—click! Only then—that is, three years after Kristallnacht, two years after the brutal invasion of Poland—"*now* there [is] a good and a bad side," and he becomes so enthusiastic about opposing the Nazis that he soon volunteers for service in the Naval Reserve (Davidson 1999, 24).

It is very hard to make sense of such an abrupt change of opinion,[1] especially because Davidson says that up till the German

---

1 How abrupt was this change of heart? This abrupt: "The story is going round that when the news of Hitler's invasion of Russia reached a New York café where some Communists were talking, one of them who had gone out to the lavatory returned to find that the 'party line' had changed in his absence" (from George Orwell's diary, on July 6, 1941). The record holder, however, is probably Michael Quill (head of the Transport Workers Union in New York), who "is reputed to have changed his line in the middle of a speech when somebody handed him a notice saying that the Soviet Union had been invaded, and he's supposed to have changed his line from calling it an imperialist war to calling it a war of liberation" (James I. Loeb, in an interview conducted for the Harry S. Truman Library).

attack on the Soviet Union, "with [his] political views in the penumbra of the Party line, [he] saw the war as a struggle for markets" (ibid.). How could a bad war (a struggle for markets) all at once become a good war (a noble fight against the evil of fascism)? The mind reels.

While the American Communist Party lost almost half its members after the Nazi–Soviet Pact of 1939 (Jacoby 2008, 89), Davidson did not waver in his loyalty to Moscow. It should be stressed that he had both relevant personal experience and close contacts with people with anti-Stalinist views, which should all have naturally protected him from Communist indoctrination and prevented him from becoming such a blind follower of the Party line. He had actually visited Germany after Hitler came to power (mind you, two years *after* the introduction of the Nuremberg Laws), so he obviously had a good opportunity to see firsthand the rise of the Nazi regime and notice that it had other goals besides getting access to new markets. And we know that around the time of his opposition to the war, Davidson had already become friends with Quine, who was resolutely anti-totalitarian, and certainly anti-Soviet. (The two of them, and another friend, drove across Mexico in the summer of 1940 or 1941.)

And despite the presence of these two potentially strong antidotes to Bolshevik brainwashing, a very intelligent person could still turn into a robotlike creature remotely controlled from Moscow, believing simply what he was "told to think." About such people Orwell said that "the Russo-German Pact...brought the Stalinists and near-Stalinists into the pro-Hitler position" (London letter to *Partisan Review*, January 3, 1941).

Notice that this is not just a case of a single individual who, by some fluke, happened to be seduced by Marxist-Leninist ideology. In all likelihood, many more philosophers would have similar stories to tell. For, as Davidson helpfully comments on his own fellow-traveler past: "[I]t is a history that quite a number of people had at that time, certainly a lot of my friends." Apparently these friends were not willing later to come forward and talk so openly about their former Stalinist sympathies. It is precisely for this reason that his own sincerity should be all the more appreciated.

And yet philosophers showed surprisingly little interest in this amazing episode. Although Davidson is one of the most prominent thinkers in twentieth-century philosophy and although he repeated several times that he and a lot of his friends were "dupes of the Communist Party," I had difficulty finding a single comment on this by any philosopher.

When Plato and Aristotle famously said that the beginning of philosophy is wonder, they meant philosophers have the ability to be surprised and amazed at many things that other people see as ordinary and uninteresting. Here, however, it is the other way around: Philosophers were those who reacted with a yawn while other people were astonished because they thought they were facing something close to "a real mystery." For example, this is Saul Bellow's comment on the scope of the political irrationality of the Communists and fellow-travelers like Davidson:

> Now there is a real mystery about Communists in the West, to limit myself to those. How were they able to accept Stalin—one of the most monstrous tyrants ever? You would have thought that the Stalin-Hitler division of Poland, the defeat of the French which opened the way to Hitler's invasion of Russia, would have led CP members to reconsider their loyalties. But no... Well, it was a deep and perverse stupidity. It didn't require a great mind to see what Stalinism was. But the militants and activists refused to reckon with the simple facts available to everybody (from a 1998 letter to Philip Roth).

These are harsh words, but then again, this is probably an appropriate description for the behavior in question: "a deep and perverse stupidity."

Imagine There's No Grades...

Another window into how leftist politics clouded Davidson's mind is provided by some of his actions during the student movement of the sixties. When the wave of student protests reached Princeton, Davidson was the chairman of the philosophy department. The philosophy students demanded that all grades be abolished because they decided "it was demeaning to be graded."

Although several members of the department were resolutely against that proposal, Davidson sided with the students. His explanation is interesting:

> *Somewhat to my own surprise* I argued that since no one knew what succeeded in education, the students would probably learn more by being allowed to take an active role in deciding educational policy than by being forced to submit to the traditional policies (1999, 47; emphasis added).

It is quite revealing that Davidson admits he was himself surprised that he argued the way he did. It is almost as if it was the *students* who now "told him what to think."

Besides, the argument he used to support the students' request is embarrassingly inadequate. It is based on a gratuitous assumption that if the students were allowed to decide about educational policies they would thereby "probably" learn more. There was no persuasive evidence then that this is true, just as there is none now.

Nevertheless, Davidson somehow managed to convince the majority of his department colleagues to support the students. As we know, many academics at the time succumbed to the pressure to be progressive and condemn the status quo. Imagine there's no grades, it's easy if you try....

The next step was to persuade the entire Princeton faculty, and this was promptly accomplished as well: "Tim Scanlon [currently a leading moral philosopher from Harvard] undertook to write the necessary brief, and he did it brilliantly. The faculty was won over, the victorious students graduated, and no discernible damage was done" (ibid.).

In the very next sentence, however, Davidson contradicts himself and concedes that some damage was indeed done. Namely it turned out that without grades students had problems getting into law, business, and medical schools. This easily predictable consequence was completely unforeseen by the Princeton faculty under the influence of Davidson and Scanlon. Anyway, there was a change of heart and the "demeaning" practice of grading was soon brought back at the request of the students.

But wasn't there also something demeaning about the university professors so suddenly and thoughtlessly changing their views all in order to please the restless students and satisfy their whims? But this was the spirit of the times. Ah, the sixties . . . As Allan Bloom said, "[S]tudents discovered that pompous teachers who catechized them about academic freedom could, with a little shove, be made into dancing bears" (1987, 315).

Princeton Philosophers and Czech Dissidents Unimpressed with Angela Davis

In another curious twist, in 1969 Davidson invested a lot of effort in trying to secure an academic job in a top philosophy department for a young radical political activist, Angela Davis:

> In one matter I failed. Princeton was undergoing another revolution: it was expanding to admit women. It was suddenly noticed that there [were] few women teaching there. I proposed that we hire Angela Davis. She was interviewed, but the department faculty was unimpressed, and she wasn't appointed (1999, 47).

There are several puzzling things here.

First, why did Davidson think that Davis was the *best* candidate for the extremely competitive academic position in what was arguably the top philosophy department in the country? After all, she didn't even have a Ph.D. at the time, nor any publications, nor apparently any other distinguishing philosophical accomplishment.

Second, Davis was mainly interested in Marxism and continental philosophy, areas in no way connected with any topics of Davidson's own research. Therefore, since he was certainly not in a good position to evaluate her work or philosophical promise, there was something awkward in the fact that he played such an active role and pushed for her to be hired.

And third, even after he failed to persuade his own department on this matter Davidson did not give up. He went on to contact the philosophy department at the University of California, Los Angeles, telling the people there about Davis and urging them to hire her (Kalish 1969), which they eventually did, although only a bare majority voted to offer her a two-year contract (Aptheker 1999, 2). Among those opposing her hiring was the logician Richard Montague, as well as most other analytic philosophers.

At the end of the 1960s, revolution was in the air. Radicalized students were asking for "relevant" courses in which Marxism would be combined with a critique of American imperialism, social injustice, alienation, consumerism, etc. For some reason the Princeton philosophy department was deficient in these offerings. But fortunately for students, the chairman was willing to accommodate their demands, although in a rather unexpected way:

> Under the new dispensation, students could petition for a course on an untaught subject, and our students asked for a seminar on the early, humanistic Marx. I agreed that they should have it, but no one in the department, several of whom could have done it competently, volunteered, so I did it myself.... I let the students do most of the preparing and talking, and they imported various famous student firebrands from Columbia and elsewhere. It was an interesting experiment but it would have been better if Angela Davis had been there to teach it (Davidson 1999, 47–48).

What Davidson implicitly but unequivocally is saying is that he was not competent to teach a course on Marx, but that he nevertheless volunteered to do it.

Would a similar arrangement have been possible with a course that went against the sentiment of the age? For instance, if, rather improbably, there had been a group of students keen on taking a course on Ayn Rand's praise of capitalism and if there happened to be no one in the philosophy department competent and willing to teach it, would the chairman have volunteered to facilitate this learning experience as well? Would he have encouraged the students to invite Randian hotheads from elsewhere to come and run the show at Princeton? Maybe in the Twilight Zone.

Finally, there are also problems with Davidson's claim that "it would have been better if Angela Davis had been there to teach [that course]." First of all, given what is known about her philosophical accomplishments at the time (and later), there is nothing to support the claim that Davis would have done a better job teaching that Marxism course than the students who in the end took charge of it.

Moreover, there is a good reason to think they might have actually been a better choice. For, in contrast to Angela Davis, it is unlikely that they would have supported the imprisonment of political dissidents for thought crimes in Communist countries, as she did. Consider the following passage from a talk given by the Czech-Canadian writer Josef Škvorecký in Toronto in 1981 (1988, 248–49):

> When Angela Davis was in jail, a Czech socialist politician, Jiři Pelikán, a former Communist and now a member of the European Parliament for the Italian Socialist Party, approached her through an old American Communist lady and asked her whether she would sign a protest against the imprisonment of Communists in Prague. She agreed to do so, but not until she got out of jail because, she said, it might jeopardize her case. When she was released, she sent word via her secretary that she would fight for the release of political prisoners anywhere in the world except, of course, in the socialist states. Anyone sitting in a socialist jail must be against socialism, and therefore deserves to be where he is. All birds can fly. An ostrich is a bird. Therefore an ostrich can fly. So much for the professor of philosophy Angela Davis.

Indeed, Jiři Pelikán's open letter to Angela Davis received a great deal of publicity in 1972 when it was published in the London *Times*, the *New York Review of Books*, and *Die Zeit.* Pelikan urged Davis to join the fight for the liberation of all political prisoners in the world, including Czechoslovakia and the Soviet Union. Davis flatly rejected the appeal, explaining her reasons through her spokesperson, Charlene Mitchell:

> Miss Davis, [Mitchell] said, did not think that people should leave socialist countries to return to the capitalist system. This was a retrograde step, and even if such people said that they were communists they were still acting in opposition to the "socialist system," objectively speaking.... Miss Mitchell, who said she was acting as a spokesman for Miss Davis, took the line that people in Eastern Europe got into difficulties and ended in jail only if they were undermining the government. Those who left to go into political exile were also attacking their own country (London *Times*, July 28, 1972).

According to Angela Davis, therefore, all those who risked (or lost) their lives in numerous attempts to escape from East Germany and (by implication) all those who in 1989 started the exodus that led to the fall of the Berlin Wall were in fact "attacking their own country"!

Davis was soon rewarded for her loyalty. Later that same year (1972) she was received by Erich Honecker, the Communist leader of East Germany, who awarded her the Great Star for International Friendship for "her extraordinary service on behalf of the German Democratic Republic." See Figure 11.1.

A few years later came the ultimate recognition, the Lenin Peace Prize, which was presented to Davis by Leonid Brezhnev himself.

It is precisely in light of these and similar facts (which Davidson must have been familiar with in 1999 when he lamented Davis's non-appointment in the sixties)[2] that we can conclude those

2 It was hard to miss Solzhenitsyn's mention of Angela Davis in his famous talk at Harvard in July 1975. He also mentioned the Czech dissidents' appealing to Davis for support and her response that "they deserve what they get. Let them remain in prison." Solzhenitsyn commented: "That is the face of Communism. That is the heart of Communism for you" (1976, 61).

FIGURE 11.1: Erich Honecker and Angela Davis

students in that newly introduced Princeton course in 1969 were in all likelihood exposed to a less crude version of Marxism and less totalitarianism-worship when they were instructed by "various famous student firebrands" than if they had been taught by Angela Davis.

Davidson is of course far from being the only major philosopher who was fascinated with Davis. But there is an unexpected name on the list of her fans: Alfred Tarski, whom the Stanford Encyclopedia of Philosophy describes as "one of the greatest logicians of the twentieth century (often regarded as second only to Gödel), and thus as one of the greatest logicians of all time."

Since Tarski was a staunch anti-Communist who even expressed his opposition to the student movement of the sixties, he was seemingly unlikely to be a Davis admirer. And yet there is evidence for this, as we learn from a highly esteemed biography written by two scholars who both knew Tarski personally:

> Given Tarski's political views, [his doctoral student Benjamin] Wells was amazed when, in the mid-seventies, Tarski showed him a scrapbook in which he kept extensive newspaper

> clippings of three women associated with revolutionary movements of the period whom he called "my heroes": Angela Davis, Bernardine Dohrn, and Patricia (Patty) Hearst (Feferman & Feferman 2004, 327).

An additional puzzling feature is that Davis kept her place on Tarski's list up to the mid-seventies, even after her cozying up to Communist tyrants in Eastern Europe and her highly publicized refusal to lift a finger to support the persecuted dissidents there, including those in Tarski's homeland of Poland.

Another person on the list of Tarski's "heroes" deserves our attention too: Bernardine Dohrn, a member of the radical leftist organization known as the Weather Underground (or the Weathermen), which conducted a series of politically inspired bombings in the United States in the seventies. Since Tarski kept "extensive newspaper clippings" of Dohrn and others, he probably could not have missed the memorable part of a long article about the Weathermen that occupied half a page of the *New York Times*'s Sunday "Week in Review" section on March 15, 1970:

> Nonetheless, it is difficult to escape the feeling that these youngsters are demented. How else explain the admiration for Sirhan Sirhan, the murderer of Senator Robert F. Kennedy, or for Charles Manson, group leader of a band of alleged murderers. Among these youngsters, there are open jokes about assassinations, and a salivating over violence. Witness Bernardine Dohrn: "Dig it, first they killed those pigs [actress Sharon Tate and her friends], then they ate dinner in the same room with them, then they even shoved a fork into a victim's stomach! Wild!"

Members of Manson's cult murdered Sharon Tate and four other people one night in August 1969, although they hadn't had any previous contact with them. Being in the ninth month of pregnancy, Tate unsuccessfully pleaded for the life of her unborn baby. After she was stabbed fifteen times the killers used her blood to write "pig" on the house's front door.

The *New York Times* got it right. Anyone who, like Dohrn, revels in this kind of bestial and gratuitous violence must be demented.[3] It is amazing, however, that apparently it was possible for a person so sick in the mind to be called a hero by one of the greatest logicians of all time.[4]

---

3 Dohrn's later attempt to present her remarks as merely a "joke" is totally unconvincing. At the 1969 Weathermen meeting where she made these remarks, Charles Manson was indeed officially proclaimed to be "a revolutionary hero," while a picture of poor Sharon Tate was displayed in the gallery of "enemies" (Barber 2008, 210, 255).

4 Later Wells, who was the source of the story, tried to make sense of Tarski's attitude toward the three women activists, but in the end he made things only more confusing: "[W]hile [Tarski] was not joking, his attitude was definitely ironic bordering on sarcastic, all the while in dead earnest. That still does not explain his motivation but makes it more likely derisive than celebratory" (Wells 2007, 984).

But how is it possible that Tarski "was not joking" and that he was "in dead earnest" and yet his attitude was "definitely ironic bordering on sarcastic"? Notice also that Wells, despite having been a student, friend, and huge admirer of Tarski, is not sure what to think about the whole episode himself. Even he takes quite seriously the possibility that Tarski's motivation here was indeed celebratory.

CHAPTER TWELVE

The American Philosophical Association: A Vehicle for Partisan Politics

"When philosophers try to be politicians they generally cease to be philosophers."

—WALTER LIPPMANN

The American Philosophical Association (APA) has three divisions (Eastern, Central and Pacific) and more than 11,000 members, including many non-Americans. It is probably the most important philosophical organization in the world. It also has a long and rich history of being drawn into leftist political activism. A brief overview follows.

Philosophers Advise: Withdraw from Vietnam with the Maximum Physical Speed!

At the business meeting of the Eastern Division of the APA in 1969, Hilary Putnam proposed that the APA adopt a resolution against the war in Vietnam. The proposed resolution said, among other things, that the war was "a direct consequence of a foreign policy whose basic aim is to make and keep a large part of the world safe for American enterprise"; that the peace negotiations in Paris actually "serve the purpose of deceiving the American people"; that "the United States economic involvement in various parts of the world—particularly in underdeveloped countries—amounts to the exploitation of the peoples of these countries and is, therefore, not in their interest"; and that "the United States economic involvement in various parts of the world necessitates the suppression of popular rebellions by acts ranging from open warfare to undercover activities by the CIA."

It is odd that despite the obvious controversiality of most of these statements, Putnam intended them to be adopted and publicized as the opinion of the whole APA. Nevertheless, the attempt to suspend Putnam's proposal failed to get enough votes. A revised version of the resolution was finally accepted, with the following main conclusion: "[W]e oppose... the claim that the United States has any right to negotiate the future of the Vietnamese people, and we advocate instead the total withdrawal from Vietnam of all American forces as fast as is physically possible."

It is unclear whether those who voted for the resolution were aware that one of the main points of those negotiations they so staunchly opposed was an attempt to prevent the expected invasion of South Vietnam by the Communists from the North as well as the massacres and massive crimes that were anticipated in the event of such an invasion. And indeed, when the eventual departure of the American troops allowed the Communists to take over, the worst fears came true: According to R. J. Rummel, an analyst of mass killings and other crimes by states, in the period between 1975 and 1987 there were at least 50,000 extrajudicial executions in Vietnam, more than a million Vietnamese people fled the country (most of them the "boat people") and in the process more than 100,000 of them died at sea, while he estimated that around 2.5 million people went through re-education camps and possibly half a million were condemned to forced labor. (The APA never considered a motion to protest any of this, or call on anyone to do something about it.)

Furthermore, the philosophers' demand that U.S. forces withdraw with the greatest speed that is *physically* possible shows their astonishing disregard of the complexity of such a political decision on multiple levels. For instance, aren't there obviously many military and political issues that would have to be considered and evaluated before a reasonable person would publicly defend this policy of lightning-speed withdrawal? And isn't it very clear that participants at the business meeting of the Eastern Division of the APA were not in a position to assess these very complex and highly relevant issues?

A good point (and pertinent in our context) was made in a discussion about another case of faculty opposition to the Vietnam War in a letter to the *New York Times* on April 2, 1967. I will only slightly change its wording: "It is not clear why people trained in [philosophy] believe their opinions on military and international problems should carry much validity. Certainly they would oppose unqualified Pentagon generals telling them how to teach their courses."

One of the severest critics of the APA's resolution against American involvement in Vietnam was Ayn Rand (1999, 48):

> The outcome was a double disgrace: (1) that a philosophical association passed a political resolution and (2) the kind of resolution it passed.
>
> (1) No professional organization has the right to take an ideological stand in the name of its members. A man's ideas, including political convictions, are exclusively his to determine and cannot be delegated to or prescribed by anyone else.... The practice of passing ideological resolutions is a futile and immoral device of pressure-group warfare. For all the very reasons that a philosopher, as a thinking individual, should take a strong stand on political issues, he should not allow it to be taken for him by a collective....
>
> (2) If movie stars give out interviews criticizing *military* tactics, no one takes it seriously. If drugged adolescents scream demands that the war in Vietnam be ended at once, regardless of means, methods, context or consequences, one wonders about the quality of their educators. But when an association of philosophers does *both*, it is a disgrace.

Ouch! A huge number of philosophers regard Rand as a crude thinker who does not deserve to be called "philosopher" at all. Besides, since philosophers strongly lean to the political left, they tend to find her political views repugnant.[1] And yet, it is hard to deny that in this particular case Rand did hit the nail on the head.

It is not that criticisms of the politicization of the APA were not expressed within the association itself. They were, but with no effect, because apparently they did not coincide with "the general will" of the association. In 1971 a group of philosophers, spearheaded by Sidney Hook, Harry Frankfurt, and Nelson Goodman, raised their voice against the recent wave of political resolutions adopted by the APA. They wrote: "A philosopher or teacher of philosophy does not join the APA in order to use it as a vehicle for his political opinion. He does not give the APA, by joining it, a mandate to make political pronouncements in his name" (reported in the *New York Times*, May 30, 1971).

But their intervention had no effect: The flood of political resolutions continued.

The APA Decrees on Abortion, IQ, Nuclear Weapons, Death Penalty, Iraq War...

In December 1971, Hilary Putnam proposed that the APA "condemn as unscientific and dangerous the views of [Harvard psychologist Richard] Herrnstein, [Nobel laureate physicist William] Shockley, and [University of California, Berkeley, educational psychologist Arthur] Jensen concerning the genetic basis of differences in mean intelligence between blacks and whites."[2] The proposal also condemned the *Atlantic Monthly, Harvard Educational Review*, and the *New York Times Magazine* on the strange ground

1 Lawrence Summers, who knows a thing or two about American universities, said in a recent talk: "Philosophy departments almost without exception boycott Ayn Rand's disciples."

2 It appears that Putnam did not even read Herrnstein's article carefully before asking the APA to condemn it, because at the time Herrnstein explicitly expressed agnosticism about the possible genetic basis of the racial gap in IQ (Herrnstein 1971, 57).

that they "irresponsibly supported" these "unfounded conclusions" merely by publishing articles in which these claims were defended. Despite complaints that the views in question should not be condemned without sufficient evidence and that the condemnation actually opposed the exercise of free speech and free research, the motion carried and was put to mail ballot. It was voted down, but a similar motion was proposed again the following year. Although it was suggested that it made no sense to push the same motion that had been defeated the previous year, without any events' occurring in the meantime that would likely change the result, the motion carried and was again put to mail ballot (with an unknown result).

In 1972 a resolution defending the pro-choice side in the abortion debate was proposed. David Lewis opposed it on the grounds that "no corporate body ever should vote on a moral issue, even on one so clear as this." Contrary to what Lewis said, there was nothing clear about this issue, unless the clarity of moral issues is understood as being determined by the majority opinion among philosophers. This was all happening immediately before the Supreme Court's decision on *Roe v. Wade,* and the nation was notoriously split on the issue. Lewis must have been well aware of this. It is possible he just wanted to signal that he also regarded the pro-choice position as clearly correct himself, but that he was still against the APA taking a side on such a divisive issue. Next it was announced that the Society for Women in Philosophy supported the resolution. After that, the majority voted in favor of the resolution.

Around that time, frustrated by the politicization of the APA, Robert Nozick proposed that some of its members be condemned "for manipulating the meeting for the sake of sectarian political interests of their own." Tellingly, his motion was not even put to a vote because no one at the meeting was willing to second it.

Later, a number of other political resolutions were adopted at the meetings of various divisions of the APA. Among other things it was concluded that "it is improper for Congress to decree by law that human life begins at conception"; that "the United States government should attempt at all cost [!?] to encourage political stability between the Soviet Union and the United States"; that the members of the APA are "to use their resources to educate their students and their communities about the negative effects the death penalty has on the social, political and spiritual well-being of the nation"; that "members of the American Philosophical Association express our serious doubts about the morality, legality and prudence of a war against Iraq led by the United States," etc.

Political activists managed to secure the majority of votes for resolutions on all these issues at the APA's meetings. However, it should be mentioned that the politicization of the association was sporadically criticized by individual philosophers who made a number of very good points, mainly in letters to the editor in the APA bulletin:

> What then could justify the APA in taking sides on the sort of broadly philosophical issues that tend to become bones of contention in the political arena? . . . Furthermore, by what principle was the death penalty chosen as the topic of an APA resolution rather than, say, partial-birth abortions? Should the APA endorse a package of positions, issuing pronunciamentos on the Balanced Budget Amendment, handgun control and ebonics? If not, why not? (William Vallicella)
>
> It is ludicrous to the point of self-parody for an APA division to give serious consideration to a resolution that tells division members what position to take (and to advocate to their students) on a philosophically controversial issue. (Felicia Ackerman)
>
> If I believed that any action of the APA could prevent nuclear war, I would of course support it. But the suggestion that such is the case does little credit to a profession whose announced aims include the advancement of rationality. (Philip E. Devine)
>
> The problem before us is whether a professional and scholarly association does not become unfaithful to its destiny, to its logic, by taking a stand on political questions. It would mean the beginning of complete politicization of our organization . . ., and this is the hallmark of totalitarianism. (Aron Gurwitsch)

But there was no indication that the APA's leadership appreciated the force of these points or that it was willing to reconsider the association's policy about its political interventions.

Some members pointed out that by getting involved in politics the APA was actually violating its own charter. They quoted Article 3.1 B of the APA Constitution, which reads: "The Association is established exclusively for educational and scientific purposes as set forth in the Articles of Incorporation."

Michael Kelly, executive director of the APA, responded to this complaint by claiming that the APA's bylaws "allow resolutions of this type to be put before its members for a mail vote, provided certain guidelines are followed." In support of his claim, Kelly extensively quoted from the APA's bylaws. Yes, Kelly is right that bylaws specify the rules for adopting resolutions, and he is also right that these rules were followed in the case of the resolution against the Iraq war. But obviously this was not the issue raised by the critics. Their point was simply that as the APA was established for *educational* and *scientific* purposes, the association's engagement in *political* affairs was clearly out of order. Kelly had nothing to say in response to this.

How Yugoslav Marxists Pulled a Fast One on the APA (and Other Philosophers)

At the meeting of the Eastern Division of the APA in December 1972, several "concerned members" proposed that the Association send a letter to Yugoslav president Tito in support of eight Marxist philosophers from Belgrade who were associated with the Yugoslav philosophical journal *Praxis* and who were at that time under political attacks. Here is the most important part of the letter:

> Dear Mr. President, Marshal Tito:
> We have been following with great interest the building and democratic development of an equitable and free society in Yugoslavia during the last two decades. We are, therefore,

> alarmed and depressed by repeated reports recently appearing both in the Yugoslav press and other journals. It is now reported that some Yugoslav publications are being suppressed, passports of Yugoslav citizens confiscated, and Yugoslav intellectuals put on trial for the expression of their views. We are especially concerned by the reports of decisions taken in local political organizations in your country to remove from their teaching positions eight professors—some of whom are internationally known...

Robert Nozick moved that the first sentence of the letter be deleted because it "implied a positive evaluation of the degree of democracy in Yugoslavia," but his motion was defeated by a very large majority.

The APA could hardly have chosen a worse moment to compliment Tito for promoting a "free society." It was only several months earlier that hundreds of students in Croatia (then a part of Yugoslavia) were arrested for their completely nonviolent political activities. Among those condemned to long prison sentences were many writers, journalists, academics, and students. A strange scene indeed: What American philosophers hailed as a "free society" in the making massively incarcerated its own citizens when they demanded freedom!

Some defended the laudatory sentence in the APA's letter, arguing that it was "not a political endorsement but a strategic appeal to the self-image of the Yugoslav powers-that-be." If so, the strategy failed miserably. Tito must have been pleased with the flattery but predictably made no concessions. When intellectuals try to outmaneuver dictators they usually only manage to make fools of themselves.

Although the political oppression in Yugoslavia in 1972 was notoriously and heavily centered on Croatia, the APA sent a copy of its letter to the Presidium of the National Assembly of the Republic of *Serbia*, but not Croatia. So the APA was "especially concerned" about the fate of the eight philosophy professors in Belgrade who were not even removed from university at the time, while it was not concerned at all about many more people in Croatia (some of them philosophers and philosophy students) going to prison for years just for expressing their political opinion.[3]

APA members obviously relied on the *Praxis* philosophers for information about the situation in Yugoslavia, uncritically accepting the highly biased political narratives of their Yugoslav Marxist colleagues. The *Praxis* philosophers always presented themselves as staunch critics of any nationalism. Their professed cosmopolitanism appealed to their brethren in the West, but in reality it was only a façade behind which lurked a thinly hidden Serbian nationalism.

What gave the game away was when in 1972 *Praxis* published a protest against a court decision in which a Belgrade philosopher (a member of the advisory board of *Praxis*) was convicted of *Serbian* nationalism and received a two-year prison sentence (soon to be commuted to nine months). In contrast, the *Praxis* philosophers were all eerily silent when around the same time a philosopher and two philosophy students received longer prison terms for *Croatian* nationalism. So from the *Praxis* perspective one nationalism (Serbian) was to be protected as a matter of free expression, while the other nationalism (Croatian) was deservedly punished as a dangerous criminal act. The irresistible conclusion was that the *Praxis* philosophers were in fact Serbian nationalists in cosmopolitan clothing.

This was soon further confirmed when the main witness for the prosecution in a 1972 Stalinist trial of two Croatian philosophy students joined the editorial board of *Praxis* only a few months after his appearance in court. This was widely perceived as a reward for his help in securing a conviction for the political opponents of the *Praxis* group. (The two philosophy students spent three and four years in prison, respectively.)

---

3 According to the section on Yugoslavia in the Amnesty International's report for 1972, eleven Croatian intellectuals were sentenced to terms of imprisonment from one to six years, while about twenty Croatian students were sentenced to up to four years' imprisonment. No other part of Yugoslavia is mentioned in the report. In later reports Amnesty International singled out 1972 as the year with an especially high number of trials for political offenses in Yugoslavia "when there were widespread arrests and convictions, *in particular in Croatia*" (emphasis added).

It would have been extremely easy for American philosophers to learn about these or similar episodes and realize the extent of *Praxis*'s political bias and untrustworthiness. They only had to ask for "a second opinion" from someone in former Yugoslavia from the opposite side of the political spectrum, or at least someone who did not belong to the hard left. But they apparently did not. So being way out of their depth in this matter they were not only easily drawn into a web of deception but also managed to involve the APA in this shady affair. In the end, the same ill-advised letter was sent to Tito on behalf of a group of Fellows of the American Academy of Arts and Sciences, which included distinguished philosophers like Carl G. Hempel, John Rawls, Willard V. Quine, Wilfrid Sellars, Patrick Suppes, and Ernest Nagel.[4]

In another open letter to President Tito (*The New Humanist*, March 1975) signed by a number of British academic luminaries, including some eminent philosophers (like Bernard Williams, Alfred Ayer, and Peter Strawson), the issue was again made *only* of the case of the Belgrade *Praxis* philosophers and their teaching positions being in jeopardy, as if this had been the worst violation of academic freedom in communist Yugoslavia in the mid-1970s. Besides ignoring the plight of those professors in Croatia who were at that time not only fired but were serving sentences of up to seven years' imprisonment, the letter writers expressed admiration for the Yugoslav system and said that "the inner organization of universities, with its self-managing, autonomous faculty councils, had seemed to be one of the most democratic in the world."

Is it possible that people like Williams, Ayer, and Strawson really believed in the "self-management" fairy tale? Did they not realize that the so-called "autonomy of the faculty" was a complete sham and that universities in Yugoslavia were tightly controlled by ideologues from the Communist Party? Furthermore, it is bewildering that Bernard Williams, once described by *The Times* as the "most

4 See "Yugoslav philosophers under fire," *Index on Censorship*, 2, 1972, pp. 63–64. A note appended to the letter says that the letter was sent to the scholars on the list for their signatures, but one of them confirmed to me by email that all of them had signed it.

brilliant and most important British moral philosopher of his time," publicly praised the organization of universities in a one-party communist country as being among "the most democratic in the world," while only several years later "he left Britain for Berkeley in protest at the impact of the Thatcher government's policies on British universities" [Chappell 2013]. His message with respect to universities appeared to be: Communist tyrant (before the *Praxis* incident) good; elected conservative government intolerably bad.

A similar open letter to Tito in defense of the "Belgrade eight" was sent by another group of Western academics (mostly philosophers) and published in the *New York Review of Books* in 1975. What these academics—including Ayer, Chomsky, Føllesdal, Habermas, Hintikka, Ricoeur, and von Wright (Wittgenstein's successor at Cambridge)—found "particularly shocking" was the newly introduced law for the Republic of Serbia authorizing the parliament to suspend university teachers from their positions. Again, how come they were so shocked about that new law in Serbia but none of them were shocked by the simultaneous persecution of Croatian academics that was much more severe and on a much larger scale? Again, a part of the explanation is that many of these Westerners were simply too naive and easily hoodwinked by their main sources of information, whose extreme bias and mendacity they never recognized.

In 1978, three Princeton philosophers (Richard Rorty, Richard Jeffrey, and Robert C. Tucker) wrote a letter to the president of Princeton urging him to support the Inter-University Center (IUC) in Dubrovnik, Croatia:

> Our principal motive in making this proposal is the need to support Yugoslavian scholars who are under pressure from their government, and for whom the IUC is a haven. In particular, the so-called 'Belgrade Eight'—a group of philosophers and sociologists who have been discharged from their teaching positions because of their defense of academic freedom and human rights generally—are still able to use the IUC as a sanctuary (quoted in Gross 2008, 230).

So in the eyes of the Princeton philosophers *the main value* of the IUC consisted in its serving as a "haven" or "sanctuary" for the "Belgrade eight." But when thirteen years later two most prominent representatives of the "Belgrade eight," Mihailo Marković and Svetozar Stojanović, got top positions in the Serbian government around the time it ordered the shelling of Dubrovnik (during which the IUC building was destroyed), Rorty, Jeffrey, and Tucker had nothing to say publicly about that event nor about the complicity of some of their Belgrade protégés in the politics that led to that attack on their previous "sanctuary."

Two more letters in support of the *Praxis* group were published in the *New York Review of Books* in 1980 and 1984. A number of philosophers were among the signatories, including Sidney Morgenbesser, Thomas Kuhn, and Donald Davidson. Some, like Adolf Grünbaum and Richard Rorty, signed both letters. It turned out that out of fourteen people whose cases were mentioned as examples of repression in Yugoslavia, *all* were Serbs. Although the American philosophers must have known that Yugoslavia was a multiethnic country, they did not find anything odd in this total lack of ethnic diversity. Surely they could not have believed that only Serbs were victims of political repression.

One of these "victims" was Vojislav Šešelj, who only a few years later—not unpredictably—took part in persecution of non-Serbs during the war in Yugoslavia, for which he was later charged by the International Criminal Tribunal with crimes against humanity, murder, forced deportation, illegal imprisonment, torture, and property destruction.[5] It is also notable that Chomsky, Davidson, Grünbaum, and Rorty were appalled by "the unusually harsh penalty of eight years in prison" that Šešelj received in 1984, but they remained unfazed by an even "more unusual" case when, a few years earlier, a Croatian university professor was sentenced to eleven

5 Speaking about war criminals, it is noteworthy that two principal members of the *Praxis* group (Mihailo Marković and Ljubomir Tadić) signed a petition in 1996 in which Radovan Karadžić, the infamous leader of Bosnian Serbs, was proclaimed to be innocent of any crime and was called "the true leader of all Serbs." Eventually the Tribunal in the Hague convicted Karadžić of genocide, persecutions, extermination, murder, deportation, forcible transfer, terror, unlawful attacks on civilians, and hostage taking. He was sentenced to forty years' imprisonment.

years of imprisonment because of an interview he gave to a foreign journalist.

Although all these philosophers probably believed that they were defending a noble cause of human rights in a troubled country, in reality they were sucked into a world they did not understand and manipulated into defending only one side in an ethnic conflict. Ironically it was the side that was soon going to bear by far the greatest responsibility for the bloody war and atrocities against civilians in Croatia and Bosnia.

Even later, on the brink of war in former Yugoslavia, when the Serbian nationalism of the leading members of the *Praxis* group was expressed much more freely on the international scene, some Western philosophers were still unable, or unwilling, to believe what their eyes were telling them. For instance, in 1990 (at the time it was publicized that Marković, the doyen of the *Praxis* group, became the vice president of Slobodan Milošević's militantly nationalist and war-mongering party in Serbia), the journal *Praxis International* (the international successor of *Praxis*) published Marković's paper about the Serbian-Albanian conflict in Kosovo in which he defended a preposterously biased view and blamed only the Albanian side.[6]

It was only two Hungarian editors (Agnes Heller and Ferenc Fehér) who were outraged and resigned in protest, saying, "We do not sit in the same board with a Serbian nationalist, it is against our principles" (Agnes Heller, personal communication). Heller later commented: "Americans did not understand, they believed that we were overreacting. They wanted to persuade us to return, but we answered that they had no idea about the context."

Heller was spot on: Americans did not understand nor did they have any idea about the context. It took them considerable time to realize the truth. The Yale philosopher Seyla Benhabib, a longtime fan of the *Praxis* group and one of the editors-in-chief of *Praxis International*, eventually wrote in 1995: "Many of us felt that

---

6 Although around that time Amnesty International reported that "in recent years, the majority of people charged with political offences have been ethnic Albanians from Kosovo province," Marković argued that "the Albanian nationality in Yugoslavia already *enjoys more rights and privileges than any other minority in the world,* therefore it is unreasonable and not acceptable to demand even more" (Marković 1990, 412; emphasis added).

the wool was being pulled over our eyes by our colleagues in former Yugoslavia in what they were or were not publishing in the pages of the journal about conditions in their own country" (Benhabib 1995, 675).

Indeed. At long last Western philosophers started coming to their senses. But too little, too late.

The Stanford Encyclopedia of Philosophy and the Politics of Citation

There are many other examples, besides the APA, of important philosophical institutions undertaking political actions that are not only unreasonable but also occasionally harmful to the profession. A good recent illustration is the jumpy reaction of the editors of the Stanford Encyclopedia of Philosophy (SEP) to a reported gender disparity in philosophy and their hasty and ill-considered attempt to correct it.

To see how the mere numerical fact of gender disparity—unaccompanied by any understanding of its origins or awareness of potential consequences of meddling with the existing situation—can move prominent philosophers to rush to a conclusion and galvanize them into urgent action, consider the following sequence of events. On June 19, 2013, the sociologist Kieran Healy publishes data on his blog showing that of all recent citations in four prestigious philosophy journals, female authors get only 3.6 percent of the total. Although Healy warns that "this is exploratory work" and that there are unanswered "questions about the underlying causes of any patterns that show up in the data" as well as "various comparisons that sound straightforward... but are actually quite complicated to answer properly, or imply a lot more data collection and analysis than I can do here," when Edward Zalta and Uri Nodelman, the editors of the SEP, learn about Healy's data they decide the issue needs immediate attention. On July 12 (just three weeks after Healy's posting), they send an email with the subject "SEP request concerning citations" to all SEP authors, subject editors, and referees, which includes a link to Healy's text, informing the

SEP collaborators that the editors take the issue of undercitation of women philosophers seriously. Although they don't explain why the issue is so pressing or what their objective is (besides pushing some numbers up), they announce that they want to "encourage our authors, subject editors, and referees to help ensure that SEP entries do not overlook the work of women or indeed of members of underrepresented groups more generally." Furthermore, the collaborators are also urged to write to the editor "any time [they] notice a source missing from an SEP entry (whether or not it is [their] own entry)."

There are at least five problems here. First, Zalta and Nodelman seem to assume, without providing any evidence, that the "undercitation" of women is at least partly the result of philosophers' bias, i.e., their tendency to "overlook" women's publications more often than men's. Second, the way the editors try to address the problem of the low citation of women looks very much like an attempt to cure a disease without knowing its cause. Third, their action will have a perverse effect as well. Namely, de facto pushing (or nudging) so many scholars to cite more female philosophers (and to report on those who fall behind in this task) may distort genuine citation patterns in the discipline and undermine the integrity of a bibliometric analysis of philosophical publications. Fourth, there might be another perverse effect: If the SEP initiative to boost the citation of women's publications becomes more widely adopted in philosophy, then philosophers who do not believe that the "undercitation" is due to sexist bias might react to the new situation by correcting for what they perceive as the citation inflation for one group. As a consequence, they might start to take the number of citations of a woman's work as being, on average, a less reliable sign of scholarly quality than the number of citations of a man's work. And fifth, it should be expected that other demographic groups would soon follow suit and demand that their "unfairly" low citation rate be similarly jacked up.

Given the SEP's importance to the discipline—in many ways it serves as a standard-bearer for philosophy as a research field—it is odd how unconcerned the editors were about making such crude and blatantly political considerations a part of their official editorial policy. Even odder is that of hundreds (thousands?) of philosophers who have been acquainted with the new citation guidelines for more than two years, no one has decided to start a public discussion about that issue.

For another indication about how far the SEP editors have been willing to give in to the political pressure of the feminist lobby, look at Table 12.1, which shows the number of articles in the encyclopedia that have the word *feminism* or *feminist* in the title, compared to the number of articles about some other, historically much more important, philosophical positions.

Table 12.1: Article Titles in the Stanford Encyclopedia of Philosophy

Term	*Number of Times Used*
Feminism, feminist	36
Empiricism, empiricist	1
Materialism, materialist	1
Idealism, idealist	0
Rationalism, rationalist	1
Naturalism, naturalist	5

The number of the SEP article titles that contain *feminism* or *feminist* is *more than four times higher* than the number of *all* articles *combined* whose titles mention the foundational philosophical isms of empiricism, materialism, idealism, rationalism, and naturalism. Given that feminism is a relatively new arrival to the philosophical scene and is still far from being a core area of philosophical research, there is simply no way the comparatively exorbitant attention it has received could be justified by invoking ordinary criteria of the profession.

This whole section draws heavily on the article "Women in Philosophy: Problems with the Discrimination Hypothesis" (Sesardić & De Clercq 2014). We argue there that although many philosophers and philosophical associations claim that women are underrepresented in philosophy largely due to discrimination, the evidence for this accusation crumbles under examination. At the very least it seems safe to say that even those who support the discrimination hypothesis ought to concede that their case is not open-and-shut. But they do not.

Hume famously said, "A wise man proportions his belief to the evidence." It appears, however, that today most philosophers live by a less epistemically responsible dictum: "Believe in discrimination."

CHAPTER THIRTEEN

Left-Wing Bias: An Infantile Disorder of Contemporary Philosophy

"In intellectual circles conservatives move quietly and discreetly, catching each other's eyes across the room like the homosexuals in Proust, whom that great writer compared to Homer's gods, known only to each other as they move in disguise around the world of mortals."

—Roger Scruton

Just as fish are not aware of the water they swim in, so too philosophers tend to be oblivious to their collective political bias while basking in the warm sun of campus leftism. The leading contemporary political philosopher, Tim Scanlon, from Harvard University, acknowledges this (at least in the abstract), writing that "it is easy to see intolerance in one's opponents and harder to avoid it oneself" (Scanlon 2003, 256).

But Scanlon seems to be unaware that it was in the very preceding paragraph that he himself exhibited that same ideological one-sidedness and intolerance. Speaking about "examples of intolerance [that] are all around us," he gave more than four instances of this regrettable phenomenon, and *all* of his illustrations come from the political right. He did not feel any need to show at least a semblance of impartiality and objectivity by citing, for the sake of symmetry, a single case of intolerance originating from the left.

But am I not open to a similar charge myself? For how can I explain that practically all the examples discussed in this book are associated with the excesses of left-wing politics? Even Michael Dummett, who had conservative views on some issues (e.g., abortion), is here represented by the opinions that strongly aligned him with the far left of British politics. Why did I not, for the sake of fairness (and balance), provide at least some examples of prominent analytic philosophers blundering politically in the right-wing direction? Is this a reflection of my bias?

There is a bias for sure, but I suggest that it is in philosophy, not me. Academic philosophy, like other disciplines in the humanities and social sciences, has a notoriously strong leftist tilt (see, e.g., Gross 2013, 299; Maranto et al. 2009, 16, 22). Therefore, it should not be surprising that there is a dearth of right-wing examples in my sample.

In particular, within the highly exclusive group of the most eminent analytic philosophers (the main focus of this book), I managed to find only one case of a conservative who made the cut. But upon analysis, as the reader will see on pp. 188–193, even that single case of a "right-wing deviation" provides additional evidence of the leftist bias in the philosophical community.

Robert Nozick Loses His Nerve

There is something else at work here that makes the effect of political bias even stronger. Consider an academic discipline in which the ratio of left-wing to right-wing individuals is, say, 10 to 1 (such a ratio, and even higher, has been reported in some studies of the politics of academic philosophers). Would you expect that in that discipline the ratio of those who publicly expressed *extreme* leftist views versus those who publicly expressed *extreme* rightist views would stay around the same value (10 to 1)?

A moment of thought points to the negative answer. Other things being equal, there is reason to think that the ratio would rise significantly. Look at how different the situation would be for the two kinds of extremists. On one hand, the leftist extremists would be considered by a huge majority of their colleagues (who share their basic political opinion) as being (a) correct or almost correct; or (b) perhaps too radical but still "having their heart in the right place"; or (c) profoundly wrong but nevertheless not remotely as condemnable as the right-wing extremists. On the other hand, the right-wing extremists would be considered by the majority of scholars in their own discipline as irrational or dangerous or beyond the pale or evil (or most, or all, of the above).

Since one has to communicate on a daily basis with colleagues in one's discipline and find a basic *modus vivendi* with one's professional peers, it is clear that in such a situation the pressure against the minority extremism would be enormous.[1] Under the circumstances, many people who would otherwise be inclined toward extreme right-wing views would probably adopt a more moderate stance while others might start having doubts and would realize they would be better off just keeping their opinion to themselves. This would result in the left–right ratio of the extreme views rising to a value much higher than 10 to 1. And the left–right ratio of *publicly expressed* extreme views would be even higher.

According to a 2013–2014 study by the Higher Education Research Institute at the University of California, Los Angeles, the ratio of university professors who described themselves as politically "far left" vs. those on the "far right" was between 30 to 1 and 50 to 1 (Eagan et al. 2014, 112). The ratio for philosophers, however, must be considerably higher than that figure, which is the average across all academic disciplines.

I think these facts must be a large part of the explanation for why so many leading analytic philosophers were Stalinists or Soviet sympathizers, whereas there is no single instance of anyone of a similar stature having publicly supported the supposed right-wing equivalent—a fascist leader, say, or even much less odious right-wing politicians such as, for example, Pinochet.

---

1 Authors of a new book about the position of conservative professors report an extreme case in which one of their subjects said: "It is dangerous to even think [a conservative thought] when I'm on campus, because it might come out of my mouth" (Shields & Dunn 2016, 87).

A nice illustration of the effect of ideological majority pressure in philosophy is the case of Robert Nozick. He admitted that at one point he went along with the *incorrect* representation of his views just because he expected it would make his colleagues view him more favorably:

> [I]t was so nice for people to be slapping me on the back and telling me that they had faith in me and they believed in me. Because they hadn't been saying that for years. And they started welcoming me back into the fold. And you know, God help me, but I just liked to not be vilified for a change. I liked to not be a pariah in my own department. And so I went along with it. I could have done the snarky thing and said, No, your approval of me is based on a misunderstanding. I could have said that, but I just didn't. I was tired and I just let it go (reported in Schmidtz 2012).

It should be pointed out that at the time (the end of the eighties), Nozick was a tenured full professor at Harvard widely admired for his intellectual brilliance. If despite his very high standing in the profession he still felt "like a pariah in his own department," it is not hard to guess how much worse the position must be for those younger, less accomplished, and much more vulnerable scholars who share his political views. They would be much more motivated to let their opinions be misrepresented in the left-wing direction, not to mention that many of them might under pressure genuinely migrate away from beliefs that could sound outrageous to most of their colleagues. This is one of the mechanisms via which the high left-wing ratio might reinforce itself and increase further.

Those Dumb Conservatives

Sometimes the political imbalance in academia is attributed to a putative correlation between being a conservative and having low intelligence. For example, in 2004 the Duke Conservative Union protested the underrepresentation of their ideological brethren among the Duke faculty: In the humanities and social sciences departments the Democrat–Republican ratio of registered voters was higher than 17 to 1. Robert Brandon, then chair of the philosophy department and a prominent philosopher of science, gave the following explanation:

> We try to hire the best, smartest people available. If, as John Stuart Mill said, stupid people are generally conservative, then there are lots of conservatives we will never hire. Mill's analysis may go some way towards explaining the power of the Republican party in our society and the relative scarcity of Republicans in academia. Players in the NBA tend to be taller than average. There is a good reason for this. Members of academia tend to be a bit smarter than average. There is a good reason for this too (quoted in the Duke *Chronicle*, February 10, 2004).

Although Brandon made the claim about a connection between conservatism and stupidity in his official capacity as the head of a highly ranked philosophy department, other philosophers did not have a problem with his statement nor did they (publicly) criticize his argument.

But several non-philosopher commentators wondered whether Brandon would be willing to extend the same logic to another context where it would seem to apply with no less force. John Zimmerman, a Duke alumnus, wrote:

> Prof. Robert Brandon's arrogant, bigoted tantrum makes the lofty suggestion that conservatives are underrepresented because they're all stupid. The logic of his statement is incredible—is he suggesting that Duke's Black Faculty Initiative proves that blacks are stupid? Is there a quote from Mill to hide behind on that subject? (Duke *Chronicle*, February 13, 2004)

Zimmerman was unfair to Brandon because Brandon neither said nor implied that *all* conservatives are stupid. But Zimmerman's main point was a good one: If it is legitimate to invoke the putative average difference in intelligence between two groups to explain the underrepresentation of one of them (conservatives), why then not explore whether the underrepresentation of blacks could be accounted for in the same way?

The idea that a black–white difference in average intelligence might play some explanatory role cannot be dismissed out of hand. After all, the authoritative report "Intelligence: Knowns and Unknowns" issued by the American Psychological Association states that "the Black mean is typically about one standard deviation (about 15 points) below that of Whites" (Neisser et al. 1996, 93).

I am not taking sides here in either of the two debates. I am only interested in the strikingly different attitudes of philosophers toward two similar empirical hypotheses. While the suggestion that the low percentage of conservatives among university professors is due to their lower intelligence tends to produce agreement, amusement, or a disinterested shrug, the same idea about blacks is met with immediate rejection, outrage, and condemnation.

A good illustration is the case of the philosopher Michael Levin, who in 1990 published a short letter in the *Proceedings and Addresses of the American Philosophical Association* (62–63) in which he suggested this explanation for the low proportion of blacks in philosophy. In the next issue the editor of the bulletin reported that Levin's letter "has provoked the largest and most impassioned outpouring of letters I have yet received." The members of Levin's philosophy department at City College of New York published a letter distancing themselves from his views. Eighteen reactions were published, all of them negative, with some authors expressing strong disagreement and others condemning the APA for publishing Levin's letter and calling it "racist propaganda." Needless to say, Levin was not invited to respond to this barrage of attacks, although this is a customary courtesy extended to authors who generate a controversy.

A similar case (in which a prominent philosopher makes a late appearance) involves Frank Ellis, a former lecturer in Russian and Slavonic studies at the University of Leeds, who publicly expressed agreement with Richard Herrnstein and Charles Murray's claims, made in their controversy-generating book *The Bell Curve* (1994), about the black–white difference in intelligence and its social effects. In response, the student union urged the administration to fire Ellis. The vice-chancellor of the university suspended him from his duties pending the outcome of a disciplinary process.

At a meeting of the Association of University Teachers (AUT), which was supposed to decide whether to offer assistance to Ellis in his attempt to keep his job, a delegate from Leeds, Gavin Reid, said "he wished Dr Ellis would crawl back into the pond from which he came" and "let us hope Leeds does the right thing and kicks this bastard out." What is most interesting for us is that the AUT stance was defended by Steven French, a philosopher of science who at the time happened to be the vice-president of the AUT/University and College Union. Here are his words:

> Leeds AUT/University and College Union concurs that the university, as a public body, has a duty under the law "to promote equality of opportunity and good relations between persons of different racial groups"; it also agrees that the university should place appropriate responsibilities upon its staff as part of its wider race equality policy. The bottom line is: why should we have to work and study with racists and homophobes? The answer is: we should not (*Times Higher Education Supplement*, June 9, 2006).

Notably, French is currently editor-in-chief of the *British Journal for the Philosophy of Science*, a top journal in the discipline. Given his treatment of Ellis, could French be expected to show minimal fairness as an editor if he had to evaluate an article that took seriously or, God forbid, defended the ideas from *The Bell Curve*? Possible, but that's not the way to bet.

In contrast to French, who argued (in his role as a union member!) that Ellis deserved to be fired for his "offense," here is the opinion of David Bernstein, a law professor and expert on issues related to freedom of expression:

> Note that there was no finding of academic misconduct, no finding that Dr. Ellis had engaged in bad scholarship, and no finding that he had harassed, discriminated against, or even addressed his comments to, any student. Rather, he is being "disciplined" solely because students found his views offensive, and thus a breach of the university's obligation to promote "racial harmony" (which sure seems to imply a heckler's veto for any controversial statements related to race). Troubling, indeed (published on the legal scholars' blog The Volokh Conspiracy, March 26, 2006).

The Curious Case of Gottlob Frege

Another illustration of the ideological bias in philosophy is the treatment of the person who is generally regarded as the father of analytic philosophy, the German philosopher and mathematician Gottlob Frege (1848–1925). Especially relevant here is the contrast between the philosophers' vehement condemnation of Frege's political views and the almost total lack of criticism of no less contemptible political opinions of some other prominent philosophers. Why did the dogs bark so loudly just in this one case? The most salient factor that makes Frege stand out from all those other philosophers discussed in this book, and might explain the asymmetry, is that he has been castigated for supporting what is regarded as an extreme right-wing view.

The Stanford Encyclopedia of Philosophy entry on Frege states: "Unfortunately, his last years saw him become politically conservative and right-wing. His diary for a brief period in 1924 show[s] sympathies for fascism and anti-Semitism."

Why is it deemed "unfortunate" that in his last years Frege became "politically conservative and right-wing"? What exactly is unfortunate about that? The word *unfortunately* could be appropriate if it referred to "the brief period in 1924" when Frege expressed extreme and generally unacceptable political views, but it seems hardly justified if it refers (as it apparently does) *merely* to the fact that in his last years (plural!) Frege became politically conservative and right-wing. Leftists might find this regrettable, of course, but why would this kind of partisan disapproval find its way into the most important reference work in philosophy? It is hard to imagine an article in the SEP (or any other high-profile philosophical publication) in which a biography of a famous philosopher would contain a similar sentence but with the following left-right inversion: "Unfortunately, X's last years saw him become politically progressive and left-wing."

What makes this example particularly striking is that the article on Frege, with this gratuitous political comment, was authored by Edward Zalta, the principal editor of the SEP.

It was Michael Dummett who first drew public attention to the diary notes in which Frege, a year before his death, defended strongly anti-Semitic views. Upon discovering this, Dummett called Frege's political views "very distasteful" (in Klement 2014, 26) and was "deeply shocked" (Dummett 1973, xii) and "very, very upset" (in an interview for a Philosophy Bites podcast). Notice, again, that no one has used the word "distasteful" (let alone "very distasteful") and no one has been "shocked" (let alone "deeply shocked") nor "upset" (let alone "very, very upset") over any of the aforementioned cases of leading philosophers publicly supporting murderous totalitarian regimes of the left.

Dummett (1973) says he regrets that the editors of Frege's *Nachlass* "chose to suppress" the part of the diary containing the controversial political views. As one commentator observed, the "charge of suppression always has odious connotations, and in a scientific and scholarly context smacks of an accusation of intellectual dishonesty" (Kluge 1977, 520–21). The editors justifiably protested and, in response to Dummett's accusation, said the diary entries in question were left out simply because they contained statements of political attitudes "which cannot be counted as part of the scientific *Nachlass*" (in Frege 1991, 263). After all, other parts of the diary were also omitted for the same reason of being considered irrelevant (such as Frege's thoughts about the life of Jesus, the notion of justice, his teacher Professor Abbe, etc.).

Besides, Dummett failed to notice that in Frege's *Nachgelassene*

Schriften, which he criticized so harshly, the editors explicitly wrote that their goal was to prepare a complete edition of Frege's "extant *scientific* writings and letters."[2] So a very clear and pertinent reason was given at the time for not publishing Frege's political thoughts from his diary—no one "suppressed" anything.

The UC Berkeley philosopher Hans Sluga makes an even stronger charge: "In his diary Frege also used all his analytic skills to devise plans for expelling the Jews from Germany and for suppressing the Social Democrats" (1995, 99). I cannot discuss Sluga's accusation here more closely, but I think it is not supported by Frege's text either. I am not alone in this judgment. In the opinion of Richard L. Mendelsohn, a Frege expert and the translator of his diary, "Sluga's final sentence presents a gross distortion of the content of the diary" (1996, 304).

Sluga (op. cit.) went further and claimed, also relying on Frege's diary, that one of Frege's "heroes" at the end of his life was Adolf Hitler. In fact there is no textual evidence to support this accusation.

Similarly, the philosopher Avrum Stroll stated (2000, 76) that "something close to admiration" is implied in the following sentence from Frege's diary: "Adolf Hitler writes correctly in the April [1924] issue of *Deutschlands Erneuerung*, that Germany no longer had a clear political goal after the departure of Bismarck." But Stroll's comment is patently false: Agreeing with Hitler's claim about a political disorientation in post-Bismarck Germany in no way implies support for Hitler's politics, and certainly not "something close to admiration" for him.

The well-known and widely respected ethicist Jonathan Glover quotes (1999, 377) the same sentence from Frege's diary that mentions Hitler. Since Glover presents this quote without any comment, it very much seems that, in the context of his strong condemnation of Frege's political views, the function of the quote is to make it appear that Frege supported Hitler. But, again, in this particular

---

2 This is from an English translation of the 1969 editors' introduction (Frege 1991, xiii, emphasis added).

instance what Frege agreed with was Hitler's rather innocuous and probably true statement about Germany (see above). It had nothing whatsoever to do with National Socialism. Moreover, immediately before that passage Frege expressed *disagreement* with the Beer Hall Putsch of 1923, Hitler's most important political action up to that time. Oddly, Glover failed to mention this statement by Frege, although it would clearly help the reader to get a truer and more balanced picture about Frege's relation to Hitler.

Glover is also grossly unfair to Frege when he writes, "Because of Frege's merit as a philosopher, his failure in the face of Nazism is more troubling [than Heidegger's]." I agree that Frege is a much greater philosopher than Heidegger, but it is hard to see how this can make his politics more troubling than Heidegger's. For, in contrast to Heidegger, who publicly supported the Nazi Party for years after it came to power and after its policies left no doubt about its true goals and methods, Frege was jotting notes in his private diary nine years before Hitler became the chancellor of Germany and more than one year before *Mein Kampf* was published.

Frege's chief sin was anti-Semitism, but we should not forget that historically anti-Semitism has not been exclusively a right-wing phenomenon. In Frege's time, in particular, negative attitudes toward Jews were widespread across the political spectrum, not only in Germany but also in other European countries: "Like the left in France and Germany, the British left played a *central* role in the popular dissemination of anti-Semitism in late nineteenth and early twentieth-century Britain" (Brustein 2003, 89; emphasis added).

Some scholars say that the degeneration of the left in this respect already started with "the 19th-century seedbed of antisemitic socialism" (Wistrich 2012, xii), while others argue that "the widespread repugnance of the left toward Jews" had several roots, one of which was the historically documented affinity between anticapitalism and anti-Semitism (Brustein & Roberts 2015, 5).

This affinity dates back at least as far as Karl Marx's essay "On the Jewish Question" (first published in 1844) and has been preserved among a number of contemporary leftists. One of many examples is the following statement of Ulrike Meinhof, the well-known German terrorist and cofounder of the Red Army Faction (RAF):

> Auschwitz meant that six million Jews were killed, and thrown on the waste-heap of Europe, for what they were considered: money-Jews. Finance capital and the banks, the hard core of the system of imperialism and capitalism, had turned the hatred of men against money and exploitation, and against the Jews... *Antisemitism is really a hatred of capitalism*" (quoted in Cowen 1997; emphasis added).

In light of such statements, it should not come as a surprise that after the end of the Baader-Meinhof group, some of its former members made a smooth transition to the extreme right and joined neo-Nazi groups.

All this shows that in the end, despite appearances to the contrary, even Gottlob Frege fails to be an example of a leading analytic philosopher whose reason went on holiday because of the support for a *distinctly* right-wing political idea.

The uncharitable approach to Frege by Dummett, Sluga, Glover, Zalta, and others may be a reflection of a widespread and familiar phenomenon: What is perceived as a right-wing deviation is not easily forgiven in contemporary philosophy. In contrast, much worse left-wing sins are typically passed over and excused.

A good illustration of this bias is again Glover's book *Humanity* (1999). More than a third of the 464-page book is taken up by parts 5 ("Stalin and His Heirs") and 6 ("The Nazi Experiment"). The part about Nazism has an entire chapter, titled "Philosophers," in which Glover criticizes the political views of Heidegger and Frege as well as those of some obscure philosophers like Alfred Bäumler and Lothar Tirala.

In contrast, Glover did not include a "Philosophers" chapter in the part about Stalinism and Maoism, although it would have been easy to produce a much longer list of well-known philosophers who had fallen under the spell of Communist totalitarianism. The names that come to mind include Sartre, Merleau-Ponty, Badiou,

Lukács, Bloch, and many others, not to mention any of the analytic philosophers shown here to have also succumbed to the same totalitarian temptation from the left (Neurath, Russell, Wittgenstein, Lakatos, Cohen, Putnam, Davidson). Yet that chapter remained unwritten, and Glover never explained why philosophers deserved a whole chapter in one case but not in the other.

Nixon or Cleaver, That Is the Question

In their academic (nonpolitical) work, philosophers become successful when they present arguments their colleagues find persuasive or worth discussing. As a rule, one is rewarded for presenting *good* arguments.

With political views it is different. The opinions here tend to be held passionately, judicious arguments do not have so much force, and animosity is often freely expressed. Since there is strength in numbers, it is leftists who mainly resort to invective. For instance, here is what the well-known philosopher Richard Rorty said in an interview for the *Believer* in 2003: "I think all that September 11 changed was to give the fascists a chance. The Republicans saw that if they could keep us in a state of perpetual war from now on... they could keep electing Republicans more or less forever."

Notice how *fascists* at the end of the first sentence becomes *Republicans* at the beginning of the next sentence. Rorty surely could not have believed that Republicans are fascists, but he nevertheless dropped the F-word, probably expecting (with good reason) that many of his readers, including his philosopher colleagues, would appreciate the barb.

Elsewhere Rorty associated Republicans with Hitler and the Nazis:

> When I heard the news about the Twin Towers, my first thought was: "Oh, God. Bush will use this the way Hitler used the Reichstag fire" (interview in the *Progressive*, June 2007).
>
> My first thought on hearing the news of 9/11 was the Bush

> administration would use this as the Nazis used the Reichstag fire. And that, I think, is pretty much what has happened (in a talk in Potsdam, March 4, 2004, posted on YouTube).

So Rorty's reaction on hearing about 9/11 was an intense fear that Bush would use the murder of three thousand of his compatriots as a welcome opportunity to behave like Hitler. I find it odd not only that he had this thought at all but in particular that this was his *first* thought after learning about such a catastrophic event.

I assumed initially that reasonable people—or reasonable philosophers—would have to agree that comparing Bush to Hitler is simply over the top. But I soon discovered (in 2007) that this was not true. In an email correspondence with a distinguished New York philosopher (whose academic work I very much admire), at one point our conversation turned to politics. I mentioned Rorty's comparison of Bush to Hitler as an example of how prominent philosophers can make wild and evidently untenable political claims. Surprisingly, my correspondent defended the comparison and argued that, in view of what he regarded as Bush's consistent record of anti-democratic moves, serious people could justifiably fear that Bush might attempt to hold on to power illegally, even after the completion of his second term. Now this would indeed be an important similarity with the Führer! But I remember that at the time, despite considerable effort, I just couldn't picture Bush appearing on Fox News (where else?), announcing that the election of 2008 was to be canceled. That someone's distrust of Republicans could go so far that they would take seriously the possibility of a Bush coup d'état is of course stunning, particularly because this came from an extremely subtle thinker who is otherwise a model of rationality.

In contrast to Rorty's statements quoted above that illustrate the leftist political bias in philosophy, Rorty was sometimes only a witness to such bias. In the already mentioned 2003 interview with the *Believer*, he recalls the political climate in the philosophy department at Princeton in 1968:

> I remember sitting around the Princeton philosophy department lounge in '68, and I turned out to be the only person in the room who was voting for Humphrey. The question was whether to vote for Eldridge Cleaver or Jesse Jackson. I suggested that perhaps one should vote by figuring out who one thought would do the best job as president, and everybody just smiled at me.

Correction is in order here: Jesse Jackson was not running for president in 1968. But who was Eldridge Cleaver? He emerged from prison in 1966 after spending nine years there for rape and assault with intent to murder. He then joined the Black Panthers and became a presidential candidate of the Peace and Freedom Party in 1968.

Rorty's story should not be immediately accepted as true, especially because it is well known that he had serious conflicts with many of his colleagues at Princeton before he left that department. Yet it seems to me unlikely that what he reported is a total fabrication. After all, he knew that many of the people involved in the story were still alive and that they could dispute it vigorously if it were untrue.

So I decided to check. I contacted a few philosophers who were listed on the Princeton website as having been members of the philosophy department in 1968. I asked them for their opinion about Rorty's claim. The most interesting response came from "XY," one of the most influential philosophers today. (It would be inappropriate to give his name since this was a private email exchange.)

XY's first comment was: "I can't recall knowing of any of my colleagues voting for Cleaver, and it seems to me unlikely." In fact, the unlikely did happen: Out of the three replies I received from former Princeton philosophers from 1968, a very prominent one did confirm that he himself had voted for Cleaver. And the last respondent, also a highly esteemed philosopher, expressed some doubt about Rorty's statement but still conceded that it may well be that in 1968 more members of the Princeton philosophy department voted for Cleaver than for Nixon. This would in itself confirm the stunning left-radicalization of Princeton philosophers and would indicate that there was indeed a huge political rift between the Princeton philosophical community and the rest of the American population. Since Nixon received more than 43 percent of the vote, versus Cleaver's 0.05 percent, this would imply that the Nixon–Cleaver voting ratio among Princeton philosophers would have been, at the very least, about 1,000 times lower than the same ratio in the general electorate!

XY's second comment: "If any did [vote for Cleaver], it would have just been as a protest vote, not expressing the view that he was suitable to be president." This response, I think, tells us much about the political mindset of many contemporary philosophers discussed here.

Casting a vote for Cleaver merely in protest against the candidates who had a real chance of being elected in 1968 (Nixon, Humphrey, and perhaps Wallace) would make political sense only if the "protest" candidate embodied some values that would point a way out of the allegedly hopeless politics represented by the main contenders for the presidency. But it is hard to see how Cleaver, with his rape conviction, could have embodied the hope of representing these new political values. He did not even deny the deeds that landed him in prison. On the contrary, he described them, and their political rationale, in his autobiographical book *Soul on Ice*:

> I became a rapist. To refine my technique and modus operandi, I started out by practicing on black girls in the ghetto—in the black ghetto where dark and vicious deeds appear not as aberrations or deviations from the norm, but as part of the sufficiency of the Evil of the day—and when I considered myself smooth enough, I crossed the tracks and sought out white prey. I did this consciously, deliberately, willfully, methodically.... Rape was an insurrectionary act. It delighted me that I was defying and trampling upon the white man's law, upon his system of values, and that I was defiling his women.

Although Cleaver renounced his rapist past in the book, it remains inexplicable how voting for a person with such a heinous record could be regarded as a meaningful protest against anything. It should be stressed that Cleaver's book came out in February 1968, more than eight months before the election, so the information about his raping career—including both its "practicing stage" (when black women were the victims) and the "insurrectionary" stage (when the prey were white women)—was publicly available information at the time. How could people on the left, with their strong identification with feminism, be recruited to support a former sexual predator for president? The simplest answer is that for many leftists, race trumps sex.

But Cleaver's "negatives" were not related just to his distant past. His political program openly announced mayhem. Seven months before the election Cleaver said in a speech: "Now there is the gun and the bomb, dynamite and the knife, and they will be used liberally in America" (quoted in O'Neill 1971, 230). And these were not empty words. Soon Cleaver and twelve other Black Panthers ambushed policemen in Oakland, California (apparently in "retaliation" for the assassination of Martin Luther King). In the exchange of fire that followed, one Panther was killed while two policemen and Cleaver were injured. Oddly, even this violent criminal act in broad daylight did not discourage some people (and apparently a number of philosophers) from supporting him in the election.

On the contrary, the campus newspapers of two Ivy League universities recommended to its readers that they vote for Cleaver rather than for any of the major presidential candidates. *The Harvard Crimson* advised that "one should vote to the left of the major three candidates—whether it be for Eugene McCarthy, Eldridge Cleaver, Dick Gregory, Fred Halstead (Socialist Worker), or Henning Blomen (Socialist Labor)," and that "in states like Massachusetts where no left wing candidates qualify for the ballot or for a legal write in, one should refuse to vote for the Presidency."

The *Columbia Daily Spectator* went even further and officially endorsed Cleaver. Notably, the editors did not envisage this as "a protest vote"; rather, they claimed that "the mindful American" should cast a vote only if there is "a candidate whose character and philosophy are intellectually and morally sound." And they said that in their opinion "such a man indeed exists; his name is Eldridge Cleaver." The day the newspaper endorsement was published the candidate gave a speech on the Columbia campus in front of an enthusiastic audience and revealed his "sound" character and philosophy:

> "We'll burn this motherfuckin' town all the way everywhere if we can't get the programs to reconstruct it," he said. "We don't need anymore [sic] wars on poverty. We need a war on the rich." The crowd in Wollman interrupted Cleaver's speech several time[s] to applaud his comments and, at the close of the talk, most of the students rose from their seats and clapped for several minutes for the fourth-party candidate. Throughout his speech, Cleaver denounced the "pigs of the power structure"—a term he uses freely at his public appearances to refer to the police and other officials....
>
> At the close of his speech, Cleaver led the crowd in Wollman in three verses of his "campaign song." While the candidate directed the verses from the stage, students yelled, "Fuck Ronald Reagan;" "Fuck Cordier;" and "Fuck all the pigs" (*Columbia Daily Spectator*, October 15, 1968).

What conclusions can we draw from all this? First, that (contrary to XY's claim) Cleaver was certainly not the sort of public figure for whom a reasonable person could ever cast even a protest vote. How could one explain such a "protest" to the many women who were raped by Cleaver? Or to the policemen who were seriously wounded in an unprovoked attack that was organized by Cleaver? Or to those who were disgusted by the fact that after the assassination of Robert Kennedy the *Black Panther Journal* published a drawing of him as a dead pig?

And second, it seems clear that the support Cleaver received in American universities arose from much more than a mere protest mentality. As we saw, there was a lot of genuine enthusiasm and excitement about someone who was finally breaking with a politics widely perceived as offering no "real" choice.

According to studies of the political attitudes of American professors at the time, the proportion of the professors' vote for the far-left candidates (including Cleaver) in the 1968 presidential election was about ten times higher than in the general population (Ladd & Lipset 1972, 44). Taking into account that the discipline of philosophy (as most other areas in the humanities) leans much further to the left than the professoriate in general, the proportion of philosophers who voted for the extreme left (including Cleaver) was probably substantially higher.

This is one of many illustrations of very clever people behaving very foolishly. Why does this happen?

And Then He Started to Cry...

A possible explanation draws on two facts: on one hand, the strong leftist bias in philosophy, and on the other hand, the philosophers' ability to concoct seemingly good arguments even for rather implausible, or sometimes even preposterous, views. Living in a bubble and spending most of their time with politically like-minded leftist colleagues will cause even very clever people to start hyperbolizing the dangers and bad effects of right-wing politics to such an extent that it may reach comical proportions—such as seriously worrying that George W. Bush might cancel the election and appoint himself dictator. Another good illustration is David Albert's account of his 1992 conversation with Sidney Morgenbesser, an iconic figure in analytic philosophy and one of the sharpest minds in that whole tradition:[3]

> I remember Sidney and I sitting together in my office in 1992, on the morning after Clinton was elected. Neither of us had any illusions about Clinton, but both of us were caught up just then in the immense relief of Bush's having lost. We were laughing and happy, and all of a sudden Sidney starts to kvetch.

---

3 Referring to his studies at Columbia University, Robert Nozick once said that he "majored in Sidney Morgenbesser."

> He said, "I can't tell you what it's been like for me, I can't tell you how I have suffered, these past 12 years under Reagan and Bush." And then he started to cry. At that, the floor just sort of came out from under me. I didn't quite know what I was in the presence of, and I didn't quite know what to do (Albert 2005).

Obviously Morgenbesser must have sincerely felt these powerful emotions that brought him to tears. But it is equally obvious that Albert, his close friend and apparently a fellow liberal, could not make any sense of this reaction. And the reason he could not is simply that in objective terms the reaction made no sense at all. For what on earth could Morgenbesser have imagined himself to have suffered so much under those two Republican presidents?

If you are mainly surrounded by people who strongly lean to the left[4] and who, living largely in the political echo chamber, tend to radicalize themselves more and more in the same direction, there will be a social reward for producing a new argument for distancing oneself even further from those on the other side of political spectrum. Indeed, on LeiterReports.typepad.com, the most-visited philosophy blog on the Internet—which most philosophers check regularly to get professional news about their discipline (new hirings, changes in the expert ranking of top philosophy departments, professional gossip, etc.)—conservatives have been routinely referred to as "repugs," "morally depraved," "morally deranged," "crackpots," "lunatics," "idiots," "twits," "nuts," "slimy," "stupid," "crazies," "villains," "moral monsters," "fools," "fascistic psychopaths," "Neanderthals," "despicable Neanderthals," "sociopaths,"

---

4 The philosopher Eric Schwitzgebel has collected data on the political affiliation of university professors in California, Florida, and North Carolina (which is publicly available information in these states). The left–right ratio among 375 *philosophers* turned out to be higher than 10 to 1, whereas the same ratio in a random sample of professors from all other departments was around 3 to 1 (http://schwitzsplinters.blogspot.hk/2008/06/political-affiliations-of-american.html). Schwitzgebel comments that this confirms his feeling that "if there's one thing that's a safe dinner conversation topic at philosophy conferences, it's bashing Republican Presidents." Here is another confirming instance: At a gathering after a philosophy talk I gave at an American research university in 2003, someone went to the department office and brought a doll that made fun of George W. Bush, which all the philosophers in attendance found immensely amusing. When I asked them whether they also kept a doll that mocked Bill Clinton, I received blank stares.

"threats to humanity," "morons," "dishonest scumbags," "right-wing slime artists," "noxious right-wing creeps," and "brainless fascist thugs." The blog's hostility to conservative politics is hard to describe. It once went so far that the blog owner, University of Chicago professor Brian Leiter, linked in a 2007 post to a list of "the 50 most loathsome people in America," and after recommending crude and insulting descriptions of a few politicians disliked by the extreme left he drew the readers' attention to "apt" comments about the popular talk show host Rush Limbaugh, which contained the following sentence: "It's hard to believe this repulsive shit fountain is even human, until you remember that we share 70% of our DNA with pigs." Another comment, also called "apt," about the conservative columnist Ann Coulter, is so tasteless that it is simply unquotable.

The fact that the philosophical community had no problem at all, until recently, with enabling such an extremely intolerant and politically unhinged person to play an important role in the profession tells us enough about how bad the situation is.[5] All those scholars who served as evaluators for the ranking of philosophy departments or who provided other disciplinary information for the blog were apparently unbothered by the fact that the results of their professional efforts would later be presented and mixed together with wild and uncontrolled outbursts against public personalities and colleagues with different political views. It would be unimaginable for philosophers to agree to cooperate in the same way with, and give so much power to, someone who would use his blog to repeatedly call leading Democrats "threats to humanity" or "morons," describe Paul Krugman as "a moral monster," or find it appropriate to refer to Michael Moore as "this repulsive shit fountain."

For all we know, some of Leiter's collaborators may have been put off by his frequent political fits but, if such people existed, their irritation did not reach the level that would lead them to

---

5 Not without reason was it said that Leiter "had become the clearing house for news and information about academic philosophy around the world" (Wolff 2013). In September 2014 the well-known philosopher Richard Heck called Leiter "arguably the most powerful single person in our profession."

publicly voice concern, or issue public criticism. Since most of them are liberals who often share the same antipathy toward conservatives, they apparently don't realize how bizarre it will look to an impartial outside observer that one whole academic discipline, claiming to carry the torch of Plato, Aristotle, and Kant, allows its key source of professional information to be constantly marred by childish name-calling and gratuitous insults of people with certain political views.

The recent massive criticisms of Leiter and requests that he stop playing such an important role in philosophy only strengthen my point. For they were triggered by his email exchange with a female colleague in which he, many thought, threatened to harm her career in retaliation to what she had written about him on her blog. As a result, more than six hundred philosophers signed a statement of protest and pledged not to provide volunteer work for the Philosophical Gourmet Report (Leiter's popular ranking of philosophy departments) as long as it stayed under his control (September Statement 2014).

Consider the asymmetry: A single *private* email from Leiter, followed by a Twitter post, started this avalanche of outrage among hundreds of philosophers, but his years-long uncontrolled torrent of *public* insults directed at his conservative colleagues and Republicans was never seen as a problem. Also, while the philosophical community rose up in outrage over his (comparatively) slight rudeness toward a female philosopher, did anyone find anything objectionable when in 2007 Leiter publicly praised an extremely vulgar attack on a right-wing female columnist which (among other things) made fun of her breasts? No. Apparently feminist sensibilities are not activated when crass and witless insults are being hurled at conservative women.

One thing is undeniable: Without the support of a huge number of philosophers, Leiter would certainly not have been able to turn his blog into such a prominent platform for his political paroxysms. Some of his readers may have merely tolerated his vitriol, but many obviously reveled in it.

Are All Rich People Thieves?

Now back to the general theme and our attempt to explain why some philosophers act so foolishly when they enter politics.

If people are largely exposed to only one point of view for a long time, it should not be surprising if they start uncritically rejecting other perspectives and if they fail to realize the weakness of some of the arguments for their own opinion. Therefore, the strong leftist bias among philosophers is certainly a part of the explanation of how some leading scholars in the field could have defended political positions that were, and are, manifestly unreasonable. But it seems this cannot be a completely satisfactory explanation. There must be something else at work as well.

Consider first an interesting example involving Derek Parfit, one of the most influential living philosophers. It would be very hard to find an analytic thinker today who is held in higher regard.

In June 2015, Parfit gave a talk at the invitation of the Oxford organization Giving What We Can, which tries to promote "the most cost-effective poverty relief, in particular in the developing world." As has already been richly documented in these pages, it is exactly such occasions of political activism that tend to bring out the worst in philosophers, leading them to make extravagant feel-good statements and also to throw logic to the wind.

At the beginning of his talk Parfit says that according to William Godwin, if you walk past a beggar and you don't give him your coins, you're stealing; the money doesn't belong to you, because the beggar needs it more than you, so you're stealing ("Derek Parfit—Full Address," YouTube, 8:15–8:39). Immediately after citing Godwin's eccentric opinion that not giving to a beggar equals stealing from him, Parfit surprisingly goes on to agree with it enthusiastically: "Well, that is actually what I feel we rich people . . . in the world today are doing. We're not entitled to our vast wealth." And a minute later he adds: "If people from sub-Saharan Africa came and started removing my property, I wouldn't feel that I had a right to stop them."

So Parfit is arguing, first, that rich people are not entitled to their wealth (even if it is the result of their hard work), and second, he is making a much stronger claim: that rich people are actually stealing from poor people. The charge of stealing appears to be based only on Godwin's rather flimsy reasoning (which Parfit seems to endorse) that if X needs "your" money more than you do, this by itself establishes that you are stealing it from X.

What is the justification, though, for the weaker claim that rich people are not morally entitled to their wealth? Here is the way Parfit appears to reach that conclusion (the relevant sections are numbered for easier reference, and the two key terms are in italics):

> (1) It seems to me fairly clear that the great wealth that we rich people have isn't in a moral sense ours to give. It's legally ours, but it's not morally ours.
> (2) I'm not *entitled* to my vast wealth compared with these two billion people in Africa.
> (3) There's no way in which I've come to *deserve* it and they haven't (ibid., 6:55–7:19).

Since (2) is what Parfit is trying to prove and (3) says something at least superficially similar to (2), it very much looks as if Parfit is offering (3) in support of (2). But this is a fallacy. For even if the truth of (3) were established, this would not imply that (2) is true.

In ordinary English, the primary meaning of "being entitled to X" (which coincides with Parfit's central interest here) is *having a right to keep X.* On the other hand, saying that someone "deserves X" usually means that *one is worthy of X by virtue of some action or personal characteristic.* Obviously these are two very different things. And there is simply no way one can validly infer that one is not entitled to X from the mere fact that one does not deserve X.

For example, if I win a million dollars in a lottery or if I inherit this amount from my rich parents, arguably I do not *deserve* this money (for I did nothing to really earn it) but this by no means proves that I am not *entitled* to it (i.e., that I don't have a moral right to keep it).

To recapitulate: Parfit's statement (2) says something very radical and very controversial, namely that rich people don't have a moral right to keep their wealth. But why should we accept (2)? Parfit apparently tries to support it by adding statement (3), that the rich do not deserve their wealth,[6] presumably because their wealth (especially compared to the poverty of those in Africa) is largely due to their pure luck of having been born in environments full of opportunities.

The problem with Parfit's logic is twofold. First, he provides no real evidence (let alone compelling evidence) for the sweeping assertion (3), and second, even if he did, (2) would still not follow.

Another question: If Parfit genuinely believed that he had *stolen* his house, car, money, etc., from others, isn't it clear that he wouldn't continue to hold on to all those things? He is obviously not the kind of person who would keep something he himself regarded literally as stolen. Hence the very fact that he has been unable to renounce his possessions indicates that in his heart of hearts he does *not* truly believe that he stole them.

If Parfit did believe this, though, it would have been extremely easy for him to restore justice in his own case. For after having publicly announced that he wouldn't stop the poor if they came to his place to remove his property, the only thing that remained for him to do in order to facilitate a quick and rightful restitution was to disclose to the world the address of his Oxford residence. Which he has not done.

Notice, however, that Parfit is not talking only about Parfit. He is talking about *all* well-to-do people in the West. Consequently the import of his statement is far-reaching. His view implies that if millions of sub-Saharan Africans came to the United States, Canada, Australia, England, France, Germany, and Italy, not only would they have a moral *right* to remove property from rich and well-off households in those countries, the local people would have a moral *duty* to invite these newcomers into their homes and ask them to take away all the stuff that the current "owners" had stolen from the needy.

---

6 It's not clear why (3) would be introduced at all if not to support (2).

Such a radical approach to economic redistribution is almost unheard of. In terms of ordinary political taxonomy, it is best classified as belonging to the extreme fringe of the extreme left.

To conclude, here is a concise evaluation of Parfit's view: very high on compassion for the downtrodden, very low on logic.

"Let the Massacre Begin!" Said the Ethicist

Another example is provided by the philosopher Jeremy Waldron, professor at the New York University School of Law and until recently Chichele Professor of Social and Political Theory at All Souls College, Oxford. Waldron participated in the debate "Is Torture Ever Permissible?" at Columbia University on April 21, 2005. (In the meantime the video of the debate disappeared from the Internet, but I saved the file on my hard disk.)

Since Waldron is well known for his absolute condemnation of torture under any circumstances, he was inevitably asked about the notorious "ticking bomb scenario": What would Waldron's advice be if a nuclear device were planted in New York City and if the only way to save *millions* of innocent people from a certain and horrible death were to torture an arrested terrorist who knew the location of the bomb?

He replied that the answer is clear: Since morality tells us there are certain things that must not be done *under any conditions*—and torture is one of those things—then it follows that in that kind of situation we should "take the hit" and let all these millions of people die.

I find Waldron's response astonishing. I expect you do too. Notice that he is not saying merely that there should be an absolute and unconditional *legal* prohibition of torture (which would be a rationally defensible position). And he is not taking the cop-out approach of claiming that the ticking bomb scenario is implausible and for that reason refusing to give an answer, or claiming that we could never be in an epistemic position to know that torture would be necessary to save lives. Rather, he is talking about the strict *moral* prohibition that is binding in any imaginable case, without exception. He is saying that if he had to choose between (1) saving millions of lives in the only way possible, by applying rough treatment (say, waterboarding, which he regards as torture) to one of the organizers of the impending nuclear attack on New York, and (2) protecting the perpetrator from any mistreatment, with the result that millions of people would die, he would choose (2). Furthermore, he insists that in that situation, it would be *immoral* not to make that choice.

Now, I simply do not believe that even an Oxford philosopher could be so out of his mind as to be really capable of choosing (2) if confronted with the above dilemma in actuality. Surely at the critical moment the proper priorities would kick in and Waldron would come to his senses and do the right thing. Outside of philosophical fantasies and back in the real world, no humane person could refrain from causing a murderous terrorist some physical discomfort if this were the only way to avoid the apocalyptic massacre.

Excellently Wise and Excellently Foolish

Question: How could a highly intelligent person like Waldron publicly and persistently defend such a nutty idea in the first place? Before trying to give an answer, let us first expand the question.

Drawing on the episodes described earlier in this book, there are more puzzles of the same kind: How was it possible that other extremely smart people managed to believe—despite all the evidence to the contrary—that, among other things, the existence of the Iron Curtain was to be blamed on the United States; that Enver Hoxha's regime in Albania was great; that all rich people in the West are thieves; that those convicted in the Moscow show trials were guilty as charged; that an appropriate reaction to the collapse of Soviet Communism was "a feeling of loss"; that there was no reason to join the war against Hitler until June 22, 1941; and that the United States in the 1950s was as much a police state as Hitler's Germany?

Perhaps we should challenge the premise of these questions. The assumption here seems to be that what is especially odd about all these examples is that such highly intelligent people held such absurd opinions. But what if, on the contrary, it is precisely such very smart individuals who are especially prone to exhibit certain types of irrationality? What if there are follies that often spare ordinary people while more easily afflicting exactly those who are exceptionally bright, highly educated, and presumed to be extraordinarily sophisticated? This possibility was first suggested in the seventeenth century by Thomas Hobbes in the following remarkable passage:

> For between true science, and erroneous doctrines, ignorance is in the middle. Natural sense and imagination are not subject to absurdity. Nature itself cannot err: and as men abound in copiousness of language; so they become more wise, or more mad, than ordinary. Nor is it possible without letters for any man to become either excellently wise or (unless his memory be hurt by disease, or ill constitution of organs) excellently foolish (1651, 23).

Notice the contrast Hobbes draws between two kinds of people: those with "natural sense and imagination" who are "not subject to absurdity" and those who "abound in copiousness of language" and who will tend to become either "excellently wise" or "excellently foolish." The expression "abound in copiousness of language" happens to connect very well with some of the main characteristics of analytic philosophers, or at least the characteristics they try to inculcate in themselves. Analytic philosophers are supposed to be able to make subtle semantic distinctions, follow and evaluate convoluted arguments, excel in conceptual analysis, notice hidden ambiguities, detect fallacies and sources of linguistic confusions, exhibit verbal fluency, and so on.

In accordance with what Hobbes says, philosophers are also good both at becoming "excellently wise" (in their strictly philosophical area of specialization) and "excellently foolish" (in politics, as numerous examples in this book illustrate). The fact that they are excellently wise (in their domain of research) requires no explanation. Philosophers tend to be very clever, so there is nothing surprising about the best of them being very successful when they apply their formidable abilities to solving philosophical problems.

But the second part is puzzling. Why would very smart people tend to be "excellently foolish"? One answer is that they can simply get away with it. Being foolish in philosophy is immediately followed by a heavy penalty (loss of reputation), but being foolish in politics often incurs no cost at all, assuming of course that the foolishness is of the leftist variety. It can even be rewarded, as one may be cheered on by politically like-minded colleagues for displaying "courage" and willingness to stick it to the other side.

And it is those most accomplished philosophers whose descent into politics will be especially appreciated, perhaps because their high intellectual prestige, earned in their philosophical work, will automatically add credibility to their political pontifications.[7] It will be natural to assume that they arrived at their political views with the same reasonableness and critical spirit demonstrated in their academic publications. Moreover, crazy views, when they are defended by highly esteemed philosophers, will often start looking less crazy than they should. Many colleagues may be inclined to reason in the following way: "I don't find their arguments very convincing, but perhaps I should rethink the issue: After all, they are very smart people, so there is possibly something more in what they say than I can see."

As a result, radicalism will spread further or encounter less resistance. Besides, there will be no real disincentive for prominent philosophers to go out on a limb and advocate extreme leftist opinions without giving a lot of serious thought to these matters. Defending loony views will not have any immediate harmful effects because usually no one outside of academia will pay attention to

7 It seems that psychological research supports the claim that those with higher cognitive sophistication are more vulnerable to ideological bias: "[W]e should expect those individuals who display *the highest reasoning capacities* to be the ones most powerfully impelled to engage in [*ideologically motivated reasoning*]" (Kahan et al. 2013; emphasis added). Also, the so-called bias blind spot (difficulty in detecting one's own biases) is more pronounced in people with higher cognitive ability (West et al. 2012).

what these philosophers are saying anyway, or these reactions will not matter much. It all becomes a game enjoyed by those inside the ivory tower but largely irrelevant to the outside world.

Nevertheless, it is a game that corrupts the mind. This is a betrayal of reason that, oddly, your philosopher colleagues will not hold against you. The philosopher F. H. Bradley famously defined metaphysics as the finding of bad reasons for what we believe upon instinct. The sin of the metaphysicians, according to Bradley, is that they bring in bad reasons to break the deadlock in a debate in which they should have remained agnostic.

What the philosophers I've discussed in these pages did was worse. They actually had excellent and easily accessible reasons to be *against* the positions they adopted and which they continued to support with grossly inadequate arguments. So it is not that they should have remained merely agnostic. Given the readily available evidence, they should have *rejected* the views they so passionately defended. But they did not. On the contrary, they have been invoking logic, rationality, and critical thinking, all in the attempt to present their strongly held political delusions as the voice of reason.

CHAPTER FOURTEEN

Conclusion

> "Have we eaten on the insane root that takes the reason prisoner?"
>
> —WILLIAM SHAKESPEARE

Is there hope that the dreary situation in philosophy described in these pages could be changed for the better in the near future? And if yes, how exactly could the ideological unanimity and self-righteousness that accompanies it be undermined? Is there an antidote for those who have eaten on that "insane root" of liberal extremism and intolerance? Many are pessimistic. Some tend to despair, maintaining that leftist orthodoxy is cemented in academia to such a degree that arguments can no longer work and that it can now be attacked only with mockery and humor.

I do not think this is the best, and it is certainly not the only, way to respond. What then do I hope to achieve with this book? It would be naive, of course, to expect that it will have a huge impact on contemporary philosophers and their attitude toward politics. It is extremely hard to change people's way of thinking about these issues, especially when it has been widely shared and entrenched for a long time. Yet it would be sufficiently satisfying if the arguments presented here eased the grip of groupthink on philosophers at least a little and if some of them woke up from what Francisco Goya strikingly called "the sleep of reason that produces monsters."[1]

1 The cover of this book is a reproduction of Goya's famous work. One of its many intriguing features is four owls, which here apparently symbolize neither wisdom (their standard meaning) nor philosophy (remember Hegel's famous statement about Minerva's owl) but exactly the opposite: "In eighteenth-century Spain the owl was not a symbol of wisdom but rather of folly, stupidity, and acts committed under cover of darkness" (Ilie 1991, 53).

And why shouldn't they? For despite the enormous pressure of leftist orthodoxy, surely there are philosophers who would find the whole "history of infamy" presented here alarming and who may conclude that the current ideological imbalance with all its excesses is intolerable. And if enough such people raise their voices, perhaps there would be some chance of change.

But the step from becoming aware that a change is needed to publicly campaigning for that change and helping it to come about is not always as straightforward and smooth as some seem to think. When John Silber, former president of Boston University, was asked whether people in the position of making politically sensitive changes in higher education are scared of taking measures in this direction, he responded: "Many are. But ask why. They're not going to be shot at or put in prison. They're probably not going to be fined. They're not going to lose their jobs. Why does it take courage when there is no risk?" (*Boston* magazine, May 2006).

Silber was wrong, of course, and he knew it. No, the people he is talking about are obviously not afraid of being shot or being put in prison. Nor are they afraid of (immediately) losing their jobs. What they *are* afraid of is their own colleagues. Making public statements that deviate from the dominant political views on campus carries the high risk of condemnation, isolation, and ostracism. Under the circumstances, the decision to keep silent does not look entirely unreasonable. Why speak your mind if doing so can lead to very unpleasant consequences, with little chance of any good ones?

Sometimes, however, being silent is not enough to guarantee being left alone. One must also express support for the right causes and publicly condemn those who have gone over to the dark side. And many academics do accept this kind of herd mentality and are happy to join in denouncing the views the majority regards as unacceptable.

Paradoxically, the academic environment in some Communist regimes of Eastern Europe was in fact far more tolerant of challenges to the prevailing leftism than is the case with many of the best universities in the West today. In Croatia and other parts of former Yugoslavia in the 1970s and 1980s, for instance, although a lot of professors, especially in the humanities and social sciences, were careerists or true believers who all vehemently opposed the slightest criticism of Communism or socialism, there were nevertheless quite a number of others who were fed up with the officially imposed ideology and who were very glad to see an anti-Marxist article occasionally make it into print. So while the Party sycophants would condemn the author of such a "reactionary" text, many of his own colleagues would pat him on the back.

In contrast, try going to Harvard, Princeton, or Stanford nowadays and doing something equivalent, i.e., publicly attacking leftist sacred cows such as affirmative action, gay marriage, multiculturalism, feminism, social justice, etc. Remember that speakers with politically incorrect views sometimes need bodyguards during their campus visit.

So the change of mentality will not come easily, and if it ever happens it will take some time. And a lot of effort and persuasion.

There are two main reasons why philosophy badly needs a recovery program. First, it is embarrassing for a discipline that advertises itself as a paragon of reason to have so many of its leading minds often champion nutty leftist views (including the support for the most appalling political regimes), while hardly any of their colleagues bat an eye. There are no enemies to the left, as the saying goes. Or better still, the implicit principle behind the philosophers' typical behavior appears to be: Leftist ideas should be endorsed or perhaps ignored, if they become too extreme, but never criticized with the same intensity as conservative views.

Here is a quick bullet-point reminder of some of the many such examples involving the crème de la crème of contemporary philosophy. One of the leading logical positivists spends more than two years doing propaganda for Stalin while millions die in the government-caused famine. Reactions? None. One of the most highly esteemed philosophers joins a militant Maoist party and is very active in it for four years, during the horror of the Cultural Revolution. Any interest among his colleagues in knowing more about the episode or understanding how this was possible? Nonexistent. A hugely influential thinker describes in his autobiography and several interviews how he suspended his opposition to Hitler after the Nazi–Stalin Pact and then reversed himself miraculously on the day of the German attack on the Soviet Union. Reaction? Yawn. A person who is widely regarded as the greatest philosopher of the twentieth century did basically the same thing. Ever discussed? Not really. A preeminent philosopher is knighted for service to philosophy *and racial justice* despite giving a platform at All Souls College, Oxford, to a notorious and vicious racist. Comments? None. (Apparently this is regarded as not worth even mentioning or it did not register at all.) A scholar in one of the top philosophy departments in the UK defends for years the brutal Soviet oppression of the Hungarian Revolution of 1956 as a completely justified response to a "fascist rebellion." Response? A total lack of interest, followed by his being elected to the prestigious Chichele chair of *political theory* at Oxford. A renowned philosopher of science was in his youth an ultra-Stalinist as well as a police informer and also gratuitously forced a young woman to commit suicide. Response? An attempt to distort some of these facts and present them in a positive light, plus naming a university building and the highest award in the field after him. And so on, and so forth.

There is another reason a change of heart in philosophy would be very welcome. Many people have lately questioned the wisdom of so much public spending for higher education, especially in the humanities. Ominously, it is philosophy departments that are often mentioned as the first candidate for cuts or even elimination when universities face funding problems. What is worse, some excellent and respected philosophers actually agree their departments should be high on the list for discontinuation:

> Were I a university administrator facing a contracting budget, I would not look to eliminate biosciences or computer engineering. I would notice that the philosophers seem smart, but their writings are tediously incestuous and of no influence except among themselves, and I would conclude that my academy could do without such a department (Glymour 2011).

With such doubts about the value of philosophy gaining momentum, the last thing we need is to project a picture of a politically unbalanced discipline that is largely unaware of its unyielding leftist bias and in which leading scholars have been for decades either rewarded for their unhinged ideological views or have encountered almost no opposition from their peers. As long as this situation continues, public announcements by philosophers that they teach students how to think critically and logically will inevitably ring hollow.

But let me end on a positive note. Despite the fact that in philosophy, reason has so often gone on holiday, we may still be hopeful. As a friend of mine remarked, the word *holiday* implies that reason might come back.

References

Agarossi, E., & Zaslavsky, V. (2011). *Stalin and Togliatti: Italy and the Origin of the Cold War.* Stanford: Stanford University Press.

Albert, D. (2005). "Facing the Fear: Remembering Sidney Morgenbesser," *Columbia College Today.*

APA (1992). "Statement on the Major," https://apaonline.site-ym.com/?major

APA (2014). www.apaonline.org/news/180699/Letter-from-the-APA-in-Response-to-A-College-Major-Matters-Even-More-in-a-Recession.htm

Andrew, C., & Mitrokhin, V. (2000). *The Sword and the Shield: The Mitrokhin Archive and the Secret History of the KGB.* New York: Basic Books.

Applebaum, A. (2012). *Iron Curtain: The Crushing of Eastern Europe, 1944–1956.* New York: Anchor.

Aptheker, B. (1999). *The Morning Breaks: The Trial of Angela Davis.* Ithaca, N.Y.: Cornell University Press.

Arntz, G. et al. (1979). *Symbols for Education and Statistics: 1928–1965*, Vienna-Moscow-The Hague. The Hague: Spruijt.

Ayer, A. J. (1936). *Language, Truth and Logic.* Harmondsworth: Penguin.

Ayer, A. J. (1977). *Part of My Life.* Oxford: Oxford University Press.

Bandy, A. (2009). *Chocolate and Chess: Unlocking Lakatos.* Budapest: Akadémiai Kiadó.

Bandy, A. (undated). "György Lukács and Gábor Kovács." Retrieved June 22, 2014, from http://web.phil-inst.hu/lua/archivum/Lukacs125/Alex Bandy_Lukacs and Lakatos.pdf

Barber, D. (2008). *A Hard Rain Fell: SDS and Why It Failed.* Jackson: University Press of Mississippi.

Barnett, S. M., & Ceci, S. J. (2002). "When and Where Do We Apply What We Learn? A Taxonomy for Far Transfer," *Psychological Bulletin* 128, 612–37.

Belfrage, C. (1973). *The American Inquisition, 1945–1960.* Indianapolis: Bobbs-Merrill.

Benhabib, S. (1995). "The Strange Silence of Political Theory: Response." *Political Theory* 23, 674–81.

Berkman, A. (ed.). (1925). *Letters from Russian Prisons.* New York: Albert & Charles Boni.

Berlin, I. (1973). "Austin and the Early Beginnings of Oxford Philosophy." In I. Berlin (Ed.), *Essays on J. L. Austin.* Oxford: Clarendon Press.

Berlin, I. (1998). *Personal Impressions.* London: Pimlico.

Berlin, I. (2011). *Enlightening: Letters 1946–1960.* London: Pimlico.

Birchall, I. H. (2004). *Sartre against Stalinism.* New York & Oxford: Berghahn Books.

Bloom, A. (1987). *The Closing of the American Mind.* New York: Simon & Schuster.

Blumberg, A. E., & Feigl, H. (1931). "Logical Positivism." *Journal of Philosophy* 28, 281–96.

Böhler, J. et al. (eds.). (2014). *Legacies of Violence: Eastern Europe's First World War* (vol. 120). Oldenbourg: De Gruyter.

Born, M. (1971). *The Born–Einstein Letters.* London: Macmillan.

Borradori, G. (ed.). (1994). *The American Philosopher.* Chicago: University of Chicago Press.

British Philosophical Association (2016). "Why Study Philosophy." www.bpa.ac.uk/resources/why-philosophy

Brustein, W. (2003). *Roots of Hate: Anti-Semitism in Europe Before the Holocaust.* Cambridge: Cambridge University Press.

Brustein, W. I., & Roberts, L. (2015). *The Socialism of Fools? Leftist Origins of Modern Anti-Semitism.* Cambridge: Cambridge University Press.

Budenz, L. F. (1950). *Men Without Faces: The Communist Conspiracy in the USA.* New York: Harper.

Burgess, A. (2010). "Make Reasoning Skills Compulsory in Schools." www.gopetition.com/petition/37997.html

Carmichael, S. (2003). *Ready for Revolution: The Life and Struggles of Stokely Carmichael.* New York: Scribner.

Carnap, R. (1963). "Intellectual Autobiography." In P. A. Schilpp (ed.), *The Philosophy of Rudolf Carnap.* La Salle, Ill.: Open Court.

Cartwright, N. et al. (2008). *Otto Neurath: Philosophy Between Science and Politics.* Cambridge: Cambridge University Press.

Cassidy, D. C. (2009). *Beyond Uncertainty: Heisenberg, Quantum Physics, and the Bomb.* New York: Bellevue Literary Press.

Caute, D. (1988). *Sixty-Eight: The Year of the Barricades.* London: Paladin Books.

Chamberlin, W. H. (1935). "Soviet Taboos." *Foreign Affairs* 13, 431–40.

Chappell, S. G. (2013). "Bernard Williams," *Stanford Encyclopedia of Philosophy.*

Chi, H. V. (1964). *From Colonialism to Communism: A Case History of North Vietnam.* New York: Praeger.

Childs, D. (1977). "The British Communist Party and the War, 1939–41: Old Slogans Revived." *Journal of Contemporary History* 12, 237–53.

Chizlett, C. (1992). "Damned Lies. And Statistics. Otto Neurath and Soviet Propaganda in the 1930s." *Visible Language* 26, 298–321.

Churchman, C. W. (1984). "Early Years of the Philosophy of Science Association." *Philosophy of Science* 51, 20–22.

Clark, K. (2011). *Moscow, the Fourth Rome: Stalinism, Cosmopolitanism, and the Evolution of Soviet Culture 1931–1941.* Cambridge, Mass.: Harvard University Press.

Cohen, G. A. (1978). *Karl Marx's Theory of History: A Defence.* Oxford: Oxford University Press.

Cohen, G. A. (1995). *Self-Ownership, Freedom, and Equality.* Cambridge: Cambridge University Press.

Cohen, G. A. (2001). *If You're an Egalitarian, How Come You're So Rich.* Cambridge, Mass.: Harvard University Press.

Cohen, G. A. (2009). *Why Not Socialism?* Princeton, N.J.: Princeton University Press.

Cohen, G. A. (2013). *Finding Oneself in the Other.* Princeton, N.J.: Princeton University Press.

Congdon, L. (1997). "Possessed: Imre Lakatos' Road to 1956." *Contemporary European History* 6, 279–94.

Cornish, K. (1998). *The Jew of Linz: Wittgenstein, Hitler and Their Secret Battle for the Mind.* London: Century.

Courtois, S. et al. (1999). *The Black Book of Communism: Crimes, Terror, Repression.* Cambridge, Mass.: Harvard University Press.
Cowen, T. (1997). "The Socialist Roots of Modern Anti-Semitism." *FEE: Foundation for Economic Education.*
Dahrendorf, R. (1995). *LSE: A History of the London School of Economics and Political Science 1895–1995.* Oxford: Clarendon Press.
Dallin, D. J., & Nicolaevsky, B. I. (1948). *Forced Labor in Soviet Russia.* London: Hollis & Carter.
Davenport-Hines, R. (1996). *Auden.* London: Minerva.
Davidson, D. (1999). "Intellectual Autobiography." In L. E. Hahn (ed.), *The Philosophy of Donald Davidson.* Chicago: Open Court.
Dawson, J. W. (1997). *Logical Dilemmas: The Life and Work of Kurt Gödel.* Wellesley, Mass.: A K Peters.
De Gaynesford, M. (2006). *Hilary Putnam.* London: Acumen.
Deery, P. (2013). *Red Apple: Communism and McCarthyism in Cold War New York.* New York: Fordham University Press.
DeJong-Lambert, W. (2012). *The Cold War Politics of Genetic Research: An Introduction to the Lysenko Affair.* Dordrecht: Springer.
Devine, T. W. (2013). *Henry Wallace's 1948 Presidential Campaign and the Future of Postwar Liberalism.* Chapel Hill: University of North Carolina Press.
Dickstein, M. (2009). "Review of Christopher Bigby's Arthur Miller: 1915–1962." *Times Literary Supplement,* July 24.
Dilman, I. (ed.). (1984). *Philosophy and Life: Essays on John Wisdom.* Dordrecht: Kluwer.
Dummett, M. (1973). *Frege: Philosophy of Language.* London: Duckworth.
Dummett, M. (1981). "Ought Research to Be Unrestricted?" *Grazer Philosophische Studien* 12–13, 281–98.
Dummett, M. (1996). *Origins of Analytical Philosophy.* Cambridge, Mass.: Harvard University Press.
Dummett, M. (2001). *On Immigration and Refugees.* London: Routledge.
Dummett, M. (2004). "The Nature of Racism." In M. P. Levine & T. Pataki (eds.), *Racism in Mind.* Ithaca, N.Y.: Cornell University Press.
Dummett, M. (2007). "Intellectual Autobiography." In R. E. Auxier & L. E. Hahn (eds.), *The Philosophy of Michael Dummett.* Chicago & La Salle: Open Court.
Dyson, F. (2012). "What Can You Really Know?" *New York Review of Books,* November 8.
Eagan, K. et al. (2014). *Undergraduate Teaching Faculty: The HERI Survey.* www.heri.ucla.edu/monographs/HERI-FAC2014-monograph-expanded.pdf
Eastman, M. (1959). *Great Companions: Critical Memoirs of Some Famous Friends.* New York: Farrar, Straus and Cudahy.
Einstein, A. (1944). "Our Goal Unity, but Germans Are Unfit." *Free World,* October 8.
Elster, J. (2011). "Hard and Soft Obscurantism in the Humanities and Social Sciences." *Diogenes* 58 (1–2), 159–70.
Elster, J. (2014–15). "Cohen, Gerald Allan." *Oxford Dictionary of National Biography.*
Engelmann, P. (1967). *Letters from Ludwig Wittgenstein: With a Memoir.* Oxford: Blackwell.
Fara, R. (1997). "Interview with Donald Davidson." London: Philosophy International, Centre for the Philosophy of the Natural and Social Sciences, London School of Economics and Political Science.

Fay, L. E. (2000). *Shostakovich: A Life.* Oxford: Oxford University Press.

Feferman, A. B., & Feferman, S. (2004). *Alfred Tarski: Life and Logic.* Cambridge: Cambridge University Press.

Feuer, L. S. (1988). "A Narrative of Personal Events and Ideas." In S. Hook et al. (eds.), *Philosophy, History and Social Action: Essays in Honor of Lewis Feuer with an Autobiographic Essay by Lewis Feuer.* Dordrecht: Kluwer.

Fisher, R. A. (1948). "What Sort of Man Is Lysenko?" *Listener* 40, 874–75.

Fitzpatrick, S. (1999). *Everyday Stalinism: Ordinary Life in Extraordinary Times: Soviet Russia in the 1930s.* Oxford: Oxford University Press.

Flett, K. (ed.). (2007). *1956 and All That.* Cambridge: Cambridge Scholars Publishing.

Flew, A. (2001). *Crime, Punishment, and Disease.* New Brunswick, N.J.: Transaction.

Føllesdal, D. (1997). "Analytic Philosophy: What Is It and Why Should One Engage in It?" In H.-J. Glock (ed.), *The Rise of Analytic Philosophy* (pp. 1–16). Oxford: Blackwell.

Frank, P. (1937). "The Mechanical versus the Mathematical Conception of Nature." *Philosophy of Science* 4 (1), 41–74.

Frank, P. (1947). *Einstein: His Life and Times.* New York: Knopf.

Frank, P. (1950). *Modern Science and Its Philosophy.* Cambridge, Mass.: Harvard University Press.

Frank, P. (1997). *The Law of Causality and Its Limits* (Vol. 22). Dordrecht: Kluwer.

Frege, G. (1991). *Posthumous Writings.* London: Wiley-Blackwell.

Friedman, M. (2001). *Dynamics of Reason.* Stanford, Calif.: CSLI.

Frey, M. C., & Detterman, D. K. (2004). "Scholastic Assessment or *g*? The Relationship between the Scholastic Assessment Test and General Cognitive Ability," *Psychological Science.* 15, 373–78.

Gilbert, A. (2016). "Hilary Putnam: Compassion and Questioning as a Guide to Life," *3:AM Magazine* (www.3ammagazine.com/3am/hilary-putnam-compassion-and-questioning-as-a-guide-to-life).

Glock, H.-J. (2001). "Wittgenstein and Reason." In J. C. Klagge (ed.), *Wittgenstein: Biography and Philosophy* (pp. 195–220). Cambridge: Cambridge University Press.

Glover, J. (1999). *Humanity: A Moral History of the Twentieth Century.* New Haven & London: Yale University Press.

Glymour, C. (2011). Manifesto. (June 24). http://choiceandinference.com/2011/12/23/in-light-of-some-recent-discussion-over-at-new-apps-i-bring-you-clark-glymours-manifesto/

Gödel, K. (2002). *Wahrheit und Beweisbarkeit 1.: Dokumente und Historische Analysen.* Vienna: ÖBV+ HPT Verlagsg. GmbH.

Godfrey-Smith, P. (2009). *Theory and Reality: An Introduction to the Philosophy of Science.* Chicago: University of Chicago Press.

Goldstein, R. (2005). *Incompleteness: The Proof and Paradox of Kurt Gödel.* New York: Norton.

Gotesky, R. (1947). "Review: John Somerville's *Soviet Philosophy.*" *Russian Review* 7, 115–17.

Graham, L. R. (1985). "The Socio-Political Roots of Boris Hessen: Soviet Marxism and the History of Science." *Social Studies of Science* 15 (4), 705–22.

Graham, L. R. (1993). *Science in Russia and the Soviet Union: A Short History.* Cambridge: Cambridge University Press.

Griffin, N. (ed.). (2002). *The Selected Letters of Bertrand Russell, Volume 2: The Public Years 1914–1970.* London: Routledge.
Gross, N. (2008). *Richard Rorty: The Making of an American Philosopher.* Chicago & London: The University of Chicago Press.
Gross, N. (2013). *Why Are Professors Liberal and Why Do Conservatives Care?.* Cambridge, Mass.: Harvard University Press.
Grundmann, S. (2005). *The Einstein Dossiers.* Berlin: Springer.
Hacker, P. S. (2014–15). "Wittgenstein, Ludwig." *Oxford Dictionary of National Biography.*
Hacking, I. (1996). "The Disunities of the Sciences." In P. Galison & D. J. Stump (eds.), *The Disunity of Science: Boundaries, Contexts, and Power.* Stanford, Calif.: Stanford University Press.
Hacking, I. (2000). "Mitteleuropa am Aldwych." *London Review of Books* 22, 28–29.
Hahn, H. (1980). *Empiricism, Logic and Mathematics: Philosophical Papers.* Dordrecht: Reidel.
Hampshire, S. (1992). "J. L. Austin." In R. Rorty (ed.), *The Linguistic Turn: Essays in Philosophical Method.* Chicago: University of Chicago Press.
Hampshire, S., & Berlin, I. (1972). Conversation in *Logic Lane,* a series of six films by Michael Chanan. www.youtube.com/watch?v=kgR85uAe7u8
Hand, M., & Winstanley, C. (2009). *Philosophy in Schools.* London & New York: Continuum.
Harman, O. S. (2003). "C. D. Darlington and the British and American Reaction to Lysenko and the Soviet Conception of Science." *Journal of the History of Biology* 36 (2), 309–52.
Haynes, J. E., & Klehr, H. (2000). *Venona: Decoding Soviet Espionage in America.* New Haven, Conn.: Yale University Press.
Hecker, R. (ed.). (2000). *Erfolgreiche Kooperation: Das Frankfurter Institut für Sozialforschung und das Moskauer Marx-Engels-Institut (1924–1928).* Hamburg: Argument Verlag.
Herrnstein, R. J. (1971). "I.Q." *Atlantic Monthly,* September.
Herrnstein, R. J., & Murray, C. (1994). *The Bell Curve: Intelligence and Class Structure in American Life.* New York: Free Press.
Hirschfeld, K. (2009). "Show Trials and the Ritual Purification of Hypermodernity." In I. L. Horowitz (ed.), *Culture and Civilization,* vol. 1. New Brunswick, N. J.: Transaction Publishers.
Hitchens, C. (2011). *Hitch-22: A Memoir.* New York: Twelve.
Hobbes, T. (1651). *Leviathan.* London: Andrew Crooke.
Holyoak, K. J., & Morrison, R. G. (eds.). (2005). *The Cambridge Handbook of Thinking and Reasoning.* Cambridge: Cambridge University Press.
Hook, S. (1987). *Out of Step: An Unquiet Life in the 20th Century.* New York: Harper & Row.
Howe, I. (1947). "Why Stalin Needs Slaves." *New International* 13 (December), 264–67.
Hyde, D. (1950). *I Believed: The Autobiography of a Former British Communist.* London: Heinemann.
Ilie, P. (1991). "The Literary Substrate of Goya's Owl Iconology." *Bulletin of Hispanic Studies* 68 (1), 53–66.
Isaacson, W. (2007). *Einstein: His Life and Universe.* New York: Simon & Schuster.

Ivanitsky, I. P. (ed.). (1932). *Pictorial Statistics and the Vienna Method* (in Russian). Moscow & Leningrad: OGIZ & IZOGIZ.

IZOSTAT (1933). *On Building Socialism: Accomplishments of the First Five-Year Plan* (in Russian). Moscow: OGIZ & IZOGIZ.

Jacoby, S. (2008). *The Age of American Unreason.* New York: Random House.

Jaschik, S. (2015). "Marco Rubio vs. Aristotle." *Inside Higher Education* (www.InsideHigherEd.com, August 20).

Jensen, A. R. (1991). "Spearman's *g* and the Problem of Educational Equality." *Oxford Review of Education* 17, 169–85.

Joravsky, D. (1970). *The Lysenko Affair.* Cambridge, Mass.: Harvard University Press.

Judt, T. (1992). *Past Imperfect: French Intellectuals, 1944–1956.* Berkeley: University of California Press.

Kadvany, J. (2001). *Imre Lakatos and the Guises of Reason.* Durham, N.C.: Duke University Press.

Kadvany, J. (2012). "Review of A. Bandy, Chocolate and Chess (Unlocking Lakatos)." *Philosophy of the Social Sciences* 42 (2), 276–86.

Kahan, D. M. et al. (2013). "Motivated Numeracy and Enlightened Self-Government." *Social Science Research Network* 2319992.

Kalish, D. A. (1969). "A Statement of Facts Concerning the Appointment and Threatened Dismissal of Professor Angela Davis, Provided by the UCLA Department of Philosophy." Los Angeles: Online Archive of California.

Kanterian, E. (2007). *Ludwig Wittgenstein.* London: Reaktion Books.

Kaube, J. (2015)."Martin? Edmund!" www.faz.net/aktuell/feuilleton/streit-um-heidegger-lehrstuhl-martin-edmund-13452086.html

Kennedy, J. (2007). "Kurt Gödel. Das Album—The Album." *Mathematical Intelligencer* 29 (3), 73–76.

Kenny, A. (2006). *Wittgenstein.* Oxford: Blackwell.

Kinross, R. (1994). "Blind Eyes, Innuendo and the Politics of Design: A Reply to Clive Chizlett." *Visible Language* 28, 68–78.

Klement, K. C. (2014). "The Russell–Dummett Correspondence on Frege and His Nachlaß." *Bertrand Russell Society Bulletin* (Fall).

Kline, G. L. (2012). "Discussions with Bocheński Concerning Soviet Marxism–Leninism, 1952–1986." *Studies in East European Thought* 64, 301–12.

Kluge, E.-H. W. (1977). "Some Reflections on *Frege: Philosophy of Language.*" *Dialogue,* 16 (3), 519–33.

Kojevnikov, A. B. (2004). *Stalin's Great Science: The Times and Adventures of Soviet Physicists* (vol. 2). London: Imperial College Press.

Köstenberger, J. (2013). "Otto Neuraths 'Wiener Methode' im Dienste der sowjetischen Propaganda." In J. Köstenberger et al. (eds.), *Gegenwelten: Aspekte der österreichisch-sowjetischen Beziehungen* (275–82). St. Pölten—Salzburg—Wien: Residenz Verlag.

Kreisel, G. (1980). "Kurt Gödel. 28 April 1906–14 January 1978." *Biographical Memoirs of Fellows of the Royal Society,* 149–224.

Ladd, E. C., & Lipset, S. M. (1972). "Poisoned Ivy: McGovern's Campus Support." *New York* (October 16), 43–46.

Lepore, E. (2004). "Interview with Donald Davidson." in D. Davidson, *Problems of Rationality.* Oxford: Clarenon Press.

Levin, M. (1990). "Letter to the Editor." *Proceedings and Addresses of the American Philosophical Association* 63.

Levine, I. D. (1973). *Eyewitness to History*. New York: Hawthorne.

Litten, F. S. (1991). "Einstein and the Noulens Affair." *British Journal for the History of Science* 24, 465–67.

Long, J. (2002). "The Unforgiven: Imre Lakatos' Life in Hungary." In G. Kampis et al. (eds.), *Appraising Lakatos: Mathematics, Methodology and the Man*. Dordrecht: Springer.

Lutz, R. H. (1922). *The German Revolution, 1918–1919*. Stanford, Calif.: Stanford University Press.

Malcolm, N. (2001). *Ludwig Wittgenstein: A Memoir.* Oxford: Clarendon Press.

Malisoff, W. M. (1934). "Editorial." *Philosophy of Science* 1, 1–4.

Malisoff, W. M. (1939). "Virtue and the Scientist." *Philosophy of Science* 6, 127–36.

Malisoff, W. M. (1947a). "Note on J. R. Baker's Science and the Planned State." *Philosophy of Science* 14, 171–72.

Malisoff, W. M. (1947b). "Note on J. Somerville's *Soviet Philosophy*." *Philosophy of Science* 14, 172.

Maranto, R. et al. (2009). *The Politically Correct University: Problems, Scope, and Reforms.* Washington, D.C.: AEI Press.

Marcuse, H. et al. (1969). *A Critique of Pure Tolerance.* Boston: Beacon Press.

Marković, M. (1990). "The Tragedy of National Conflicts in 'Real Socialism': The Case of the Yugoslav Autonomous Province of Kosovo." *Praxis International*, 9, 408–24.

Martins, H. (2011). "Dear LSE: Notes on an Academic Disaster." *Society* 48 (4), 286–89.

Maynard Smith, J. (1992). "J. B. S. Haldane." In S. Sarkar (ed.), *The Founders of Evolutionary Genetics.* Dordrecht: Kluwer.

Mayr, E., & Schreder, G. (2014). "Isotype Visualizations." *eJournal of eDemocracy & Open Government* 6 (2), 136–50.

McGinn, C. (2002). *The Making of a Philosopher: My Journey through Twentieth-Century Philosophy.* New York: HarperCollins.

McGuinness, B. (2002). *Approaches to Wittgenstein.* London: Routledge.

McGuinness, B. (ed.). (2012). *Wittgenstein in Cambridge: Letters and Documents 1911–1951.* New York: Wiley.

Medvedev, R. A. (1989). *Let History Judge: The Origins and Consequences of Stalinism.* New York: Columbia University Press.

Melgunov, S. P. (1924). *The Red Terror in Russia 1918–1923.* Berlin.

Mendelsohn, R. L. (1996). "Translator's Preface (to Frege's Diary)." *Inquiry* 39, 303–05.

Menger, K. (1982). "Memories of Moritz Schlick." In E. T. Gadol (ed.), *Rationality and Science.* Vienna & New York: Springer.

Menger, K. (1994). *Reminiscences of the Vienna Circle and the Mathematical Colloquium.* Dordrecht: Kluwer.

Mitin, M. (1944). "Twenty-Five Years of Philosophy in the USSR." *Philosophy* 19, 76–84.

Monk, R. (1990). *Wittgenstein: The Duty of Genius.* London: Penguin.

Monk, R. (2000). *Bertrand Russell: The Ghost of Madness, 1921–1970* (vol. 2). London: Jonathan Cape.

Moran, J. (1972). "Wittgenstein and Russia." *New Left Review* 1, 85–96.

Muggeridge, M. (2010). *Time and Eternity: Uncollected Writings.* London: Darton, Longman and Todd Ltd.

Muller, H. (1934). "The Views of Haeckel in the Light of Genetics." *Philosophy of Science* 1, 313–22.

Naimark, N. M. (2010). *Stalin's Genocides.* Princeton, N.J.: Princeton University Press.

Naipaul, V. S. (1980). *The Return of Eva Perón; with The Killings in Trinidad.* New York: Knopf.

Napolitano, G. (2007). "Sraffa and Gramsci: A Recollection." *Review of Political Economy* 17, 407–12.

Neider, H. (1999). "Persönliche Erinnerungen an den Wiener Kreis." In K. R. Fischer (ed.), *Österreichische Philosophie von Brentano bis Wittgenstein: Ein Lesebuch.* Vienna: WUV.

Neisser, U. et al. (1996). "Intelligence: Knowns and Unknowns." *American Psychologist* 51 (2), 77–101.

Nemeth, E. et al. (eds.). (2008). *Otto Neurath's Economics in Context.* Vienna: Springer.

Nemeth, E., & Stadler, F. (1996). *Encyclopedia and Utopia: The Life and Work of Otto Neurath (1882–1945).* Dordrecht: Kluwer.

Neurath, O. (1973). *Empiricism and Sociology.* Dordrecht: Reidel.

Neurath, O. (2004). *Economic Writings: Selections, 1904–1945.* Dordrecht: Kluwer.

Norton, J. D. (2010). "Philosophy in Einstein's Science." http://philsci-archive.pitt.edu/9108/1/Phil_in_Einstein.pdf

Noske, G. (1920). *Von Kiel bis Kapp: Zur Geschichte der deutschen Revolution.* Berlin: Verlag für Politik und Wirtschaft.

Nussbaum, M. S. (2003). "'Don't Smile So Much': Philosophy and Women in the 1970s." In S. Bartky et al. (eds.), *Singing in the Fire: Stories of Women in Philosophy.* Lanham, Md.: Rowman & Littlefield.

O'Grady, J. (2016). "Hilary Putnam Obituary." *Guardian,* March 14.

O'Neill, D. J. (ed.). (1971). *Speeches by Black Americans.* Encino & Belmont, Calif.: Dickenson.

Paul, D. B. (1983). "A War on Two Fronts: JBS Haldane and the Response to Lysenkoism in Britain." *Journal of the History of Biology* 16, 1–37.

Pedersen, V. L. (2001). *The Communist Party in Maryland, 1919–57.* Urbana & Chicago: University of Illinois Press.

Popovsky, M. (1984). *The Vavilov Affair.* Hamden, Conn.: Archon Books.

Popper, K. (2008). *After the Open Society: Selected Social and Political Writings.* London: Routledge.

Potier, J.-P. (1991). *Piero Sraffa, Unorthodox Economist (1898–1983): A Biographical Essay.* London: Routledge.

Putnam, H. (1970). "Liberalism, Radicalism and Contemporary 'Unrest.'" *Metaphilosophy* 1, 71–74.

Putnam, H. (1992). *Realism with a Human Face.* Cambridge, Mass.: Harvard University Press.

Putnam, H. (2015). "Intellectual Autobiography." In Auxier, R. E. et al. (eds.). *The Philosophy of Hilary Putnam.* Chicago: Open Court.

Radosh, R. (2001). *Commies: A Journey through the Old Left, the New Left and the Leftover Left.* San Francisco: Encounter Books.

Rand, A. (1999). *The Return of the Primitive: The Anti-Industrial Revolution.* Harmondsworth: Penguin.

Read, C. (2013). *Lenin: A Revolutionary Life.* London: Routledge.

Redman, J. (1958). "The British Stalinists and the Moscow Trials." *Labour Review* 3 (2), 44–53.
Redpath, T. (1990). *Ludwig Wittgenstein: A Student's Memoir.* London: Duckworth.
Reisch, G. A. (2005). *How the Cold War Transformed Philosophy of Science: To the Icy Slopes of Logic.* Cambridge: Cambridge University Press.
Rhees, R. (ed.). (1984). *Recollections of Wittgenstein.* Oxford: Oxford University Press.
Ritchie, D. A. (ed.). (2011). *Congress and Harry S. Truman: A Conflicted Legacy.* Kirksville, Mo.: Truman State University Press.
Rogers, B. (1999). *A. J. Ayer: A Life.* London: Chatto & Windus.
Rosefielde, S. (2009). *Red Holocaust.* London: Routledge.
Rosen, M. (2010). "Jerry Cohen: An Appreciation." http://scholar.harvard.edu/files/michaelrosen/files/jerry_cohen_-_an_appreciation.pdf?m=1360039747
Ross, J. (2004). *Murdered by Capitalism: A Memoir of 150 Years of Life and Death on the American Left.* New York: Nation Books.
Rowe, D. E., & Schulmann, R. (eds.). (2013). *Einstein on Politics: His Private Thoughts and Public Stands on Nationalism, Zionism, War, Peace, and the Bomb.* Princeton, N.J.: Princeton University Press.
Russell, B. (1912). *The Problems of Philosophy.* London: Williams and Norgate; New York: Holt.
Russell, B. (1918). "German Peace Offer." *Tribunal* (January 3).
Russell, B. (1951). "Democracy and the Teachers: Using Beelzebub to Cast Out Satan." *Manchester Guardian* (October 30).
Russell, B. (1967–69; 2009). *Autobiography.* London & New York: Routledge.
Sandner, G. (2014). *Otto Neurath: Eine politische Biographie.* Vienna: Paul Zsolnay Verlag.
Scanlon, T. M. (2003). *The Difficulty of Tolerance: Essays in Political Philosophy.* Cambridge: Cambridge University Press.
Schmidtz, D. (2012). "Schmidtz on Rawls, Nozick, and Justice." www.econtalk.org/archives/2012/05/schmidtz_on_raw.html
Schulte, B. (2015). "Das Ende des Heideggerianertums." www.badische-zeitung.de/literatur-und-vortraege/das-ende-des-heideggerianertums–99384125.html.
Searle, J. S. (2015). "Oxford Philosophy in the 1950s." *Philosophy* 90, 173–93.
September Statement (2014). https://sites.google.com/site/septemberstatement.
Sesardić, N., & De Clercq, R. (2014). "Women in Philosophy: Problems with the Discrimination Hypothesis." www.nas.org/articles/women_in_philosophy_problems_with_the_discrimination_hypothesis
Shields J. A., & Dunn J. M. (2016). *Passing on the Right: Conservative Professors in the Progressive University.* Oxford. Oxford University Press.
Siegel, F. (2013). *The Revolt Against the Masses: How Liberalism Has Undermined the Middle Class.* New York: Encounter Books.
Sigmund, K. (2015). *Sie nannten sich Der Wiener Kreis: Exaktes Denken am Rand des Untergangs.* Wiesbaden: Springer.
Sigmund, K. et al. (2006). *Kurt Gödel: Das Album.* Wiesbaden: Vieweg.
Škvorecký, J. (1988). *Talkin' Moscow Blues.* Toronto: University of Toronto Press.
Sluga, H. D. (1995). *Heidegger's Crisis: Philosophy and Politics in Nazi Germany.* Cambridge, Mass.: Harvard University Press.
Soames, S. (2003). *Analytic Philosophy in the Twentieth Century, vol. 1: The Dawn of Analysis.* Princeton, N.J.: Princeton University Press.

Solzhenitsyn, A. (1976). *Warning to the West.* New York: Farrar, Straus & Giroux.

Solzhenitsyn, A. (2011). *Apricot Jam: And Other Stories.* Berkeley, Calif.: Counterpoint.

Somerville, J. (1945). "Soviet Science and Dialectical Materialism." *Philosophy of Science* 12, 23–29.

Somerville, J. (1946). "Basic Trends in Soviet Philosophy." *Philosophical Review* 55, 250–63.

Stadler, F. (1992). "The 'Verein Ernst Mach'—What Was It Really?" In J. T. Blackmore (ed.), *Ernst Mach—A Deeper Look: Documents and New Perspectives.* Dordrecht: Kluwer.

Stadler, F. (1993). *Scientific Philosophy: Origins and Development.* Dordrecht: Kluwer.

Stadler, F. (2015). *The Vienna Circle: Studies in the Origins, Development, and Influence of Logical Empiricism.* Vienna: Springer.

Stadler, F. (ed.). (1982). *Arbeiterbildung in der Zwischenkriegszeit: Otto Neurath-Gerd Arntz.* Vienna: Löcker Verlag.

Stroll, A. (2000). *Twentieth-Century Analytic Philosophy.* New York: Columbia University Press.

Tchernavin, V. V. (1935). *I Speak for the Silent Prisoners of the Soviets.* Boston & New York: Hale, Cushman & Flint.

Todd, O. (1997). *Albert Camus: A Life.* London: Chatto & Windus.

Topping, K. J., & Trickey, S. (2007). "Collaborative Philosophical Enquiry for School Children: Cognitive Effects at 10–12 Years." *British Journal of Educational Psychology* 77 (2), 271–88.

Tormey, S. (2009). "Interview with Gerald Cohen." *Contemporary Political Theory* 8, 351–62.

Uebel, T. (1991). *Rediscovering the Forgotten Vienna Circle: Austrian Studies on Otto Neurath and the Vienna Circle.* Dordrecht: Kluwer.

Usdin, S. T. (2005). *Engineering Communism: How Two Americans Spied for Stalin and Founded the Soviet Silicon Valley.* New Haven, Conn.: Yale University Press.

Valentinov, N. (1968). *Encounters with Lenin.* Oxford: Oxford University Press.

Wallace, H. A. (1952). "Where I Was Wrong." *This Week* (September 7).

Wallace, H. A., & Steiger, A. J. (1946). *Soviet Asia Mission.* New York: Reynal & Hitchcock.

Wang, H. (1990). *Reflections on Kurt Gödel.* Cambridge, Mass.: MIT Press.

Wang, H. (1996). *A Logical Journey: From Gödel to Philosophy.* Cambridge, Mass.: MIT Press.

Warburton, N., & Edmonds, D. (2010). Philosophy Bites Interview with Michael Dummett. http://philosophybites.com/frege/.

Wechsler, J. A. (1953). *The Age of Suspicion.* New York: Random House.

Wells, B. (2007). "Alfred Tarski, Friend and Daemon." *Notices of the American Mathematical Society* 54, 982–84.

West, R. F. et al. (2012). "Cognitive Sophistication Does Not Attenuate the Bias Blind Spot." *Journal of Personality and Social Psychology* 103, 506–19.

Williams, B. (2006). *Ethics and the Limits of Philosophy.* London: Routledge.

Wistrich, R. S. (2012). *From Ambivalence to Betrayal: The Left, the Jews, and Israel.* Lincoln: University of Nebraska Press.

Wittgenstein, L. (1967). *Philosophical Investigations.* Oxford: Blackwell.

Wolff, R. P. (2013). *A Life in the Academy.* Wellington: Society for Philosophy & Culture.

Worrall, J. (1976). "Imre Lakatos (1922–1974): Philosopher of Mathematics and Philosopher of Science." In R. S. Cohen et al. (eds.), *Essays in Memory of Imre Lakatos* (1–8). Dordrecht: Reidel.

Worrall, J. (2003). "Lakatos in Disguise." *Metascience* 12, 79–83.

Zimán, M. (1989). "A Memorial of Words for Éva." www.johnkadvany.com/GettingStarted/Kadvany_Design/Assets/Downloads/A_MemorialOfWordsFor_Eva.pdf

Index